19.95
80P

# CLASSROOM APPLICATIONS OF MICROCOMPUTERS

Robert V. Bullough, Sr.
LaMond F. Beatty
University of Utah

MERRILL PUBLISHING COMPANY
A Bell & Howell Company
Columbus   Toronto   London   Melbourne

Cover Photo: David Strickler

Published by Merrill Publishing Company
A Bell & Howell Company
Columbus, Ohio 43216

This book was set in Baskerville

Production Coordinator: Mary Harlan
Art Coordinator: Lorraine Woost
Cover Designer: Cathy Watterson
Text Designer: Martha Morss

Library of Congress Catalog Card Number: 86–61507
International Standard Book Number: 0–675–20525–5
Printed in the United States of America
   2 3 4 5 6 7 8 9—91 90 89 88 87

# PREFACE

The purpose of this book is to provide educators with the concepts and skills that will enable them to deal effectively with the computer and its many associated implications and applications. We believe that teachers who are familiar with computers, and who do not feel intimidated by them, constitute the most promising force for realizing the technology's instructional potential.

The microcomputer is being acquired in increasing numbers by every sector of the educational establishment, but merely buying equipment is not enough—teachers must be willing and able to make good use of it. The importance of preparing teachers to use computers was highlighted when representatives of the National Education Association and the National School Boards Association went on record before Congress as opposing any legislation that furnishes hardware to the schools unless it includes a provision for training those who will use it.

Another indication of the need to train teachers to use the technology is the move to make computer literacy mandatory for every graduating teacher. In some institutions this effort has taken the form of compulsory classes. School districts and universities offer workshops and classes for those already in the classroom who need to upgrade their knowledge and skills in microcomputer technology. This book will serve as the basis for a course in educational uses of microcomputers or as a useful supplement in established courses or preservice or inservice workshops.

There can be no substitute for hands-on experience; the skills acquired by reading a chapter must be honed at the microcomputer keyboard. It is thus assumed that the reader will have access to a microcomputer to benefit from the various exercises provided.

The operation of the microcomputer system is but one focus of the book. Most workshops and many college classes emphasize equipment operation but ignore or gloss over other important considerations. We have attempted to strike a balance by including a broad range of topics that address not only system-related matters but also social and ethical issues.

The book is arranged to be used sequentially, chapter by chapter; however, selected chapters can be pulled out to be used in a workshop or a course tailored by an instructor. It is designed with pre- and inservice teachers in mind, but it can also be of interest to those using computers in the home or desiring an overview of the technology.

Chapter 1 provides the student with a historical sense of instructional computing and includes a discussion of trends and a look at some of the research in the field. Chapter 2, the hardware chapter, provides a description of the equipment, including both the microcomputer and its peripherals. Because maintenance is always a problem, some suggestions are offered on how to keep the system operating. In chapter 3, on selecting a system, we match different kinds of hardware and programs to specific needs and outline a five-step model for system selection.

Educational software is covered extensively in chapter 4, which describes the kinds of computer-assisted instruction programs. Some attention is also given to computer-managed instruction, as well as to software evaluation, which is simplified by the inclusion of a sample evaluation form. The three primary kinds of applications programs—word processors, spreadsheets, and data base management programs—are discussed in chapter 5, on tool software, and suggestions are offered on how these might be used in the classroom.

In chapter 6 you will learn how to "hook your computer to the world" using a modem and the telephone lines and how to make use of local area networks, which enable several computers to communicate with each other or with common printers and mass storage devices. The following chapter presents the arguments for and against making programming a part of the curriculum. Chapter 7 offers an introduction to BASIC and Logo, including classroom activities involving these languages, along with a discussion of the PILOT authoring language.

The important concerns in formulating and successfully implementing a school microcomputer program are addressed in chapter 8, including suggestions for acquiring funding and support. Finally, chapter 9 examines such concerns as computer crime, privacy in the computer age, the impact of computers on jobs, and computer equity. It develops a scenario of the future and concludes with suggestions for approaching the subject of ethics in the classroom.

The extensive appendixes provide a glossary; lists of software publishers, sources of free or inexpensive software, software guides, catalogs, and reviews, computer magazines and newsletters, and user groups; telecommunication information; word processing exercises and descriptions of several word processing programs; and a BASIC programming exercise and sample PILOT program.

So many people have helped in the preparation of this book that we would be hard-pressed to name them all. Dolores Bullough and Lois Beatty deserve our thanks for their diligent efforts at proofing the manuscript and for their endless support. Bob Bullough, Jr., offered helpful criticism on organization and structure. Our colleague Tom Callister gave ideas, help, and encouragement. Betty DeMond was a critical reviewer of the text and did much to field test it.

We wish to thank our colleagues who reviewed the manuscript and made many useful comments and suggestions:

John C. Arch, Shippensburg State College
Bill Baird, University of Texas at Austin
Deborah A. Bott, University of Kentucky
Philip East, University of Oregon
Louis A. Gardner, Georgia State University
Judith E. Jacobs, Educational Consultant, Oakton, VA
Gerald Kulm, U.S. Department of Education
Michael Milone, Jr., American Research and Development Group, Honesdale, PA
Robert V. Price, Texas Tech University
Nancy Roberts, Lesley College
Ted Singletary, University of Wisconsin—Parkside
David Tanner, California State University, Fresno
Jim Thompson, University of South Alabama at Mobile
Brent Wholeben, University of Texas at El Paso

Finally, we extend our sincere gratitude to the hundreds of education students and others who endured the numerous revisions of the course units that ultimately came together to form this text.

# CONTENTS

# 1

# AN OVERVIEW

## INTRODUCTION

Using microcomputers for instructional purposes has become routine for many educators. Others are rapidly catching up as they enhance their skills and knowledge by taking college courses or by participating in workshops offered by their schools and districts. The result of this is a growing corps of capable educators who will be able to manage what some have called a "microcomputer revolution."

Surveys by publications such as *Electronic Learning* and organizations such as Quality Education Data, Inc. indicate that the acquisition and utilization of microcomputers will continue to increase into the foreseeable future as the technology becomes more capable and the programs more diverse and powerful. The trend toward requiring all undergraduate teachers to successfully complete a class on instructional uses of microcomputers will help them feel comfortable with the new equipment and will enable them to take advantage of its unique characteristics.

Used properly, the computer holds great promise. Its potential far surpasses that of such prior instructional innovations as television, teaching machines, and projectors. Although better visual images can be obtained with films and slides, and better sound from audio equipment, there are things the computer can do that are beyond the capabilities of other mediums.

Among the attributes that make computers unique is the ability to encourage students to try new things without the fear of making mistakes. Making mistakes is a natural occurrence in the learning process, but traditional classrooms are set up in such a manner that an illogical response or incorrect answer may bring with it consequences that can be out of all proportion to the magnitude of the mistake. Many contemporary instructional microcomputer programs are highly tolerant of incorrect responses. Experimentation is actually encouraged as students explore different approaches to the solution of a problem until they discover the best one. In programs of this type, the exercise of logic and the use of problem-solving techniques are emphasized over the simple memorization of spelled-out facts.

Another highly desirable feature is the self-paced characteristic that computers provide. Students can truly progress at their own speeds—a feat that even the most accomplished human teacher has great difficulty achieving under prevailing conditions. Also, students are given immediate feedback regarding their performance so they can move on to the next set of activities without undue delay.

A related attribute is the ability to bring more interactive learning into the crowded classroom. Due to the large numbers of students with which a teacher must deal, she gets few opportunities to actually interact with them on a one-to-one basis. Interaction with a machine might appear to be less desirable than that with a human being, but it is infinitely better than virtually none at all. There is also an increased potential for the teacher to do more one-on-one instruction where it is most needed if the computer takes over some of the responsibility for many of the other instructional chores (fig. 1.1).

**FIGURE 1.1  Computers Can Enhance Learning** (Courtesy of Commodore Electronics Limited)

The computer also has powerful socializing effects on students and can change attitudes in positive ways. Studies such as those conducted by Johns Hopkins University indicate that students tend to be more cooperative and more social when working with computers. They exhibit greater independence and require less frequent assistance from teachers. They also tend to work together to solve problems, and they tend to share knowledge and information more freely. Students eagerly look forward to classes in which computers are used effectively and, rather than attempting to miss sessions, often spend more time in class than is required.

Computers can also monitor a student's progress in great detail and with precision. A human teacher can do this too, but various constraints generally prevent such an effort from being fully carried out. Diagnosis and prescription are integral and essential parts of the on-going monitoring process; these activities are tedious and time-consuming for the teacher, but not for the computer. On the basis of the student's performance, a good computer-based program will spot problem areas and supply the appropriate remedial activities with great efficiency.

With so many positive claims being made for computer-based learning it would seem that all teachers should be clamoring to get their students busily working with it. For several reasons, however, the promise hasn't been fully realized. For one thing, although the numbers are growing, there aren't as yet enough trained persons to implement widescale computer-oriented curricula. And, although many teachers are embracing the concept, resistance continues from various sources, one of which is the teaching profession itself.

There is also the financial problem—lean budgets won't permit the wholesale acquisition of the technology. But conditions are changing for the better. Master's programs have been established at many universities to train professionals who can manage a school's computer facility. Teacher resistance decreases as familiarity with the equipment and programs increases. And those in charge of budgets are beginning to recognize that money spent on computers and software is money well spent.

The trend is clear and there is no turning back—the technology is here to stay. Statistics such as those cited later on in this chapter indicate that the numbers of microcomputers are increasing in both the home and the school, and that support for computer-based learning continues to grow at an accelerated pace.

Indeed, the dissemination of the technology has been so rapid that educators have been taken unaware to a large extent and find themselves ill-prepared to deal with the phenomenon. Seemingly, computer-assisted instruction (CAI) and the systems that made it possible suddenly appeared from out of nowhere—a case of spontaneous generation, so to speak. However, as with other innovations, computer-based instructional systems developed over time; they have a history.

It would be nice if we could say that this development was the result of a carefully executed strategy, a sort of "technological five-year plan," but this was not the case. Indeed, the manufacturers of large computers showed little interest in the early microcomputers, and with good cause. They were used to thinking in terms of very powerful machines that processed vast amounts of data at extremely high speeds. What good was a miniature computer with a tiny memory that did its work in relative slow motion? It would make an interesting toy perhaps, but little else—or so they thought.

The common perception that CAI simply evolved as a consequence of the widespread availability of the microcomputer is also a misconception. CAI was practiced in a limited fashion long before the innovations that made the microcomputer possible were invented.

Although this text is about modern microcomputers and contemporary computer-related educational practice, we would be remiss if some mention weren't made of those creative pioneers and their innovative projects that contributed so much to the current state of the art. By presenting a short survey of the twenty-five-year history of CAI we hope to establish a point of departure for subsequent discussion.

In addition, information on trends in the acquisition and use of microcomputers will be presented in this chapter. A recent trend is the subtle shift away from an emphasis on programming (writing the instructions that run the computer) and toward the use of applications or "tool" programs such as word processors, data base management programs, and spreadsheets. This trend prompted us to decrease the amount of information on programming in the text and to include an entire chapter on tool applications.

A survey of selected research studies is also included. The fact that many studies point up the effectiveness of CAI should lend support to efforts aimed at broadening its use and should give encouragement to those teachers who are using the technology in their classes. While it is true that more studies are needed before a universal stamp of approval can be given to the CAI concept, the widespread research efforts currently underway will most certainly clarify many of the questions being asked about this controversial movement.

## THE DEVELOPMENT OF COMPUTER-BASED INSTRUCTION

Today more than ever before people involved both directly and indirectly with the educational enterprise are caught up in efforts to introduce and integrate computers into the curricula of the nation's schools. The concept involved, that of using computers for instruction, is referred to as novel, innovative, and new, but what is not generally known is that instructional computing has been around for quite awhile. Table 1.1 traces some of the notable events that contributed to the development of computer-based instruction.

Early efforts dating back to the late 1950s and early 1960s were hampered by a number of factors, one of which was a lack of suitable hardware (the computers and electronics that support them). The first computers were large, expensive, and used primarily for large-scale mathematical calculation ("number crunching"). Thousands of vacuum tubes organized into clusters produced the on-off code that the computer used (fig. 1.2). Because of the costs involved in building and maintaining such machines, only well-endowed organizations, such

**TABLE 1.1** Notable Developments: From Vacuum Tubes to Computer Literacy

| | |
|---|---|
| 1946 | First generation computers, based on vacuum tubes, introduced |
| 1959 | Second generation all-transistorized computer introduced by IBM |
| 1960 | The PLATO project begins at Illinois |
| 1963 | The Stanford Project begins |
| 1964 | Third generation computers, based on integrated circuits, appear; BASIC developed at Dartmouth |
| 1965 | Digital Equipment Corporation markets the inexpensive PDP-8 minicomputer; teaching of classes at the University of Illinois using PLATO |
| 1967 | The New York plan; expanded use of computer-assisted instruction in the public schools |
| 1968 | Logo introduced |
| 1969 | The first microprocessor chip developed by Intel |
| 1972 | Fourth generation begins with the introduction of expanded microchip by Intel |
| 1975 | First widescale marketing of a microcomputer (Altair 8800) |
| 1977 | Commodore Pet, Apple II, and TRS 80 microcomputers introduced |
| 1980s | Widescale adoption of microcomputers by the schools; computer literacy movement |

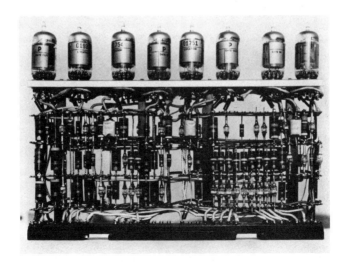

**FIGURE 1.2 A Bank of Vacuum Tubes** (Courtesy of IBM Corporation)

as departments of government, could afford to purchase them. The prototype of these "first generation" computers operated until 1955, but not even the most far-seeing visionaries recognized in the machines anything but a rather restricted potential for educational applications.

With the advent of the "second generation" computers, which used transistors (see fig. 1.3) rather than vacuum tubes for creating the coded signals, reliability was improved and the size and cost came down dramatically. Among the companies addressing the problems of cost and size was Digital Equipment Corporation, which introduced its first computer, the PDP-1, in 1957 (fig. 1.4). This machine was used in several of the early pioneering CAI projects. An increasing number of institutions began to purchase or rent computer systems, and although commercial data processing remained the major application, it wasn't long before the idea of developing computer science courses in departments of engineering was implemented. But this was a far cry from the universal utilization of computers as teaching devices, a futuristic scenario envisioned by a mere handful of professors in a few universities.

### The Advent of the Chip

In 1959 both Texas Instruments and Fairchild Semiconductor devised ways to place electronic components, such as miniaturized transistors, on a single, thin piece of silicon. These integrated circuits (ICs) on a chip would ultimately make

FIGURE 1.3   A Transistor (Courtesy of IBM Corporation)

**FIGURE 1.4 The PDP-1** (Courtesy of Digital Equipment Corporation)

possible the widescale manufacture of inexpensive and reliable microcomputers of the kind that schools could afford to buy.

These diminutive marvels, known as chips, have no soldered junctions that might break. They also generate little heat, use minuscule amounts of power, and are extremely reliable. They can be produced in great numbers at low cost from materials that are readily available. Figure 1.5 shows a chip (the tiny speck on the right) in comparison with a transistor and a vacuum tube. Computers built around collections of various kinds of chips were referred to as "third generation" computers.

The third generation was ushered in with the introduction in 1964 of IBM's System 360 family of computers (see fig. 1.6). These powerful machines used IC chips exclusively. The new generation of machines caught the public's fancy, and those who were able purchased or rented them in increasing numbers.

In an effort to provide a range of choices to those who wanted the technology but couldn't afford it, Digital Equipment Corporation, in 1965, marketed a smaller, cheaper machine that came to be known as the minicomputer. The introduction of this innovative system made possible the purchase of computers by small companies and educational institutions that never dreamed they might afford such an apparent luxury. While the larger systems commonly sold for prices that ranged into the millions, the PDP-8 minicomputer (fig. 1.7) sold for the unheard-of low price of $20,000.

**FIGURE 1.5   Comparative Sizes of the Vacuum Tube, Transistor, and Chip**
(Courtesy of IBM Corporation)

**FIGURE 1.6   An IBM System 360 Computer** (Courtesy of IBM Corporation)

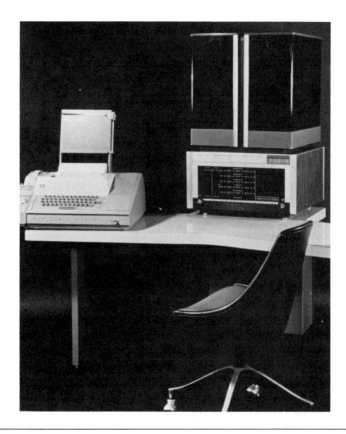

FIGURE 1.7 The PDP-8 Minicomputer (Courtesy of Digital Equipment Corporation)

## The Stanford Project

During the 1960s various computer-oriented instructional programs were developed. The needed monetary support came from the federal government, which pumped large sums of money into the school system (through such vehicles as the Elementary and Secondary Education Act of 1965) in an effort to upgrade certain areas of the curriculum. Proposals that held promise for better instruction in general, and for better math and science instruction in particular, were readily funded. Thus, computer-assisted instruction, with its technological underpinnings, was to enjoy a period of sustained support.

Among those who continued their research with federal support were Patrick Suppes and Richard Atkinson of Stanford University, who implemented the Stanford Project in 1963. Although this project received its initial support from the Carnegie Foundation, it was a grant from the U.S. Office of Education that made long-term development possible.

The Stanford effort was directed toward the development of mathematics and reading programs, with Suppes involved with the former discipline and Atkinson with the latter. Suppes saw in CAI the potential for realizing the age-old dream of teaching students in a one-on-one tutorial approach. His goal was to individualize instruction for every student; however, the magnitude of the task caused him to redirect his resources and energies toward the teaching of selected groups of students, such as those who were working below grade level.

The Stanford program was based on three levels of interaction. At the first level was drill and practice. The exercises could be varied according to a five-tiered hierarchy of difficulty that reflected varying levels of competence. The second level was the tutorial system, in which the emphasis was placed on concept attainment. The lessons progressed from the initial introductory segment through progressively more complex interactive activities until the concept was mastered. The tutorials were self-paced and included what was known as a "teacher-call." If the student, after having worked through the program, was unable to meet the performance requirements, a teacher would be called to assist in whatever ways were deemed necessary.

The third system was referred to as the dialogue system. This was an attempt to involve the student in a less structured and more open-ended computer-based activity. In this system the student would ask a question of the computer, just as would be the case if human teachers were involved. The problem in the sixties, as now, was programming the computer to understand the question completely. Suppes recognized that although a computer might be capable of understanding a question posed in standard English, it might not respond to the same question if a dialect were involved or if the speaker didn't enunciate the words clearly. The problems of using the spoken word for input were not sufficiently resolved to make this a viable option. Indeed, the concept of the dialogue system remained largely undeveloped, and the drill-and-practice and tutorial approaches predominated. Though speech recognition has progressed markedly over the intervening twenty-five years, problems encountered in the early days of the Stanford Project remain even today.

The system employed over five hundred pages of prepared information that could be selectively displayed on a screen where the student had access to it via a light pen (a small device used to point to a portion of a screen display). Information could also be entered using a keyboard; a standard cathode ray tube (CRT—similar in concept to a TV monitor) was the display medium. This system was widely tested using remote CRTs located in the schools. The approach was mainly involved with the drill-and-practice component of the program. Mention should be made of the fact that during these early experimental and developmental days, much wider use was made of supplemental noncomputerized equipment than is currently the case. Today the CRT is the standard output device and the keyboard (and certain less-used devices, such as the mouse and joystick) represents the primary input device. But during the 1960s it was not uncommon for a CAI system to employ not only a rear projection screen and voice output but also such specially designed equipment as slide projectors, tape recorders, "electronic blackboards," and filmstrip projectors. A common procedure during this period was to display visual materials via a projection medium (such as a filmstrip) while using the computer to respond to the material in the projected images.

The typical configuration of a CAI system was a number of stations consisting of a monitor (or CRT) and a teletype hooked to a central computer where all of the processing took place. This was referred to as a "time-sharing system" (fig. 1.8).

The development of time-sharing was one of the most important factors in the early evolution of CAI because it permitted large numbers of students to participate concurrently in individualized learning activities. Time-sharing refers to the ability of a single central computer to handle almost simultaneously the demands of a host of users. The processor operates at such a high rate of speed that the waiting time experienced by users is virtually imperceptible. Once such systems had been perfected, the economics of CAI were much less prohibitive than

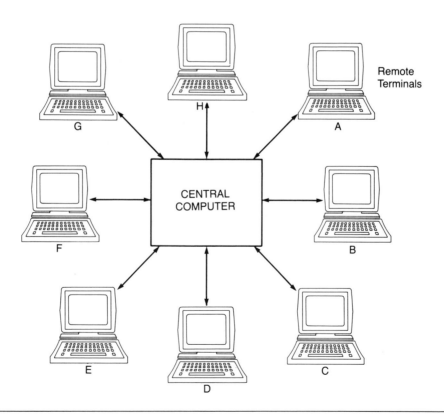

**FIGURE 1.8   A Time-Sharing System**

was formerly the case. Obviously, one student at a single work station interacting with one computer was an unacceptable arrangement for anything but an experimental session.

With the refinement of materials, such as those from the Stanford Project, and the availability of time-sharing came the opportunity to implement CAI in the public schools. The experience gained from classroom-oriented activities added to the expanding store of knowledge that was to be of immense value when interest in CAI was revived with the introduction of the microcomputer.

## The PLATO Project

Another notable project, implemented in the early 1960s at the University of Illinois, was PLATO—Programmed Logic for Automatic Teaching Operations. The first prototype system of 1960 consisted of the computer and a single student learning station. An expanded system followed, which consisted of the central computer and a network of twenty individual terminals equipped with video displays and keyboards. The system was highly interactive, providing an environment in which the student and computer often engaged in an on-going dialogue of a tutorial nature. The PLATO system was quite sophisticated for its time, utilizing such innovations as touch screens in place of the traditional teletypes as the primary terminal device for communicating ("inputting") with the main computer. A touch screen is a monitor (similar in concept to a TV receiver) that permits the user to input information by touching the screen at various selected points. For example, rather than having to type in the answer to a multiple choice question, the student need only touch the answer of his choice on the screen; the display then changes in response to the action.

PLATO continued to expand with support from the National Science Foundation until, by 1965, the programs and other materials had been refined to the point that the teaching of regular university courses was undertaken at Illinois. Because a powerful central computer was used (there were no microcomputers), the programs could be sophisticated, extensive, and complex. Also, the larger computer permitted the creation of excellent graphic displays and even animation. But all of this had a price—PLATO was very expensive.

The inexpensive microcomputer gave educators an affordable alternative to networked, time-sharing systems like PLATO. Although microcomputers weren't able to do many of the things the more powerful systems were capable of, they were at least obtainable. Whereas few educators were aware of the truly remarkable strides that had taken place in the development of computer-assisted instruction using large computers, the ubiquitous quality of the microcomputer stimulated an interest in this aspect of education. It would seem that the vast effort to create and field-test programs for the PLATO system was to be wasted, since they could not be used with the newer, smaller machines. But this was not the case; the effort was to pay off in a much broader fashion than was anticipated. Under the direction of Control Data Corporation, the current owners of PLATO, these excellent materials are being modified to operate on personal computers. Conversions have been made of programs in a number of areas, including foreign languages, physics, math, and computer literacy. Educators find the new versions of the PLATO programs and the print materials that go with them (collectively called "courseware") to be among the best available (fig. 1.9).

PLATO received a large infusion of federal dollars in the late seventies, which enabled development to continue at an expanded pace. A similar grant was awarded to a second project, under the direction of the Mitre Corporation, called TICCIT (Time-shared, Interactive, Computer Controlled Information Television). The hardware developed for the Stanford Project was modified and expanded for use with TICCIT. A considerable quantity of courseware was created for the system, which yielded quite positive results.

The hardware components functioned well together and constituted one of the more successful attempts to develop a true computer-based instructional system. The courseware was innovative and effective, and, perhaps most important of all, students learning with TICCIT showed significant gains in achievement. Again, despite all the positive features of the system, TICCIT, like PLATO, was a very expensive approach to CAI.

Although PLATO and some other systems based on the original networked concept are still in place and operating in several locations in the United States and foreign countries, the popular microcomputer has all but monopolized instructional computing. Nevertheless, the contributions of such pioneering efforts as those undertaken by the originators of the PLATO, Stanford, and TICCIT projects—and others not mentioned—have had much to do with the current state of the art in instructional computing, and educators continue to enjoy the fruits of these early labors.

FIGURE 1.9 PLATO Courseware for the Microcomputer

### Programming and Authoring Languages for Education

The development of a number of new computer languages was another accomplishment of those working during this exciting period of the sixties (referred to by some as "the golden age of CAI"). Two kinds of languages will be mentioned in this chapter: programming languages and authoring languages. A programming language consists of a finite set of words and symbols that are used in various combinations to instruct a computer to perform a wide range of tasks. An authoring language provides the user with a matrix or template that serves as the common format for lessons. The instructions for authoring languages are much less flexible than are those used for programming. On the whole, authoring languages are easy to use, but they have less versatility than those used for writing programs.

One of the new programming languages that was to have an influence on the "second golden age" (the age of the microcomputer) was the Beginners All-purpose Symbolic Instruction Code, or BASIC. This language was developed at Dartmouth in order to meet a specific instructional need. When the Dartmouth staff made a commitment to computer training for all students, they found that a new approach was needed. John Kemeny and Thomas Kurtz directed the efforts to find a way to provide computer training to the large numbers of students from diverse disciplines who would be involved. They conceived of the idea of using a time-sharing approach that would permit students to interact with the computer in a one-on-one fashion. This necessitated networking a large number of terminals to the central processor, which would communicate in extremely rapid fashion and in specific order with each terminal. This format required the development of a new language that would be interactive; that is, the student would receive feedback as he or she typed in the program. Various programming languages, including FORTRAN, had been developed, but these didn't lend themselves to the interactive learning of programming. The standard approach to data processing before the advent of interactive languages was to compile all the data to be processed and feed them into the computer. Punched cards were commonly used as the input medium. The results (or output) were typically printed out on sheets of fanfold paper.

The new language, which was introduced in 1964, worked very well, and it wasn't long before BASIC was adopted as the language of choice by many institutions engaged in activities similar to those being carried out at Dartmouth. But the use of BASIC was to extend beyond the time-sharing instructional systems: when microcomputers became generally available, it was selected as the language to be used with them.

Most educators have heard of Logo. The tendency is to consider this a recent innovation; however, Logo was another product of the sixties. Logo was created in 1968 by the firm of Bolt, Beranek, and Newman, Inc., under the sponsorship of the National Science Foundation. Seymour Papert and researchers at M.I.T. tested the language in a number of different settings and continued with its development. Today, Logo operates on most microcomputers and is considered by many educators potentially to be one of the most useful of instructional programs.

The development of numerous computerized instructional systems stimulated the creation of several versions of the authoring language. One of the earliest versions was known as TUTOR, which was created for use on the PLATO system. TUTOR was complex and required considerable effort to learn. The present concept of an authoring language, however, is generally to provide a teacher with a framework into which particular questions and answers can be fitted. One purpose of the simpler authoring languages is to provide educators who are not professional programmers with the necessary tools to create their own computer-based lessons.

Several of these early authoring languages survive to this day, some of them in a form that is rather close to the original versions. PILOT and the updated SuperPILOT are examples of programs developed in the 1960s that have been modified to work with microcomputers.

You may refer to chapter 7 if you are interested in more information on programming and authoring.

## The Public Schools Get Involved

Through the second half of the 1960s and into the early 1970s new technological advances, infusions of money, and a growing staff of competent people caused considerable interest to be generated, particularly in the United States, in the potential of computer-assisted instruction. Indeed, as the decade of the sixties neared its close, CAI had become a fact of life for thousands of students throughout America. The first city whose school system adopted CAI as an integral part of its overall instructional program was Philadelphia, but New York City wasn't far behind. The New York plan, which was initiated in 1967, was an ambitious one. Funded by money provided by Title III of the ESEA act, the program had as its focus the study of math, spelling, and reading in the second through the sixth grades. The materials from the Stanford Project served as the core of the curriculum. Sixteen different schools containing 192 student stations were connected to a central computer in a time-sharing arrangement. The system was widely tested, and a considerable amount of useful information was collected. The experiment proved to be effective in varying degrees, with some educators favoring the approach and others showing less enthusiasm.

Other implementations might be cited, but it is sufficient to point out that CAI had come out of the laboratory and had become a reality in certain of the nation's schools. Though not all-inclusive, the examples of work accomplished during the early days of CAI should give the reader some sense of the innovative thinking that was taking place at that time. The varied accomplishments of the sixties were ultimately to come together in a blending of ideas and technology that would erupt a decade later in the form of the microcomputer revolution.

## The Microcomputer Takes Over

As the 1970s dawned, advocates confidently predicted that CAI would become an indispensible element in the American classroom. But, optimistic as some were, others did not share this utopian point of view. These individuals cited the high costs and long implementation time involved in this approach and suggested that, rather than being a viable tool, CAI was merely an expensive frill. Interest and support had dropped to a low level by the mid-1970s, but an event occurred that was to stimulate a wave of renewed interest: the microcomputer was introduced. This compact, inexpensive, handsome little machine was to bring about a renaissance in instructional computing.

The small electronic calculators that were gaining notice in the late sixties suddenly became widely popular in the early seventies. Demand for these machines, which were based on the integrated circuit chip, provided manufacturers with the incentive to expand production and refine the technology. The calculators were made increasingly more capable, cheaper, and ever smaller through the use of chips in various combinations. The ongoing competitive efforts to refine the calculators ultimately led to the creation of the microprocessor, or the "computer on a chip." Before the advent of the microprocessor, specialized chips were combined in various ways to serve as the processing unit of the computer. Computers constructed around an array of chips were called third generation computers. When, through a process known as large-scale integration, the various functions that a processor performs were all integrated on a single silicon chip, the fourth-generation computer was born. In 1975 the first microcomputer in kit form was offered for sale, and things were never to be the same again.

The development of the microcomputer was a phenomenon not so much for the technology, which was already there for the most part, but for the manner in which the actual fabrication took place. The first microcomputers were created by hobbyists who obtained components from any available source, figured out their own circuit designs, and finally soldered everything together to form a unique and complex device that only they (and a few other like-minded individuals) could operate. They programmed the early machines in tedious ways, often using a bank of switches that permitted the 0s and 1s of binary machine language to be fed into the computer by flipping the switch one way for a 0 and the other way for a 1.

Some of the handcrafted microcomputers were considerably better than others, and soon a demand for these particular machines began to develop; a modest industry was born. Several technical periodicals evolved, dedicated to those who wished to build and program their own computers.

The first microcomputer to appear in the schools in any numbers was the Commodore Pet, introduced in the late seventies (fig. 1.10). Then came the

**FIGURE 1.10 The Commodore Pet** (Courtesy of Commodore Electronics Limited)

Apples, Ataris, Radio Shacks, TIs, and others that caught the fancy of many educators who set out to acquire one or two for their schools using any funding method available. Innovative fund-raising ventures, such as PTA cookie sales, were commonplace during this period of time.

At first, few knew what to do with the machines; it was simply fashionable to have them. But it wasn't long before serious educators began to experiment with the equipment and to learn about it. Universities began to offer classes, workshops abounded in school districts, and states began to talk about "computer literacy" as a requisite for all teachers. In the meantime, microcomputers became more sophisticated and capable (fig. 1.11). The new machines had larger memories and better displays and could perform many tasks that the earlier ones could not. Now that the first shocks have subsided, schools are getting down to the task of acquiring and integrating computers into the curriculum in a more orderly and coordinated manner. Attempts at standardization are being made, and the uses for the technology are being more carefully defined. Some trends are now becoming apparent, several of which will be discussed in the following section.

## A LOOK AT TRENDS

What is the state of microcomputer education today, and what, most likely, will be the situation tomorrow? Considerable information is available that, when

**FIGURE 1.11   A Modern Microcomputer** (Courtesy of IBM Corporation)

viewed collectively, gives a fairly good picture of the present state of affairs. A bit of interpolation is necessary in order to come up with a profile of future applications and implications; the resulting scenarios can only be classified as hypotheses, however, because the field is in such a state of flux that solid trends are difficult to identify with any kind of precision. There are those who believe that the microcomputer will, among other things, make our traditional textbooks obsolete—but this prediction is nothing new. The same pronouncement was made over sixty years ago by none other than Thomas Edison, but he was referring to the impact of another marvelous invention—his motion picture projector—and not, obviously, to the latest technological marvel, the microcomputer.

Although the primary emphasis of this section is on classroom computers, some reference will be made to the home computer (microcomputers that are located more or less permanently in private homes). The reason for this inclusion is that education is rapidly becoming one of the primary applications for these machines. Futurists such as Alvin Toffler predict that this trend will continue and that many students will actually obtain the bulk of their formal education not from classroom activities but via computers in their homes. Further, it is predicted that within the schools themselves students will study different subjects using the computer not only for remedial learning but as an adjunct to, or replacement for, established classroom techniques. Indeed, educational programs represent the most rapidly growing segment of the home software market, with a rate of increase that is approximately 70 percent per year, and the hardware picture looks much the same. The interest that families with children have in home education is reflected in the findings of a recent survey by the Minnesota Center for Social Research: a full 75 percent of computers purchased would be used for educational applications.

Home computers are presently located in about 10 percent of the private homes within the United States (fig. 1.12). This doesn't appear to be a very substantial figure until you realize that it equates to eight or nine million homes. If trends continue, up to twenty-five million home-based machines could be in place by 1990. Further, 1987 expenditures for educational hardware and software in the United States will exceed one billion dollars per year, with the larger share (70 percent) being for home use rather than for use in the schools. However, schools aren't sitting still either: they will spend over $300 million in 1988 on instructional hardware and software.

The NPD Group of Long Island conducted a poll of five thousand American households in an effort to determine who buys computers. They found that the average computer-owning family made approximately five thousand dollars more per year than did the average nonowning family. This statistic hints at a growing concern among educators: the potential for educational opportunities,

FIGURE 1.12  Computers Are Becoming More Common in the Home (Courtesy of Commodore Electronics Limited)

which are already somewhat out of balance between the haves and the have-nots, to be more radically altered than ever by the acquisition of microcomputers by those who can afford them. However, the fact that the microcomputer is being adopted by schools at a rapid rate may help offset to some extent the advantage enjoyed by those students who have equipment at home; this will only be the case, however, if decisions are made within the schools that result in an equitable user policy.

A survey by Quality Education Data, Inc., found that the percentage of school districts having microcomputers had climbed from 38.2 percent in 1981–82 to 56.8 percent in 1982–83. According to a survey and analysis by Market Data Retrieval, 94.2 percent of school districts currently use microcomputers for instructional purposes. This organization also reports that there were 630,000 microcomputers in U.S. schools in 1984, with an estimate of over one million in 1985.

The average number of students for each classroom computer tends to be greater in the elementary grades than in the higher grades. A 1984 survey by Market Data Retrieval indicated that the average number of students for each computer was 112 in the elementary schools, 92 in the junior high schools, and 77 in the senior highs.

The Johns Hopkins University's Center for Social Organization of the Schools has conducted various surveys involving a large selection of principals and computer-using teachers in more than 1,500 elementary and secondary schools in the United States and has issued six reports on the findings. Because of the large numbers of participants involved, these surveys represent perhaps the best information available on computer ownership and use. According to the Johns Hopkins reports, the schools having the least number of microcomputers in 1983 were elementary schools in the south (29 percent). These figures contrast with those for elementary schools in rural and western areas, where the ownership rate was 60 percent. The figure for all elementary schools was 43 percent. However, the lowest figure for secondary schools (63 percent for institutions in low income areas) was still higher than was the top figure for the elementary schools. According to a more recent set of figures, 1985 computer ownership at the elementary level reached the overall figure of 85 percent, while the figure was 93 percent for the secondary schools.

The effort to acquire microcomputers is vividly illustrated by the results of a 1983 Market Data Retrieval survey. The figures show that the number of public schools using computers when the survey was conducted was more than double that of one year earlier. Approximately 5,700 elementary schools had the machines at the beginning of the year, but by the end of the year the figure had risen to 13,000.

Trends are becoming apparent in the way computers are being used in the schools. There is a decreased emphasis on straight drill and practice and an increased use of tutorials (programs designed to function like a one-on-one learning session) and simulations. An increased use of applications programs such as word processors and file management programs has also been noted; in addition, problem solving software is becoming increasingly popular.

A tendency to move away from programming as a required component in computer literacy courses has developed. Many schools have implemented elective programming classes to meet the needs of those students who want to pursue the study of computer science. Additionally, many schools are now moving to integrate computers into the broader curriculum, as opposed to the practice of teaching with and about computers in a "computer as subject" awareness class.

The figures and estimates given here reflect a growth trend that will in all probability continue. One thing seems evident: the microcomputer revolution appears to be real, and educators will find themselves affected by it to one degree or another.

## RESEARCH

Most computer-using educators, when asked if they feel that computers make a difference where learning is concerned, will answer with an unqualified yes. Such an answer cannot be totally unbiased, for a teacher who uses a computer must have some degree of conviction that there is value in its use. Also, such an answer is typically subjective, because little research is available that addresses the question of computer effectiveness. Much that is reported in educational journals on this subject is based upon intuitive beliefs.

Both children and adults easily get caught up in the fascination of running the computer if the experience is so structured that it is a positive, nonthreatening one. It is natural for the instructor to assume that the expression of enjoyment indicates that learning is taking place. However, liking and learning are not necessarily correlates. Some evidence indicates that many individuals learn the most from those methods they like the least. Most people seem to enjoy computers—does this mean that entertainment is taking precedence over learning? The studies that are available, while modest in number, indicate that this is not the case. Students not only enjoy using computers; they learn from them as well.

Mention should be made, however, that the advantages for CAI tend to be present when it is used in conjunction with other instructional methods; more needs to be known about the effectiveness of the computer as the major or sole instructional medium. There is not as yet enough information to help classroom teachers determine what sort of application might best be coupled with what type of student under what circumstances to achieve the best results. A few solid studies, however, are available that provide a foundation upon which additional research is being built. Some of these are mentioned on the following pages.

James Kulik and a group of his colleagues at the University of Michigan selected and analyzed fifty-one studies. Although many were fairly current, some dated back to the early days of CAI, when the only available computers were of the large, powerful (mainframe) type. For the most part, Kulik and his staff found that students who were involved in computer-aided learning scored higher on objective tests than did those who were involved in other types of learning activities. Additionally, the studies showed that students learned the materials more rapidly and retained the information for longer periods of time when CAI was the mode of instruction.

Kulik's analysis included only studies involving secondary students (sixth grade and above), in large part due to the fact that much more research has been conducted at this level than at the elementary level. However, a recent study, conducted by the Educational Testing Service, employed disadvantaged children from grades one through six as subjects. The findings from this study were consistent with those reported by the Kulik group. One noteworthy finding was that even a modest ten minutes on the computer each day tended to increase learning, and twenty minutes doubled the learning gain (in mathematics). Though the gains in math were most noticeable, positive results were also observed and measured in other areas.

In a project implemented by Silverman and Dunn at Hempstead High on Long Island, two groups of high school students prepared for the Scholastic Aptitude Test, one group using SAT computer software and the other more traditional materials. The students were tested to determine the difference between test scores recorded at the onset of the project and those derived at the conclusion of the one-month-long study period. Those students who used the software had an average increase of thirty-five points, while the second group gained just ten points. The fact that tests such as the SAT can, in effect, determine the course of an individual's life makes it imperative that the most effective methods available be used by students who plan to participate in the testing. If computerized tutorials prove to be as useful as initial studies seem to indicate, we may be looking at a tool that can have considerable utility for bringing into balance the traditional inequity between the disadvantaged and the privileged sectors.

Certain studies have led to findings that may be useful in determining how to allocate computer-related school resources. A study conducted by Program Design, Inc., a company that publishes educational courseware, indicates that computerized instruction can be highly effective with preschoolers. Two groups of preschool children (one of which was involved with computer-based learning) were employed in the study. All came from the same socioeconomic background and all were given standardized tests at the beginning and at the conclusion of the study. Results were dramatic: the computer group showed a gain of 47.4 percent, while the control group gained a modest 13.5 percent. These results seem to indicate that computer-based learning activities should be made available to all students. On the other hand, the report of the Johns Hopkins group gave some very different conclusions. This research indicated that CAI is most effective when it is used with low achievers, implying "that CAI should possibly be targeted at specific groups of students—not provided wholesale to the entire student population." Other research indicates that CAI is also effective with high achievers, but it appears to be less effective among average students. These findings support the contentions of some that there should be no attempt to force computer literacy onto every student. Note that these studies were based upon the use of CAI in the schools; the conclusions for the less-structured approaches that involve open-ended kinds of activities and for programming-oriented applications are not so clear. In any case, the data tend to reflect a degree of ambiguity. More research is desperately needed before firm conclusions as to how computers should be integrated into the curriculum can be made.

Students sometimes learn most from methods they like least, but not necessarily where other options are available. One problem with many quantitative studies is that they consider only cognitive gain and overlook affective concerns. In the affective area computer-based learning ranks high. Students tend to be very positive when they talk about learning with computers—the unique attributes claimed for computers are precisely the ones that are mentioned by students as making this type of learning interesting.

The fact that computers can and do influence behavior was mentioned previously. According to the Johns Hopkins study the predominant role of microcomputers in schools may very well turn out to be social rather than academic. Kulik also found that teachers tend to perceive the social role of the computer in the classroom as being more important than its academic role.

Studies at the Bank Street College of Education support this point of view. Researchers at this institution found that students worked together more harmoniously when the computer was being used than they did in more traditional educational settings (fig. 1.13). Indeed, this phenomenon is being reported from numerous educators and has been, for the most part, an unanticipated bonus. In

FIGURE 1.13 Computers Encourage Cooperative Learning (Courtesy of Apple Computer, Inc.)

actuality, the anticipated outcome was that computers would become surrogate companions, thus causing students to become antisocial (such individuals are sometimes given the derogatory label "computer nerd"). Although this has happened in a few isolated instances, it certainly doesn't represent the norm.

The study of affect nearly always leads to a consideration of the much-maligned computerized game. It is unfortunate that more research hasn't been conducted in this area because games represent an approach to learning that holds great promise. The positive aspects are often overlooked—games continue to be the subject of much controversy and are frequently condemned.

Unfortunately, a large number of computer games tend to encourage aggressiveness over other more desirable kinds of expression. This is particularly true of arcade-type games, which often serve as models for their educational counterparts. Although research on violence in computer games is virtually nonexistent, such is not the case with other mediums such as television. Among the significant studies is one by Stein et al. that was based on child behavior as it relates to the viewing of violence-laden television programs. The conclusion was that "high action" and "high violence" in TV programs may indeed produce aggressive behaviors in children. This combination—high action and high violence—is employed in many computer games of both the arcade type and the instructional variety. To win the typical game, a player must be both ruthless and aggressive.

In light of the simplistic game rules involved (destroy the enemy as rapidly as you are able), it is claimed by some that such worthwhile traditional instructional activities as problem solving, concept attainment, and even social skills attainment have lost out. In place of being rewarded for achievement in such areas, the player is rewarded for behaviors of an antisocial nature.

Things are not as bad as they might seem to be, however. The new generation of games is much improved. Not only has much of the violence been eliminated, but in the process the games have been made to appeal to female players, who have, in the past, been turned away by the male-oriented "shoot-'em-ups." Field tests and further studies will provide educators with the information needed to determine just how effective the new games are; first impressions tend to indicate that they are highly so.

From the modest beginnings outlined above, educators will see an explosion of useful research studies developing over the next several years. From these will come answers to questions that are raised throughout this and succeeding chapters.

## SUMMARY

The early computers were not suited to educational applications because of high cost, large size, and a certain degree of unreliability. The absence of appropriate programs was another critical factor. Despite these shortcomings, a few educators saw in these complex systems the potential for improving instruction by using the power of the computer to provide individualized activities. Smaller, cheaper minicomputers, an infusion of federal funds, and the refinement of programmed sequences by a growing corps of experts led to the implementation of several notable projects, including PLATO and the Stanford Project. Both monetary and institutional support diminished in the early seventies, and a period of malaise prevailed. With the invention and implementation of the chip, a completely new generation of computers emerged. Placing thousands of miniature electronic components on a single piece of silicon to form a programmable microprocessor, or "computer on a chip," made microcomputers possible. The first such machines were the products of enthusiasts who tailor-made them in private workshops. When the microcomputer was finally introduced to the public in the mid-seventies, the response was overwhelming.

Statistics indicate that schools and homes are acquiring computers at an ever-increasing rate, with acquisition being correlated to socioeconomic status. Research indicates that the primary beneficial effects may well be in the area of affect rather than in cognitive areas. For instance, children working with computers tend to socialize in positive ways; for example, they help one another, offer suggestions, and collaborate to solve a problem. However, learning is also enhanced under some conditions and with certain groups when computer-assisted instruction is used. CAI appears to be most effective with the high- and low-achievement groups and least effective with average students.

Although research on the use of the computer in education continues to expand, much more information is needed before a clear picture of its place in the curriculum and the extent of its effectiveness is obtained.

## REFERENCES

Atkinson, R., and Wilson, H., eds. *Computer-Assisted Instruction*. New York: Academic Press, 1969.

Becker, H. "How Schools Use Microcomputers." *Classroom Computer Learning* (September 1983): 41–44.

_____. "Our National Report Card: Preliminary Results from the New Johns Hopkins Survey." *Classroom Computer Learning* (January 1986): 30–33.

Bushnell, D., and Allen, D. *The Computer in American Education*. New York: John Wiley, 1967.

Fisher, G. "The Social Effects of Computers in Education." *Electronic Learning* (March 1984): 26, 28.

_____. "Where CAI Is Effective: A Summary of the Research." *Electronic Learning* (November/December 1983): 82–84.

Forman, D. "Search of the Literature." *The Computing Teacher* (January 1982): 37–51.

Goodlad, J., O'Toole, J., and Tyler, L. *Computer and Information Systems in Education*. New York: Harcourt, Brace & World, 1966.

Grossnickle, D., and Laird, B. "Profile of Change in Education: Micros Gain Momentum." *Educational Technology* (February 1983): 13–16.

Johns Hopkins University. *School Uses of Microcomputers*. Baltimore: Center for Organization of the Schools, Johns Hopkins University.

Kulik, J., Bangert, R., and Williams, G. "Effects of Computer-based Teaching on Secondary School Students." *Journal of Educational Psychology* 75 (1983): 19–26.

Market Data Retrieval. *Microcomputers in Schools, 1984–1985*. Westport, CT: Market Data Retrieval, 1985.

Ryba, K., and Chapman, J. "Toward Improving Learning Strategies and Personal Adjustment with Computers." *The Computing Teacher* 10 (1983): 48–53.

Siegel, M., and Davis, D. *Understanding Computer-Based Education*. New York: Random House, 1986.

Silverman, S., and Dunn, S. "Raising SAT Scores." *Electronic Learning* (April 1983): 51–55.

Stein, A., et al. "The Effects of TV Action and Violence on Children's Social Behavior." *The Journal of Genetic Psychology* (June 1981): 138, 183–91.

"Survey Maps Computer Use." *Electronic Learning* (January 1986): 12–13.

Taylor, R., ed. *The Computer in the School: Tutor, Tool, Tutee*. New York: Teachers College Press, 1980.

"Up to Date." *Electronic Education* (April 1984): 22.

# 2

---

# THE
# MICROCOMPUTER
# SYSTEM

## INTRODUCTION

To many people the word *computer* conjures up an image of huge, intimidating machines banked in climate controlled rooms hidden away in large corporate buildings. The people who use computers are thought to be an elite group, different from ordinary people, hunched over their glowing cathode ray tubes and whirring disk drives like sorcerers gathered around a bubbling cauldron of unknown substances.

Nothing could be further from the truth. Although the manner in which a computer is constructed is highly technical, and the precise way that data and instructions are managed is complex, modern microcomputers are so designed that with a modest amount of effort and study, anyone can learn to use them effectively.

When you sit down at the microcomputer system several aspects of its physical presence are immediately apparent. The keyboard is there, with an arrangement of keys that reveals its typewriter heritage. There is a monitor, looking much like a television set but lacking a tuner and certain other controls. One or two disk drives, or perhaps a cassette drive, are off to the side. Sometimes the drives are built in, as with units such as the IBM and the Apple Macintosh. Some machines incorporate the keyboard and perhaps the monitor in a modularized system; others provide a keyboard that is movable and can be positioned either on a desk or in your lap if this is the most comfortable place to work. A printer might also be a part of the system, and other devices are often included. These add-ons are called peripherals. The one part of the system that isn't very obvious is the actual computer. It is tucked away in a case that often looks very much like a plastic or metal box. The computer, or *microprocessor* (that part of the computer that actually does the computing, a processor on a single chip), is very small, as you shall see; all of the devices mentioned above are simply there to permit you to get at the computer, use it, and store the results of its work. An Apple or Commodore has the keyboard as an extension of the case in which the computer is housed. The IBM and many others have a separate case to which the keyboard is attached with a cord. Opening the cases on those machines that permit access by the user reveals the microprocessor (a long ceramic or plastic integrated circuit with numerous pins that are engaged in matching sockets) and the various memory units, input/output circuits, power supply, and other components that are necessary to support the microprocessor.

Having seen the complex contents of the case, many people simply put the cover back on and begin to type on the keyboard or run a program. Indeed, it really isn't necessary to know how a computer is constructed and how it does its work to use one effectively. The overused analogy of the car and driver is frequently offered in support of this argument: you don't have to know how an internal combustion engine works in order to operate your automobile. As a general rule, this is a compelling argument; however, teachers are in a rather unique position when compared to computer users in general. There is a very real possibility that a teacher will be called upon to explain some of the intricacies of the computer to her students as well as to colleagues who are just learning about the technology. In addition to this, knowing something about the mechanics and the manner in which the work is done can be most useful in dispelling the mystery surrounding computers. Teachers who understand how computers operate, even at a basic level, will not be intimidated or frightened by them. They will come to know the machines for what they are—electronic devices that slavishly and logically follow the instructions of their human masters.

Just what is a computer? A computer is a tool for accomplishing the data processing functions of input, processing, output, and storage. The computer has proliferated because it processes data and delivers information in large volumes, efficiently, and at relatively low costs. Further, the computer exists because it has introduced the capacity and capability to perform data processing jobs that would have been impossible through other means. One of the impressive features of a computer is its speed. A fast, modern computer can do more arithmetic in one minute than a person using a pencil and paper could do in a lifetime. The computer thus makes it possible to solve many problems that would be completely impossible to do by hand. Most modern advances in science, engineering, and medicine are made possible by the availability of high-speed computers.

Computers come in many sizes, shapes, and colors. They range from very large computer systems called *mainframe* computers to small *minicomputers* to even smaller *microcomputers*. Regardless of size, all computers work on the same basic principles and perform the same basic functions. Mainframes and minicomputers perform the functions faster and can store and handle more data than a microcomputer; however, they all process the data in an identical manner. The similarities and differences between the three types of computers are discussed in this chapter. We briefly present the binary system used by computers and the ASCII code. Discussions are included on how the microprocessor and other units work and how the job of manipulating data is managed, and some suggestions for the maintenance of the microcomputer system are offered.

In this chapter we also discuss the peripheral devices that can be added to the computer to make up a complete system. The peripheral devices that provide both input and output capabilities for a microcomputer are detailed, along with a rationale as to why teachers should know about these devices.

## MAINFRAME COMPUTERS

Mainframe computers are very large, often taking up as much space as the average classroom (nine hundred cubic feet). They can store enormous amounts of information, billions and billions of individual pieces of data. Generally, a large mainframe computer system will cost more than one million dollars. Many large corporations, state and federal agencies, and universities use mainframe computers to assist in the daily operations of record keeping, budget preparation, payroll, personnel data, inventory maintenance, and so forth. The United States Navy uses mainframe computers to help keep track of the movements and locations of its ships and submarines. The U.S. Air Force uses these large computers to keep track of aircraft and satellites.

Mainframe computers usually have many terminals connected to them. These devices are used to send information to, and receive information from, the mainframe computer. Terminals may be in the same room as the computer, in another building, or even in another city. The terminals are interconnected to the mainframe computer via cables, through telephone wires, or by communications satellites. (For a view of a mainframe computer setup, see fig. 2.1.)

Mainframe computers, because they are so large and can store so much information, can do many jobs at one time. For example, the U.S. Air Force has a large computer in Colorado that can communicate with terminals at all Air Force bases in the United States and via satellite with all bases in the world. Large department stores have a computer system that can communicate with terminals in all branch stores around the country.

## MINICOMPUTERS

Minicomputers are smaller than mainframe computers. They usually take up only a small space on the floor; some can fit on a large table. They range in cost from $10,000 to $150,000. They can store large amounts of information,

**FIGURE 2.1  Mainframe Computers** (Courtesy of IBM Corporation)

although not as much as the mainframe computer system. Like mainframe computers, minicomputers can handle more than one job at a time and are interconnected by terminals. (See fig. 2.2.) They are used by medium and small companies as well as by some school systems. A mainframe system may be used to handle information affecting an entire company or agency, while minicomputers are used in the different departments. For example, a government agency may have several departments. Each department handles specialized data that do not concern other departments in the agency. So, rather than use the agency's mainframe system to handle this specialized work, each department has its own minicomputer.

In some medium-sized or small school districts, the minicomputer has the capacity to handle all the varied needs of the district (payroll, pupil records, attendance reports, budget information, and inventory, for example).

## MICROCOMPUTERS

Microcomputers, even smaller than minicomputers, are often called personal or home computers because many people purchase them for personal, home use. They are small and light enough to be portable, fitting on a table or desk. A complete microcomputer system usually costs less than three thousand dollars, sometimes considerably less. Microcomputers cannot store as much information as mainframes or minicomputers, and terminals are usually not connected to them. Unlike the larger, more powerful machines, microcomputers are designed to do only one job at a time. In a typical large organization, the mainframe computers and minicomputers are used to handle major computing chores and the microcomputers are called upon to solve smaller, more individual problems.

For the purpose of this text, we will concentrate on the functions and utilization of the microcomputer. Although the functions it performs are identical to those of the mini- or mainframe computer, there are differences between these machines in speed, capacity, and ability to perform more than one job at a time.

FIGURE 2.2 **Minicomputer** (Courtesy of Granite Mill, Salt Lake City, UT)

In general, a device can be classified as a computer if it:

1. performs *arithmetic* operations on data, including addition, subtraction, multiplication, and division;
2. performs *logical operations*—for instance, it can compare data items to determine whether they are equal or unequal, smaller or larger than each other;
3. can be *programmed*—that is, it can be provided with a set of instructions that processes data without human intervention; and
4. can *store* programs internally, rather than relying on wired panels or other external methods.

Basically, a computer used for data processing must be provided with two ingredients: *instructions* and *data*. The instructions (programs) are prepared by individuals known as programmers. The program is essential to the operation of the computer; it provides the precise instructions for the input, arithmetic, logic, and storage operations that the computer must carry out to complete a data processing job. A program is prepared and entered into the computer, then control is turned over to the computer, which executes, or carries out, the various instructions in the program. Under program control (prepared by a programmer), the computer processes the data without human intervention.

## BINARY IDEAS

The microcomputer is a digital device, that is, it uses discrete signals in its operation. Two states are employed which are, very simply, on and off. This is the basis for the binary (*bi* = two) system. The smallest unit of information in the binary system is called a *bit* (short for binary digit). A bit can have the value of 1 or 0; that is, it can be on or off. Although only two signals are possible, many bits can be linked up in various ways and these extensive combinations can then be used to represent different letters, numbers, and symbols.

In order for this approach to be workable, it is necessary to have some kind of code based on the various combinations of on and off. One such code is the American Standard Code for Information Interchange, or ASCII.

## THE ASCII CODE

Computers don't speak English (or Japanese or Russian) and people don't speak binary; therefore, some method of translating back and forth is essential if people and computers are to communicate with each other. The code that makes this possible is the ASCII code. The human language input at the keyboard is changed into the 1s and 0s of ASCII by electrical circuitry.

On the outside a computer keyboard looks much like the ones used on typewriters, but internally it is very different. Electronic elements are provided that, when activated by a keypress, generate the ASCII codes for specific symbols, numbers, and letters. Note that each letter and number in the ASCII chart (table 2.1) has a special combination of 0s and 1s that is distinctly its own. For example, an *A* is 01000001 (which is the number 65 in binary); and *B* is 01000010 (or binary 66). Each succeeding letter is one number higher, permitting the computer to alphabetize a list of entries quite easily, if this is desired. No two combinations in ASCII are the same; there are more than enough combinations available to represent all of the letters (both upper and lowercase), numbers, and symbols on the keyboard.

**TABLE 2.1  ASCII Code (Partial)**

| A | 01000001 | W | 01010111 | a | 01100001 |
|---|----------|---|----------|---|----------|
| B | 01000010 | X | 01011000 | b | 01100010 |
| C | 01000011 | Y | 01011001 | c | 01100011 |
| D | 01000100 | Z | 01011010 | d | 01100100 |
| E | 01000101 | 0 | 00110000 | + | 00101011 |
| F | 01000110 | 1 | 00110001 | − | 00101101 |
| G | 01000111 | 2 | 00110010 | > | 00111110 |
| H | 01001000 | 3 | 00110011 | ? | 00111111 |
| I | 01001001 | 4 | 00110100 | # | 00100011 |

## MICROCOMPUTER SYSTEM COMPONENTS

All digital computers consist of the same basic components. Let us examine the major components.

### Microprocessor

The real computer in any microcomputing system is actually no bigger than your thumbnail. It consists of thousands of transistors (electronic on/off switches) that, through the use of microphotography, have been squeezed onto a very small segment (called a chip) of silicon. This chip, encased in a piece of ceramic material, is called a microprocessor (see fig. 2.3).

There are other chips within a microcomputer; the microprocessor, however, has features that set it apart from all the others. Microprocessors differ in construction from one brand to another, but all are similar in one respect: they contain the central processing unit (or CPU), which does the actual computations, comparisons, and so on. Some microprocessors contain varying amounts of memory, and others might even add the capability to perform input and output functions; but all contain, as a minimum, the CPU. Let us examine this remarkable device.

**FIGURE 2.3**  Microprocessor

## The Central Processing Unit

The central processing unit controls the flow of instructions and data to and from memory or an input/output device. It also performs operations upon the data to change them in some way. The operation of the CPU is managed by specific instructions, which are provided by a program, the nature of which determines just how the data are to be handled. For example, the instructions intrinsic to a word processing program will cause the CPU to proceed in a manner that will be different from the way it works with a graphics program.

The CPU consists of three basic entities—the control unit, the arithmetic unit, and the logic unit. In most microcomputers, the arithmetic and the logic units are combined into one unit called the ALU. The control unit supervises the sequencing of the work—it handles or controls the operation of all the computer parts—while the ALU actually executes the instructions. It is the CPU that is the actual computer within the computer system.

## Memory

One group of chips within the microcomputer provides memory spaces within which the information that the computer is working on is stored.

The RAM (*random access memory*), like other functions within the computer, is located on silicon chips. One chip may be capable of holding thousands of bits of information, stored in the form of an on or off state corresponding to the 1s and 0s of the binary code with which computers work.

The memory cells of a computer are arranged so that they can be *written to* or *read from* as needed. Thus, memories operate in two basic modes: read and write.

One disadvantage of semiconductor RAM memory units is that they require a constant power source. Since they rely on electrical currents to represent data, all their stored data is lost if the power source fails and no emergency (backup) system exists. Thus, when you turn off your microcomputer or the power is interrupted (for even a split second), the RAM memory is lost. This is called *volatile* memory because it is not permanent.

You will recall that a character in ASCII is made up of a series of 0s and 1s; each 0 or 1 is called a *bit*. A group of 8 bits is termed a *byte*. A computer that has the capability of working with one full byte at a time is termed an 8-bit computer. The terms *bytes, words,* and *characters* are synonymous in a computer with an 8-bit word length. The capacity of RAM is generally measured in kilobytes (K), or thousands of words. Generally one K equals 1,024 units; thus a computer that has 64K of storage can store $64 \times 1,024$, or 65,536 characters.

The amount of RAM available in computers today varies from 4K to 128K in small personal computers, 64K to 512K in professional microcomputers, and all the way up to 16MB (megabytes, or millions of words) to 32MB in large mainframes and super computers.

RAM is still much more expensive than secondary storage (data on diskette, disk, or magnetic cassette tape) on a byte-by-byte basis. As a result, secondary storage is where the vast amount of computer information is held in computer-usable form until required for processing. The capacity of one diskette of secondary storage varies between one hundred thousand and several million bytes of information (more detailed information on secondary storage is presented later in this chapter).

Another group of memory chips provides a place where certain information is stored permanently. This information is built into the computer by the manufacturer and includes such things as instructions that translate a computer language such as BASIC into the only language a computer can understand, the 0s and 1s of machine-language. This type of memory is known as *read only memory* (ROM).

ROM instructions are "hard-wired"; that is, they cannot be changed or deleted by other stored program instructions. This type of memory is permanent, or *nonvolatile*. The only method of changing its contents is by altering the physical construction of the circuits.

All of the chips, RAM and ROM, are plugged into a plastic board called a *motherboard*, which provides an interconnecting network of circuitry for them. See figure 2.4 for a complete diagram of a typical microcomputer. This figure details the location of the CPU, the RAM chips, the ROM chips, the peripheral slots, the power supply, the speaker, the keyboard, and the input/output port.

## PERIPHERAL DEVICES

As we stated at the beginning of this chapter, teachers may need to know how a microcomputer works so they can, in turn, assist students as they learn about computers. The same reasoning applies to peripheral devices, with several

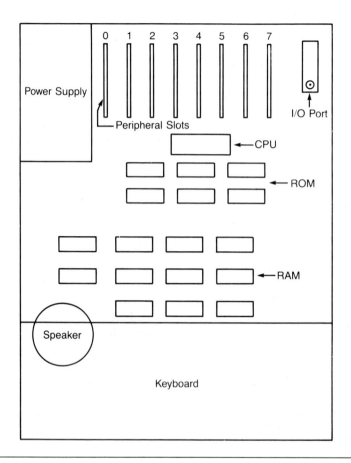

**FIGURE 2.4   Diagram of a Microcomputer**

added concerns. A teacher will need to know what devices are available, how they work, and some idea of costs in order to make wise decisions regarding purchasing peripherals to complete a basic system consisting of the microcomputer, monitor, and disk drives or cassette recorder/player. The teacher will also need to know how to hook up these peripheral devices so they can be utilized by the students (as it is unlikely that someone knowledgeable will be available to do this installation for the classroom teacher). With some basic knowledge, teachers can provide their students with a rudimentary introduction to the operation of these mechanisms.

Several basic components comprise a microcomputer system. The physical machinery (*hardware*) includes input units (such as the keyboard); processing (the actual computer) and storage units (such as disk drives and cassette recorders); and output units (such as a monitor or printer). The system enables the user to enter data into the microcomputer, allows the computer to process and store the data, and provides a means for the computer to return the processed data to the user. Even though both input and output units are mentioned in other chapters in this text, an in-depth discussion of selected units will be helpful and will provide a better understanding of how a complete microcomputer system operates.

## PERIPHERAL STORAGE

The fact that microcomputers are limited in the amount of read-write memory (RAM) that is available makes it necessary to provide for the storage of large amounts of data in some other way. External or peripheral storage devices are available for this purpose. Currently, the floppy disk is the most common mass storage medium in use in the schools, although cassette tapes are also employed. As hard disk systems drop in price, however, these are likely to become popular also.

Cassettes are losing favor because of the slow speed at which data can be accessed. The cassette recorder is less expensive than a disk drive, but it is less reliable and lacks the random access feature of the latter. Also, much more information can be stored on the diskette than on the cassette tape; and, with a disk system, files can be directly accessed just by typing in the name of the file.

The recently introduced 3½-inch disk format is destined to become popular as more companies design machines to use it. In the meantime, the 5¼-inch (commonly referred to as 5-inch) format is far and away the most popular for home and educational applications. Eight-inch floppies hold considerably more data, but the drive is quite expensive. And *hard disks* (finely machined aluminum disks coated with a magnetic material and encased in a rigid housing), capable of storing very large quantities of information, are great for record keeping on a school or district level and for other specialized functions. Although hard disks are currently very expensive to purchase, they are becoming more affordable all the time.

Most operations can be performed with a single disk drive, but there are times when two disk drives are not only handy but essential. For example, when using an authoring language such as PILOT to write lessons, a lesson disk must be in the second drive to save the program that is written. Although many two-disk programs work fine on a single drive, the inconvenience of switching back and forth from the disk containing the program to the one saving data makes the purchase of a second drive a good investment.

Disks of a common size don't always hold the same amount of information; some computer systems are designed so that they make better use of the storage space on the disk than do others. The most common way to store data is to place it on only one side of the disk in a pattern that is termed single-density. But it is possible to place twice as much data on a single side by cramming it together— this is termed double-density. In order to do this, the disk must have a higher quality ferrite (iron oxide) coating than is necessary for single-density storage, so the cost goes up.

Storage is also increased when both sides are used. This type of disk is used in drives that have two read-write heads, one for each of the two sides. Or, the disk can be flipped over and used in the traditional way in a standard drive. Double-sided disks have been certified on both sides, while the single-sided ones are certified on one side only. It is therefore possible to store four times as much data on a double-sided, double-density disk as on a typical single-sided, single-density one. Whichever type is used, the drive must be compatible with the particular disk format.

It seems appropriate at this point to discuss the care that must be exercised in handling and utilizing the disk drive system. It is very critical that the disk be inserted properly into the drive mechanism (see fig. 2.5). Note the placement of the thumb over the label and the position of the read-write opening on the diskette.

With proper care, diskettes last for a long time. Here are some suggestions that will help extend their lives.

1. Always store the disk in its protective envelope when not in use. Make sure that the read-write opening is covered by the envelope.
2. When handling the disk, do not touch the exposed surface (that portion you can see through the read-write opening). A thumb print on this portion of the diskette can cause the disk drive to misread information stored there.
3. Be careful where you place the disk—never expose it to a magnetic field. Electrical devices such as monitors and TV receivers emit magnetic signals that can damage the program on the disk.
4. When you label a disk, use a felt marker. The pressure from a ballpoint pen or pencil may destroy the data on the disk.

FIGURE 2.5   Properly Inserted Disk

5. Don't leave the disk in your car, particularly on very hot or very cold days.
6. Do not bend the disk: you may damage it.
7. Do not use alcohol to clean the disk surface. The alcohol will cause the magnetic coating on the surface of the diskette to separate from the plastic base.
8. Never attach anything to the disk with a paper clip.
9. A good rule to follow when placing the disk in the drive is the "rule of thumb." Place your thumb over the label (on the top) and carefully insert the disk (never force it) into the drive (see fig. 2.5).
10. Store the disks upright in their original boxes or in cases available commercially for this purpose.

The flexible disk, diskette, or floppy disk (it is called any one of these three names in the current literature) was introduced in 1973 to replace punched cards as a medium of data entry. It can also store programs and data files. The diskette comes in three standard sizes, 8 inches, 5¼ inches, and 3 inches. It is made of plastic and coated with a thin, precisely placed iron oxide coating; the disk is then permanently sealed in a plastic or paper jacket lined with a soft paper coating containing hundreds of small holes that absorb and contain the dust and dirt particles that may scratch and damage the disk surface.

Diskettes sell for under five dollars in most cases; they are reusable, easy to store, and weigh less than two ounces. A typical floppy disk can store the equivalent of as many as three thousand punched cards.

## HARD DISK (WINCHESTER) DRIVES

More and more large schools and many school districts are now making the switch to hard disks for storing programs and data and for "networking" systems (consult chapter 6, on telecommunication, for additional details). The hard disk devices can hold huge amounts of information, so many schools equipped with a hard disk drive can easily store their entire software collection and associated data files on one hard disk. In addition to the great convenience of having all needed information stored on a single storage device, most hard disk users find that their units are faster, easier to use, and more reliable than floppy disk drives.

Hard disk drive units, called *Winchester drives*, employ fixed cartridges containing a disk formed from aluminum and coated with iron oxide (as in the floppy disk). The fixed cartridge concept means that the heart of the Winchester system—the disk—with its associated read-write head mechanism, is sealed in a dustproof housing. Winchester head-disk assemblies are put together in "clean rooms" so microscopic dust particles do not get on the disk surface. This great care is necessary because the head, unlike that in the floppy disk drive, does not ride on the surface of the disk. The hard disk spins at 3,600 rpm and literally floats over the surface on a cushion of air.

The advantages of hard disk drive systems are in their storage capacity, speed of operation, and relative permanency of stored information. An eight-inch hard disk unit can store up to twenty megabytes (millions of characters) of information—approximately four hundred pages, single-spaced, of instantly accessible data. Hard disks can transfer data at speeds up to ten times faster than floppy drives; therefore, a hard disk unit can get needed information into a microcomputer's RAM at lightning speed. The stored information is relatively permanent, so if the system is properly designed, commonly used programs will be instantly available instead of requiring insertion of a disk, loading, and executing a desired program.

The greatest drawback to a hard disk system is cost, average cost being several times greater than for a floppy disk drive. Even with these high costs, however, many schools and school districts are finding that the speed and great storage capacity are worth the expense when networking and storage of large amounts of data are required.

## THE DISPLAY

The most common output devices used with today's classroom microcomputers are cathode ray tubes (CRTs) and printers. We will discuss the cathode ray tube first.

There are basically two kinds of CRT screens. The first is the regular television set hooked up to a special modulator adaptor that allows the TV to receive computer signals instead of television programs.

The differences between using a computer monitor and a standard television receiver coupled to your microcomputer are in speed of display, amount of data capable of being handled, and quality of the picture. With a standard television the colors tend to smear together: there is a lack of distinct edges between various colors, and the colors are not pure in hue or saturation. There is also the problem called overscan, in which the picture goes beyond the edges of the screen. This is acceptable with broadcast television but can cause important details on the edge of the picture to be blurred or even omitted in microcomputer utilization.

The slower speed of display and reduced amount of data handled by a standard television set are major drawbacks because these two factors affect color quality. The information handled corresponds roughly to dots of light on the screen; the more dots, the clearer and sharper the image. The total number of dots, or pixels (short for picture elements), that can be displayed is limited because of the TV receiver's *bandwidth* (the range of frequencies available for transmission of data). The bandwidth of a television receiver is not sufficient to accommodate all the data that can be sent to the CRT by a microcomputer. In simple terms, the standard television receiver will not handle the data fast enough or clearly enough to be legible and sharp on the screen; therefore, a user gets a poor-quality picture that can cause eyestrain and muscle fatigue after a short period of viewing the screen.

The second CRT device, and one that is much superior to the TV receiver for use with a microcomputer, is a *monitor*. A monitor is like a television receiver minus the front-end electronics. You can't tune to any channels with it, and it won't amplify signals from the antenna. It simply takes the video signal coming from the microcomputer and passes it through to the circuitry that drives the cathode ray tube. With the exception of a channel-selector knob, a monitor has all the usual controls: vertical and horizontal, brightness, contrast, tone, and (in color sets) color. Most monitors have a separate on/off switch, so they must be turned on or off independently of the microcomputer (unless you use a central control switch).

A monitor is designed to handle higher and wider bandwidths than those of a standard television receiver. The television signal that most monitors are designed to accept is called NTSC (National Television System Committee) video or *composite* video. This video signal can't be sent over the airwaves on the specific frequencies designed by the Federal Communications Commission for television stations. It is designed to be transmitted via the cable that is hooked from the monitor to your microcomputer. *Composite* means that the picture information that defines the beginning of each horizontal scan line (there are 525 lines needed to fill the entire surface of the screen) and the number of pictures per second are tied together into synchronized pulses that the monitor can understand and translate into a picture. There are thirty complete pictures/displays on the screen each second.

## MONITORS

You are likely to encounter three types of computer monitors: monochrome, composite color, and RGB. Following is a brief description of each.

### Monochrome

Monochrome means one color, usually green or amber against a black background. Amber screens have become popular because many people believe that they are easier on the eyes. There is no scientific evidence to back up this claim, however; it seems to be a matter of personal preference. Generally, amber monitors cost a bit more than green ones.

Monochrome monitors have quite sharp displays, and they are the least expensive, commonly available for less than $200.

### Composite Color

A color monitor is a bit more complex than a monochrome one. A color monitor contains three electron devices (instead of one as in a monochrome monitor) to create the scan lines on the picture tube. These devices, called "guns," generate the three colors red, green, and blue. The composite color monitors employ, basically, the same technology as used in conventional color television sets except that the speed with which they handle data and the sharpness of the picture are enhanced. This type of monitor has one composite electron signal that controls all three of the color guns; thus the beam of light that strikes the front of the picture tube is a combination of red, green, and blue. Most composite color monitors cost within the range of $250 to $400.

## RGB

The sharpest color monitors are the RGB monitors. RGB stands for "red, green, blue"—the basic colors all TVs and monitors use to produce a color picture. With RGB monitors, unlike regular TVs and composite monitors, a separate video signal is used for each of the three color guns. These discrete signals mean that color intensities can be transmitted more precisely and decoded by the monitor more rapidly, making it possible to produce sharper images than those of the composite video monitor or regular TV. The RGB monitor is more expensive than the composite, ranging in price from $400 to $5,000.

### Test for Monitor Quality

Once you have narrowed down your choice to a monochrome, composite color, or RGB monitor, you should try one out yourself before making a purchase. You may need to spend time in a few different microcomputer stores, but it will be time well spent. Many vendors will bring a monitor right to your school to let you try it out for a few days. Be sure to ask for this service; if the vendor will let you borrow the monitor you can try it out on your students.

In the store or at your school, there are a few tests you can perform to help determine how good a monitor is and how well it suits your needs.

- *Convergence* (point at which the beams of light come together in a color monitor). The critical area is around the screen's edges, where the television tube's face curves back and the electron beams are shot at their most acute angle. Fill the screen with one letter—an N, H, Z, M, or E—by pressing down on the key and holding it down. Adjust the monitor so the letters are white; this requires all three electron guns to work at full strength. Now look closely at all the letters around the screen's perimeter, especially in the corners. Are there any colored fringes? How bad are they? If such fringes are present, they are caused by poor manufacturing or design, or improper factory adjustment. The factory adjustment can be corrected; the poor workmanship or design cannot.
- *Screen loss.* With the text still on the screen, look again to see if any letters are chopped off at the screen's top or bottom edge. If there is any loss, look for another brand or manufacturer's model: the inadequacy of this model is obvious.
- *Horizontal and vertical lines.* Again, with the text still on the screen, stand about six feet back from the screen and stare at it straight on. Do all the horizontal lines of characters look horizontal? Are the vertical lines in a

vertical position? With allowances for the natural curve of the tube's face, you should not see much degree of wavering. If you do, it generally means faulty design or poor manufacturing.

- *Cursor smear.* Clear the screen and move the cursor across the screen at maximum speed. This is generally accomplished by holding down on the space bar. Do you see a trail, or smear, behind the moving cursor? If you do see this trail, the surface of the monitor may be coated with special phosphors designed to glow longer than others. These long-persistence phosphors prevent flickering but are not suitable for applications that require rapidly changing images as with CAI packages. This smear can be very frustrating to your students and can even cause eye fatigue.

- *Monitor flicker.* Place a few words on the screen or even a small figure. Does the image seem to flicker? If it does, it generally means the electron guns are not emitting rays that strike the surface of the monitor rapidly enough to prevent the flicker. In some cases your eyes may be very sensitive and you can detect this problem. In either case, this flicker is likely to get on your nerves and could cause eyestrain.

These little tests will give you a good general idea of the quality of the monitor; still, the most important consideration is your own viewing comfort. Seat yourself in the normal viewing position you would take when using the microcomputer. Now stare at the screen and decide if you like what you see. Do you like the colors or, when necessary, the lack of them? Are you satisfied with the resolution? Do you like the appearance of the characters? How is the brightness? The contrast? Are the controls conveniently located and accessible, or is the access door difficult to unlatch? Do you need to get up to adjust these controls, or are they right in front of you? Make the effort while shopping or previewing a monitor to deal with these questions seriously so you will select a monitor you will be pleased with and can live with for many school sessions.

Before we conclude our discussion on the selection of a monitor, it is important that we suggest the securing of a glare-free screen and a mechanism to hold the monitor that has the capability of being tilted or adjusted for users of varying heights. There are growing indications that the glare and difficult viewing angles experienced by users of a microcomputer monitor are the two major factors causing eyestrain and body fatigue. There are even some indications that extended use of high-phosphor CRTs seems to produce some physical problems and that the ambient radiation from extended exposure to color monitors by young children may enhance such problems as eyestrain, backache, irritability, and neck strain.

## New Monitor Technologies

Flat-panel displays are now on the market. They are the latest innovations that may change the look of the traditional CRT. They are not yet available as monitors for most standard microcomputers; however, they are being used in the latest lap-sized portable computers and most likely will become practical as monitors for microcomputers within the next few years.

We will discuss four types of flat-panel displays that seem to hold promise for use with personal computers—liquid crystal, plasma, electroluminescent, and electrophoretic. All four of the new technologies are based on solid-state electronics rather than on electron beams; therefore they are much more rugged and consume less power than a cathode ray tube. Their slim profile and light weight make them ideal for small, portable microcomputers. Another positive feature is that flat screens do not distort images around the edges as CRTs do.

**Liquid Crystal Display.**  Liquid crystal displays (LCDs) have been used in watches, calculators, and other electronic devices for some years now and are currently available on portable computers such as Radio Shack's TRS 80 model 100. To provide this kind of display, a liquid crystal material is deposited between two sheets of polarizing material; this sandwich is in turn squeezed between two glass panels containing thin wire electrodes arranged in a very closely spaced grid pattern.

In a normal state, light shines through the two polarizers and is reflected back to the viewer. When a current is passed between two crossing electrodes, the resulting electromagnetic field aligns the liquid crystals so that light cannot shine through, thus producing a dark pixel on the light background.

One drawback to a liquid crystal display panel is that because the LCDs emit no light of their own, there must be a reliance on reflected light to see what is on the screen. This limits the viewing angle to a very narrow range, requiring that the viewer observe the screen very straight on.

**Plasma Display Panel.**  Plasma display panels include two glass plates with finely spaced electric wires. Sealed between the glass plates is a mixture of neon gasses that glows with an orange color at the point where an electric field is created between two electrodes (fine wires) that cross. The Photonics Corporation is developing a plasma display for the U.S. Army that can pack two thousand pixels into each square centimeter of a two-square-meter screen. IBM Corporation is creating a plasma display that is a three-inch-thick panel intended for use as a display terminal for the IBM mainframe computers. The General Digital Corporation is offering a touch-sensitive plasma screen that is extremely sensitive and accurate.

**Electroluminescent Panel.**  As with the other flat-panel displays, the front panel of an electroluminescent display contains a set of closely spaced vertical wires that are invisible to the eye. The back panel includes a similar set of horizontal wires. A layer of zinc sulfide and manganese is sandwiched between these two panels. When a current is sent through a vertical and horizontal wire, an electrical field is set up at the point where the wires cross and an orange- or yellow-colored pixel is generated. Currently, a 12-by-21-inch electroluminescent panel can provide a resolution of 240 by 320 pixels on the monitor screen. The price has dropped dramatically in recent months, and soon this type of display may be economically feasible for microcomputer use.

**Electrophoretic Display.** Electrophoretic displays offer one unique advantage over the other three screens: the screen "remembers" the image it is displaying. Once a dot is turned on, no further power is needed to make it glow. These panels contain electrically charged particles of colored pigment suspended in a fluid of a contrasting color. As with the other panels, glass sheets on the front and back contain sets of closely spaced wires aligned in a vertical and horizontal grid pattern. When a current is passed through two crossing wires, the electric field pulls the charged pigment particles to the front surface of the screen, creating a colored dot. These particles stay in position against the front panel until the pixel is erased by reversing the electric field, which sends the particles to the rear surface of the panel where they are no longer seen.

## PRINTERS

The two major kinds of printers are impact and nonimpact. Characters are formed in the one case through physically striking the paper surface with the printing element (like a typewriter); nonimpact printers use no such physical action.

The most common type of printer is the dot matrix impact printer, which uses a matrix of tiny wires from which any character can be formed. In this type of printer, characters are not formed by a type element (such as a ball, thimble, or wheel) but are stored as a pattern or matrix of dots in a memory inside the printer. When using dot matrix technology to print, the pattern of dots is retrieved by the output device and transferred dot by dot to the impacting mechanism of the printer. Compared to printing with a formal character set (such as a daisy wheel), dot matrix printing has fewer restrictions on the size or style of characters. Since characters or images are produced by a selected pattern of dots, the software program being utilized can change the number, size, and style of characters. It can even produce graphics and draw pictures, filling in the graphs and images dot by dot. With the addition of multicolored ribbons, the dot matrix printer can produce text and graphs in several colors.

The other common type of impact printer is the daisy wheel printer, which uses an element composed of "petals" upon whose tips the raised characters are located. This style of printer is slower than the dot matrix variety and does not permit the quality production of graphics; however, the daisy wheel printer produces a typed copy that is termed "letter quality." This means that the printed document is of the same quality in terms of legibility, evenness of print, and formation of letters, symbols, and numbers as that achieved by an electric typewriter. This is the quality that is generally required for business correspondence, textbook copy, advertising layouts, magazine text copy, research papers, and so on. (See fig. 2.6 for samples of impact printing.)

Nonimpact printers use methods other than striking the printing head or matrix to form characters. Typically, they are quieter than the varieties mentioned above, and they tend to be more reliable and cheaper.

dot matrix printer

# dot matrix printer

letter quality line printer

# letter quality line printer

**FIGURE 2.6   Sample of Type from a Dot Matrix Printer and Letter-Quality Type Sample from a Daisy Wheel Printer** (©1983 Burgess Publishing Company. Used by permission.)

Thermal and electrosensitive printers burn dots into special papers. Thermal printers use heated wires to do the job, whereas the electrosensitive models employ dots of light to burn off the outer layer from a special paper to expose the darker underlayer. Both kinds are very fast in the more expensive models but relatively slow in the cheaper lines. The special papers are expensive, and the final draft is considered to be inferior to the product from other types of printers. However, as the technology improves, these options will become increasingly more attractive.

Inkjet printers release tiny globules of ink through a matrix of holes to form characters. Due to the manner in which the ink tends to fuse together, the characters are very clean and sharp. These printers have few moving parts so they are very reliable and quiet in operation. (See fig. 2.7.)

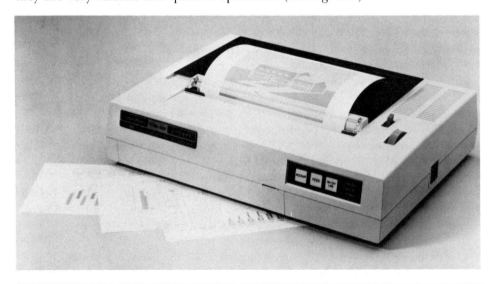

**FIGURE 2.7   A Color Inkjet Printer from Radio Shack** (Reproduced by written permission from Tandy Corporation)

Don't buy a printer before you have tried out a number of different kinds in your price range. Look for qualities such as speed, the nature of the printed character, and noise level. Be cautious that you do not purchase a printer that does not print below the line; that is, the bottom of such letters as p, g, and y needs to descend below the level of the printed line. Also, the need for subscripts and superscripts for scientific or math applications is an important consideration, as is the ability to print special characters such as Greek letters or math symbols. Good documentation is certainly an asset if you are unfamiliar with printers. A critical consideration is whether or not there are reliable repair and service agencies available locally.

Some printers produce excellent graphics and others have color capabilities, which are features to consider if such luxuries are needed and can be afforded. Even certain low-cost printers have special features such as the ability to print in boldface and to underline—always check for such things before you buy. Graphics are possible with a dot matrix printer *only* if the computer has a graphics-capable interface board. Often users buy graphics software only to discover that to use it they need to replace their text-only interface with a graphics-capable interface such as a "Grappler +."

A printer does not have to be of the same brand as the computer to work. A few modifications may be required to match up the units, such as a different connector from the computer to the printer or a different interface board, but these are normally easy to make.

Printers have different kinds of feed mechanisms. Friction feed is like the method used by typewriters where a single sheet is fed through at a time. The more common method is tractor or pin feed: in this case sprockets are provided whose pins engage the holes in the continuous supply of fanfold paper. The more versatile printers employ both kinds of feed, thereby permitting the user to print a special letter on a sheet of bond paper or to tractor feed numerous pages of cheaper paper for inexpensive hard copy.

Of the several kinds of available printers, the daisy wheel is the most practical for school use when letter-quality hard copy is needed. Most daisy wheel elements can be changed to permit a variety of typefaces and degrees of boldness to be printed.

Although the low-cost dot matrix printer is the most widely used for hard-copy printouts, the quality is not the best. On the other hand, high-resolution dot matrix machines are capable of creating copy that is very nearly as sharp and clean as that produced by character printers. They do this through the inclusion of more and finer dots in the characters. Printers of this kind have the advantage of being able to print out a wide variety of fonts without the need for element changes.

Printers not only provide hard copy, but some also have a graphics capability. It is a relatively straightforward matter to create colorful, stunning graphics on the computer screen, but it is another problem to do the same thing on paper. Graphics output devices are available, but many are far too expensive for most schools to afford. At the low end, once again, are the dot matrix printers, which constitute the most common hard-copy graphics device, using patterns of dots to create pictures rather than letters and numbers.

Printers other than impact varieties are also available for hard-copy graphics production. Inkjet printers produce nice graphics because the ink tends to blend, for a softer effect.

## PLOTTERS

A different breed of device for the production of hard-copy graphics is the plotter. These machines are quite different from printers in appearance and construction, but this seems to be an appropriate place to mention them. They contain from one to eight pens of different colors that descend and ascend in concert with signals from the computer to place marks upon a moving sheet of paper. Basically, a plotter is much like an electrocardiograph in the manner in which it works, but the signals are coming from the computer rather than from a human heart.

A plotter produces the image on paper by controlling the motion of the pen carriage that draws the lines. The output medium of paper is utilized by the plotter as a series of $x, y$ coordinates. If you were to plot similar coordinates on a piece of graph paper and then draw lines connecting the points, you would have an approximate visual metaphor of how a plotter draws lines. The microcomputer sends the plotter a series of numbers that represent $x, y$ coordinates in the desired pattern. The pen carriage then moves to the different positions while holding the pen or pens on the surface of the page. Curves are drawn by linking together a series of short straight lines, much in the same way curves are produced on the monitor screen. Figure 2.8 shows a plotter from the Houston Instrument Company.

## MODEMS

Several data base networks operating in various places around the country can provide a wealth of information to those who are set up to access them. (See chapter 6, on telecommunication, for details.) The major problem at present, at least for many schools, is the cost. There is typically an initial network membership fee and an hourly on-line fee, which varies in amount from one system to another. The Source, CompuServe, and Dow Jones are among the larger, better-known companies, but others have been established at universities and colleges that offer information of value in many subject areas.

The advantage of telecomputing for students is obvious: it's as if they had a first-class library right at their fingertips, but without the inconveniences. By hooking into the system through a modem and a microcomputer, students can access the extensive data base directly from the classroom, and the information is always as current as today.

The *modem* (for modulator-demodulator) is used to convert the digital 0s and 1s of the machine language of the computer into voice signals for transmittal

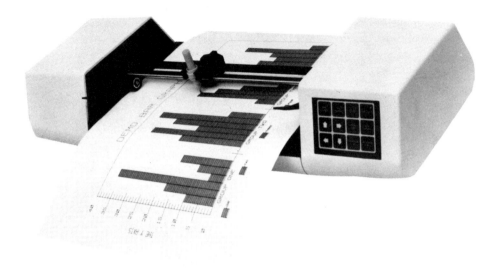

**FIGURE 2.8  A Plotter from Houston Instrument Company**

over telephone lines. There are two types of modems—the acoustic coupler and the direct-connect varieties. The acoustic coupler employs the telephone handset, while the direct-connect type is attached within the computer or between it and the telephone jack. The latter type costs more than the acoustic coupler, but the advantages are most likely worth the extra cost. Some microcomputers come with a built-in modem.

Along with the modem it is necessary to have the appropriate software to run it. The software takes care of the problem of getting information from the computer to the modem and vice versa.

## ALTERNATIVE INPUT DEVICES

The keyboard is the most common device for getting information into the computer, but a number of alternatives exist for accomplishing the same purpose without the need to know how to type. Young children can't type, and neither can many adults; also, people with various kinds of handicaps find it difficult or impossible to communicate with the computer through the keyboard. Moreover, folks who can type often find certain of these options to be highly attractive for various applications.

Alternative input devices aren't meant to replace the keyboard entirely but to supplement it. You will use the keyboard to input text for the printer or to write a program in most cases, but there are a few special devices that actually permit the input of textual material.

No attempt will be made here to describe all of the available alternative input devices; rather, a selection has been made of those that appear to have the greatest utility for the largest number of readers.

### The Mouse

An input device that was popularized when introduced by Apple's Lisa computer, the mouse is rapidly becoming the "electronics marvel" of the input function on microcomputer systems. It has been estimated that by the end of the eighties at least one-third and possibly over half of all computer work stations, and especially microcomputer stations, will utilize the mouse technology for input functions.

Why the excitement over the mouse? Simply because the mouse is a versatile cursor-mover that helps make a computer vastly easier and faster to use. With a mouse you can move the cursor to any point on the screen virtually as fast as you can point with your finger. You simply move the mouse around on your desk and with the click of the button on the top of the mouse, you can delete, move, save, scroll, or otherwise manipulate text and graphic data. You can even draw with a mouse, though not the detailed work that can be done with a graphics tablet (described later in this chapter). The mouse is a perfect tool for picking up symbols, words, sentences, figures, textures, and so forth and carrying them to other locations in your text or drawing.

Now that the mouse is being used with the popular Macintosh (Apple Computer) microcomputer, we may well see a mouse population explosion and the introduction of additional kinds, shapes, and sizes of mouse accessories that could make microcomputers totally understandable in human terms, or *user friendly.* (See fig. 2.9.)

### Light Pens

Some types of light pens work in much the same way as the mouse, but they are very different in appearance. A light pen looks like an ordinary fountain pen with a cord attached to it that connects to your microcomputer (see fig. 2.10). Some models of light pens are used to direct the cursor through movements that are traced on a surface; others are touched directly to the screen surface to do such things as draw lines, move icons, and so on.

The light pen lets you interact directly with what you see on the monitor, turning the microcomputer screen into a canvas or sketch pad for drawing or painting. Working with a light pen is very similar to coloring with a crayon or pointing a finger, thereby enabling children to interact quickly and easily with the microcomputer. Children do not need to have the ability to read or recognize shapes that utilizing the keyboard demands of them.

The quality of a light pen is usually determined by its resolution, or its degree of accuracy. One other factor that determines the light pen's overall performance is the quality and accuracy of the on/off switch. This on/off function

FIGURE 2.9   **A Mouse** (Courtesy of Apple Computer, Inc.)

FIGURE 2.10   **The Gibson Light Pen from Koala Technologies** (Courtesy of Koala Technologies Corporation)

can be either a mechanical part of the light pen or a part of the software program. With a mechanical switch, you usually push a small button on the side of the pen, touch a specific key on the keyboard of the microcomputer, or touch the tip of the pen to the monitor screen to select a location on the screen. With the on/off function as a part of the software program, the program constantly checks the screen location and assumes you have selected a specific location when you stop moving the pen.

When choosing a light pen, you will want to consider at least three factors. First is the degree of resolution the particular application requires. If the light pen will be used to create designs, play games, make menu selections, or introduce children to microcomputers, a light pen costing from forty to sixty dollars (including pen and software) will do the job very nicely.

The second factor is the quality and variety of software that works with the pen. A slightly more expensive pen that comes with plenty of software is probably a better value than a less expensive pen with only one application.

The third factor that must be considered when using the pen with elementary age children is how easy it is to use. For young users, a pen with a software switch where the pen is pointed to get a reaction may be the best. Mechanically triggered pens, however, do give more control over the input of information to the microcomputer. These pens require a child to find the correct key on the keyboard or push the trigger while aiming the pen. Although pushing a button on the side of the pen is simple to do, the act of pushing the switch may move the pen. The push-tip (push the pen tip on the monitor screen surface) is probably the most efficient method, but it is only available on the most expensive pens and can cost as much as $150.

As a teacher in the classroom, responsible for a computer literacy program, you should consider the purchase of a light pen. This can be a very worthwhile investment that can keep the lines of communication open between the students and the microcomputer.

## Touch Screens

Imagine sitting in front of the computer screen examining a list of activities that you can do. This is common practice, to be sure, but if your machine is equipped with a touch screen, the next steps are quite atypical. For example, if word processing is the choice, a simple touch of your finger on the screen at the location of the word processing option will put you in this mode.

The word processing functions are also activated by the touch of a finger. If editing is needed, this can be done without the need to type in commands. As mentioned previously, there are numerous applications for which touch screens can be used. Despite this, they are infrequently seen in the schools; perhaps the lack of fine discrimination between detailed points is a factor.

Some very interesting applications of touch screens are used in entertainment and business enterprises. For example, Walt Disney's EPCOT Center combines infrared touch technology with color video monitors to create an interactive visitor information system. Visitors to the amusement park can secure a wide variety of information about the park, its various attractions, their locations, and special features by touching one of the many video monitors located throughout the park. These monitors are a great attraction to people who visit the EPCOT Center.

The Apple Computer Corporation uses infrared touch technology to provide their dealers with an interesting electronic point-of-purchase sales technique. The dealer can place the freestanding display system in a prominent location in the store where customers can use the system to view one or more displays of information about various microcomputer systems.

Many teachers are exploring the use of the touch screen, especially with young children. This technology provides yet another way for students to bypass the keyboard while effectively inputting data into their microcomputer.

### Graphics Tablets

Electronic drawing is possible on a sensitive surface called a graphics tablet. Most graphics tablets are a one-quarter to one-inch-thick plotting board that is generally six to twelve inches on a side. Some varieties have a pen or arm attached to this plotting board that is utilized in the drawing operation. Others employ a stylus for pointing and drawing. As the pen or arm contacts the surface of the plotting board, a difference in electrical charge is detected, and the drawn image is stored in the memory of the microcomputer. (A specific device known as a digitizer converts the analog measurements into digital form.) One type of tablet contains a horizontal and vertical grid of sensor wires covered, generally, with a thin plastic overlay to protect the wires from pen or stylus movement. As the pen or stylus moves over the grid, it makes contact with specific points, and these points are correlated with points on the display screen; thus a screen graphic is created that replicates the combination of movements on the tablet. The data from the graphics are stored in memory so the completed drawing can be converted to hard copy on a printer or plotter or stored on a data disk for later use in a program.

One of the popular graphics tablets is the KoalaPad (see fig. 2.11). This is a slender, hand-held, six-by-eight-inch pad with a touch-sensitive surface. To use the pad, the student selects an option from a menu (much the same as with the touch screen mentioned above) and then proceeds to create various kinds of displays by using commands that are defined in the menu. This device emphasizes a discovery approach to learning. It permits the user to design an endless array of graphic pictures quite simply. Other kinds of activities are also possible with this affordable and intriguing device.

Another of these devices is the VersaWriter, which has an arm that can be moved about on the tablet. Commands are entered on the keyboard, and the movement of the arm causes lines to be generated that reflect the nature of the command. For example, different line widths can be selected, and, in response

FIGURE 2.11   A KoalaPad from Koala Technologies (Courtesy of Koala
Technologies Corporation)

to these, the nature of the line will vary. Routines such as circle generation and
color fills are also provided.

The VersaWriter is a digitizer consisting of a one-quarter-inch-thick plotting board with a clear plastic overlay. Attached to the plotting board is the
double-jointed drawing arm with digitizers/potentiometers at the elbow and top
locations and a magnifier lens with a dot in the center at the end of the arm.

The VersaWriter also has a two-disk software package that provides several
interesting features and capabilities. Disk one displays a menu that will allow you
to draw, calibrate the system (tablet), recall a picture from a disk, catalog the disk,
add text to a picture, calculate area and distance, and display a set of electrical
schematic symbols. The software allows you to draw in different scales ($125 \times$ to
$4 \times$), so the original drawing can be reduced or expanded on the monitor screen.
Six colors are available, and five different line widths, from a thin line to a paintbrush effect, can be chosen. Other options on the "draw" menu allow you to create a shape tablet, store a picture, or recall a picture that has previously been
drawn. The finished graphic design, including the printed text, can be produced
in hard copy on a printer or plotter and could be inserted into a software program that you have created. The plotting board, arm, and software sell for about
three hundred dollars.

We have included a rather detailed discussion of KoalaPad and Versa-
Writer, two of the more popular graphics tablets, to give you an idea of how they

work and their capabilities for producing graphic images that could be utilized in a computer literacy program or in a school-produced package.

## Voice Input Devices

Voice input technology is merely in its infancy, but some rather astounding results are being seen. Most of the voice input devices are quite expensive, but a few are within the range of affordability for many schools.

For about one thousand dollars it is possible to purchase a unit that enables the computer to learn up to one thousand words, which are divided into twenty-five groups of forty words each. This system, called Shadow/VET, is produced by Scott Instruments of Denton, Texas. The system includes a headset, a small interface box, and a peripheral card that interfaces the system to the computer. This system has its own memory on the interface board so as not to use any of the computer memory space. A master vocabulary allows the user to switch back and forth between all of these forty-word lists without even touching the keyboard.

Another device, called Apple Voice Input Module, comes complete with an interface board, a microphone, a utility desk, and an instruction manual.

Having the computer understand verbal input is termed "speech recognition." The opposite transaction—having the computer speak to the user—is called "speech synthesis." Although the latter is not an input operation, this is an appropriate place to mention it.

The categories of voice input are speech recognition and speaker verification. Most input devices are of the speaker verification type; that is, the microcomputer is only capable of recognizing a voice that has been preprogrammed into the memory of the computer. When someone talks to the computer, her speech is converted into digital information and stored in memory. When the user says that word again, the computer takes that digital data and compares it to words in memory. In essence, the computer develops a pattern for each word and then searches through the memory to see if there are any other patterns of the same size and shape. If one is found, the computer then follows the instructions associated with that word.

The uses of voice input devices in the field of special education are promising, to say the least. One use is as a reader for those who are blind, and a second application is as a voice for those who are unable to speak. Consider those who cannot speak distinctly, for example, but who can make consistent sounds. The computer will recognize those sounds just as it will recognize English, French, Russian, or Latin. Attach a speech synthesizer, such as the Votrax Type 'N Talk (Maryland Computer Services, Inc., Forest Hill, MD), and the microcomputer will translate these sounds into plain English.

The Votrax system uses a synthesizer board that is capable of producing or vocalizing sixty-four different phonemes—phonetic sounds such as *th*, *sh*, and long and short vowels. The on-board microprocessor converts letters and groups of letters into digital code corresponding to these phonemes, employing English pronunciation rules; for example, the silent *e* rule tells the microprocessor that an *e* is silent when it is followed by a space or by punctuation and preceded by a combination of one or more vowels and a consonant. Approximately four hundred such pronunciation rules enable the system to produce intelligible speech. The system provides the capability of reading aloud a single character or symbol, a full word, a line, or an entire page. Its full speech capability allows it to pronounce any word, no matter how the word is spelled.

One last consideration is for those who cannot talk at all. With any form of physical movement, they can train the microcomputer to recognize Morse code or any other combination of sounds. The possibilities are endless, and the future holds great promise for devices that will be less expensive, easier to use, and more human-sounding in character.

## Joysticks

The name *joystick* comes from the steering device used in older airplanes, but the resemblance stops there. Electronic joysticks are used to move the cursor around on the screen. When a game is involved, the cursor may be replaced by a movable configuration that can take the form of a rocket ship or just about anything else. A button on the joystick serves as a firing device, which triggers a response when the screen cursor or other symbol is in the proper position in relation to other display elements. For example, when the cursor is positioned over an option on a menu in a word processing program, a push on the button activates that option. Or, by moving the cursor to various points on the screen and pressing the button, it is possible to create graphics of various kinds. (See fig. 2.12.)

The electronic construction of joysticks is very simple. They consist basically of two channels corresponding to the $x$ and $y$ coordinates of a two-dimensional grid or graph. By moving the joystick, you move an electrical potentiometer (like the volume control on a stereo music system) that changes an electrical current from high to low voltage. These currents must be converted from analog measurements to digital form. The electronics logic for this process is built into the microcomputer, not the joystick, and is activated when the joystick is plugged into the joystick port on the computer.

A few inexpensive joystick designs do not use potentiometers. Instead, contact switches are mounted in a circle around the joystick handle. Moving the handle closes one of the switches and thus indicates the general direction of motion.

The joystick "fire" buttons are simple on/off switches. Input from the joystick can be read almost instantaneously by the microcomputer. Most microcomputers can read the button inputs 100,000 times per minute; thus the microcomputer can react very quickly to any shots a user may make while using the joystick.

## Optical Mark Readers

A device that is being utilized by many schools, the optical mark reader (OMR), has been around for many years. Optical mark readers are devices that detect marks in predetermined locations on a document (generally a card or sheet of

FIGURE 2.12 **A Joystick from Kraft Systems** (Courtesy of Kraft Systems)

paper). As the document is fed into the unit, the OMR's transport mechanism moves the document past a light source (often a laser beam). Timing marks printed in a track on one margin of the document tell the OMR when to read and examine the reflected or transmitted light. This information is fed into the microprocessor as digital data that the microcomputer can understand and process.

In test scoring, the answer key is first passed through the unit. The OMR will then compare all the rest of the documents with this key. Most marks are made as dark lead pencil marks; however, some OMRs can read punched cards.

Schools and districts have used OMRs to grade objective tests automatically. Recent developments in technology have made it possible to attach OMRs to microcomputers, eliminating the time delay previously encountered when the marked cards had to be sent to a large mainframe computer for processing—a mainframe generally located out of the city and sometimes even out of the state. By linking the OMRs to the school's microcomputer, it is possible for students to get immediate feedback about test results and for problems of individual learners to be detailed quickly. OMRs also save teachers a great amount of time in the process of paper correcting.

Connecting an optical mark reader to a microcomputer is a simple process. Some OMR models come equipped with an interface board for a given microcomputer model. In some cases, no additional equipment is necesssary. Just plug the interface board into a peripheral slot and connect the cable from the OMR to the board. If the OMR unit is not designed to interface directly with a certain microcomputer model, then a serial or parallel interface and appropriate cable must be purchased. Once the unit is connected to a microcomputer, appropriate software designed to compile the data will be needed.

In addition, you will need special cards or sheets for students to use in marking their answers to standardized tests and surveys or for other applications. Cards can be purchased that are marked for letter answers (a, b, c, d, e) and for number answers (1, 2, 3, 4, 5). Also, special-purpose cards—such as those for attendance, absence verification, ballots, inventory, scheduling, and class registration—can be obtained.

Depending on the software package purchased with the optical mark reader, other common applications (besides test checking) of OMR technology include monitoring of achievement objectives, keeping attendance, reporting grades, scheduling media equipment, keeping library records, and recording inventory for textbooks, films, and other equipment.

## MAINTENANCE AND REPAIR

Now that you have been introduced to the computer, how it does its work, and the peripheral devices that can be added to it to make a complete system, it is time to discuss some principles of computer repair and maintenance.

### Preventive Maintenance

Preventive maintenance is something that everyone can practice. This type of maintenance can prevent, or at least delay, breakdowns that can be costly and inconvenient. An ounce of prevention is worth more than five pounds of cure when working with microcomputers. When something goes wrong with a microcomputer, someone has to bundle it up and take it in for repair, where it might be tied up for days or weeks.

The first rule of preventive maintenance is to avoid causing problems by your own actions. If it isn't broken, don't tinker with the mechanism just because you think it's fun. If it is broken, find out what you should do before you start to fix it. A careful look at the operating manual that came with the computer is a good first start—be sure to read it thoroughly before you do anything else.

Cleanliness is one of the cardinal rules of prevention. *Never* permit food or drink to come near the computer. The smallest amount of coffee or cola can put the keyboard out of action. The keyboard is really a series of little switches. As you push a key, you make a contact and complete a circuit. A small drop of liquid can short out the circuit and destroy the keyboard circuitry.

If you should get a small amount of grease or oil (from fingerprints, for example) or human hairs on the surface of your diskette, that segment will be effectively isolated from the reading mechanism of the disk drive. This will prevent the data stored in that area from being accessed; you might lose thousands of words of information from one single fingerprint. Precautions in handling the disk are listed earlier in this chapter.

Try to keep the dust at a minimum in your environment. Dust is a hazard to the computer, but the main problem is a layer of dust that may collect on the surface of diskettes. If this occurs, there may well be segments from which data cannot be successfully accessed. One effective way to control the dust problem is to cover the disk drives and computer with dust covers when not in use. Such covers are inexpensive and are available from many computer stores. If you do not have the budget to purchase a dust cover, however, construct one from butcher paper, newspaper, chart paper, or something similar. Just a few minutes of your time to make or secure a dust cover may prevent problems later when a diskette, disk drive, or computer fails because of accumulated dust and dirt. Always be sure to cover your computer system before the cleaning crew comes in to stir up the dust on the floor. Chalkboard dust can also cause serious problems.

Tobacco smoke can cause a disk drive head to read and write erratically. Each smoke particle is a small ball, and it can lift the head off the diskette sufficiently to keep it from sensing the data magnetically arranged on the surface. Some commercial centers forbid smoking in computer rooms, even though the air going to their disk drive systems is filtered. Microcomputer disk drive systems do not have filters on them; these are installed at the request of the user. If you plan to use a computer extensively, this may be incentive enough for you to give up the smoking habit.

The hair of pets (as well as of humans) seems to gravitate naturally to the keyboards, as do other small particles, such as paper shavings, strands of clothing, or chalk dust. You can remove them with a strip of masking tape simply by holding the tape so the sticky side faces the offending items, pressing lightly, then pulling away. The hair or other particle will be securely adhered to the tape and your problems should be solved. Never use a liquid spray cleaner on the keyboard: the liquid will be forced into the contact areas and the keyboard will not function.

A magnetic field, which can exist in unusual and unexpected places, can raise havoc with your diskettes. Any magnet can cause problems, and all motors produce a magnetic field. A small vacuum cleaner or electric drill used in close proximity to stored diskettes, for example, has the potential to destroy the stored information. Most screwdrivers and other tools are slightly magnetic and should not be used around diskettes. Never place your diskettes on top of the television or monitor: the field within the monitor can affect the data on the diskette. If you have an auxiliary fan or a surge protector on the computer (this add-on is discussed later in this chapter), do not lay a diskette on top of the running fan; the magnetic field created by the fan motor can alter the data on the diskette.

Static electricity is another enemy of data stored on diskettes and can also be a potential destroyer of a chip. You may need to modify your classroom or other facility if you find that static electricity is a problem. For example, you may find it necessary to cover a carpet with an antistatic pad or to place the computer on a grounded antistatic pad. You may even need to obtain a pair of shoes with soles that cut down on the potential of static electricity generation. It is possible for a charge of electricity to be strong enough to wipe out data on a diskette or destroy a chip in a disk drive or microcomputer instantly. Humidifiers may be useful: moist air seems to help cut down the amount of static electricity that is generated. When you remove the cover of the computer to examine the mother-board or to place an interface board in a peripheral slot, be sure to touch the power source pack (see fig. 2.4) so you will discharge any static electricity before touching any of the RAM or ROM chips and the other interface boards. A large charge of static electricity is capable of completely destroying the CPU.

While you are examining the inside of the computer, it is important that you take off any metal rings or dangling bracelets. *Do not* allow metal jewelry to touch inside parts of the computer: it can damage chips or other parts of the microcomputer.

Some disk drives frequently damage the hole in the center of floppy disk-ettes; also, diskettes that are frequently used suffer from wear around the center hole. If the wear is excessive, the diskette will not work properly and will eventu-ally become useless. You can repair the hole with an attachable reinforcing ring that effectively extends the life of the diskette. A better approach is to attach the ring before the damage has occurred or, even wiser, to purchase only diskettes that have an attached ring already built in.

Even if you are using reinforced diskettes, it is a useful precaution to only partially close the door to the disk drive that presses the drive hub slightly in the center of the diskette, thus sliding the diskette one way or the other toward the center of the drive. After this brief hesitation, the door can be completely closed; the hub of the drive should be precisely aligned with the hole in the diskette.

Another concern in preserving your diskettes is to store them always in a vertical position. You should not stack one on top of another or allow anything heavy to press down on them. It is a good idea to store the diskettes in a strong plastic, fiber, or metal box. Your archival copies should be played at least once each year: if the diskette is not rotated slightly, there is a possibility, after pro-longed storage, that magnetic distortion may occur. An important item to add to the computer system to help prevent component breakdowns is a unit containing a surge protector, a cooling fan, and a heavy-duty switch.

During a month's time, a personal computer that is plugged into the 120-volt power outlet will be subjected to up to a hundred jolts of electricity of over 500 volts each. These power surges are devastating to a microcomputer. Power line glitches, which are very common, can be caused by such things as a storm, a refrigerator cycling on and off, or a printer being powered up. These high-intensity surges last only billionths of a second, but they measure between 400 and 25,000 volts. Sudden surges in electricity can instantly erase the computer's memory or ruin an entire diskette filled with data. About 80 percent of all microcomputer malfunctions can be attributed to power line glitches.

To protect your microcomputer from these glitches, it is critical that you purchase a safety device known as a surge protector. It is also advisable to purchase an auxiliary fan to push cool air inside the microcomputer. Microcomputers run at relatively cool temperatures when compared to mainframe computers; however, if the machine is used constantly for long periods of time, and if several interface boards are plugged into a peripheral slot in the motherboard, overheating can be a serious problem. This overheating can be aggravated by the external environment—a hot summer day, for example, or poor ventilation.

You can purchase a unit for under sixty dollars that provides a surge protector, a fan, a heavy-duty switch, and a receptacle that allows you to plug in both the computer and the monitor. This unit is a very good investment and could save the life of a chip or diskette (see fig. 2.13).

Now that we have considered several aspects of preventive maintenance, we will detail what you might do to actually fix some of the problems that could go wrong with your microcomputer.

## HANDS-ON MAINTENANCE

First, let's look at cables. Any piece of equipment connected to another by a cable is certain to experience some trouble from time to time. If a cable connector becomes unplugged, the equipment will not operate. If it becomes partially unplugged all kinds of odd happenings can occur. If your computer is acting

FIGURE 2.13  Surge Protector, Fan, Switch Unit

strangely, or if it won't function at all, check all of the connections. This sounds too simple even to mention, but often a connection that appears to be tight and sound is not, and a bit of wiggling will again mate up the two connectors and put your computer back in running order.

Most plug problems arise from lack of contact between the mating plugs, and the most frequent offender is an edge connector. Some circuit boards have notches at one edge that allow a plug to make contact with a number of circuits on the board. These circuits are manufactured from copper, which corrodes when exposed to the atmosphere. Expensive computers have gold-plated edge connector contacts, but most microcomputers use bare copper to cut down on expense. Periodically, or when a problem arises, unplug the computer from the power line, disconnect each edge connector, and check to see if any corrosion has occurred on the contact areas. If there seems to be a residue (it will look darker than the rest of the surrounding copper area), you can generally remove it by carefully rubbing a red pencil eraser (one that is clean and not covered with lead from paper erasing) over the surfaces. In effect, you are erasing the residue from the contact points. The resulting eraser crumbs must be removed before the surfaces are reunited: blow carefully on the surfaces, taking care that you do not spray moisture on the contact points as you blow away the eraser particles. A can of compressed air, available at a photo store, can be used for this purpose, as well as for removing particles from the keyboard and other areas of the computer.

You can polish the contacts by obtaining a can of Cramolin spray from an electronics supply house and applying a very small amount to the contacts. *Do not* use the ordinary oily television tuner or contact cleaner and lubricant: this cleaner picks up dust and can cause intermittent problems.

You should make it a point to check all the cables periodically to make certain that they are not bent or kinked in ways that might lead to wire breakage. Whenever you move or reroute a cable, take the time to straighten it and to smooth out any twists that might have occurred. Also, look carefully for frayed insulation, which most likely indicates damage to the wires. In some cases these frayed areas can be repaired with electrical tape, but you may need to replace the cable if the damage is extensive. Inspecting the cables regularly is the kind of preventive maintenance that can extend their life significantly.

After a microcomputer system has been in operation for several years and a number of peripheral devices have been added, you may have accumulated several different cables to connect a printer, disk drives, synthesizers, modems, extra monitors, and so forth. These cables look somewhat alike, but most of them are different—in the number of internal wires or edge connector pins they contain, for example. Sometimes these differences can lead to system failure if a cable is reversed or is plugged in at the wrong place. Also, forcing a plug into a connector could do serious damage to pins or housings. It is a good idea, to prevent any disastrous damage to a plug or component, to label both ends of each cable. If a cable can be inserted two ways, label the top or right side. If there is space on the plug, place the label directly on the plug; if not, place the label on the cable.

After you use your disk drive for a period of time, iron oxide from the surface of the diskettes will build up on the face of the read-write head. This residue buildup must be removed if first-rate operation (accurate reading or writing of data) is to be maintained. To accomplish this, a liquid cleaning solution is applied to a head-cleaning diskette made of a plastic mesh; the diskette is then rotated against the head for a few seconds (usually *only* thirty seconds). There are a few operational safeguards that you should observe when using the head-cleaning diskette. Because you cannot see when the oxide is removed, the tendency is to use the cleaner for too long a period of time; but thirty seconds is sufficient. Also, it is possible to insert the diskette upside down, which will not clean the head. The label on the cleaning diskette should be up, with your thumb on the label, just as when inserting a regular program diskette. It is good practice to read the instructions that come with the cleaning diskette carefully before using it. Incidentally, if you are using a cassette recorder rather than disk drives, you can obtain a cleaning cassette that does the same job as the diskette cleaner.

It is possible to clean the read-write heads on your disk drives by actually opening up the case and going directly to the heads. This is the best way, but it involves an element of risk. In some cases, warranties may be voided if you open the equipment, so be sure to check on this aspect. If the warranty has expired, however, this is no longer a factor.

If you intend to clean the heads directly, you will need a kit of materials—the kind used to clean audio tape recorder heads—which you can purchase from an electronics or sound store. Be sure that you know how to open the disk drive case before you begin. The technical manual provided by the manufacturer of the disk drive system will spell out precisely how to do this. Read this manual carefully so you do not damage the case or internal mechanisms of the disk drive. For most disk drive systems, the procedure is a simple matter of removing a few screws and sliding off the case.

Locate the head; if there is a red smudge on it, indicating a buildup of iron oxide, put some of the cleaning solution on one of the cotton swabs in the kit and wipe off the smudge, being careful to touch only the head with the moistened swab. The residue should come right off with little effort. Use only the cleaning solution—*not* the lubricant that comes with the kit, which is designed for tape, not for diskettes. Finally, put everything back together, being careful to line up all holes properly and to replace the screws and other parts you might have disassembled.

## Major Repairs

If you need to have repairs done to your computer beyond the simple preventive maintenance and hands-on techniques outlined above, here are a few words of advice.

If you must ship your computer for service, using commercial methods (for example, U.S. Parcel Post, United Parcel Service, or a freight line), be sure to ship it in the original boxes in which it was sent to you, along with all of the original packing material. These containers are designed to protect the equipment from damage while in transit. Many hundreds of microcomputers are damaged each year because they were packed inadequately. Be sure to send all the parts that may be giving you trouble. In case of doubt send everything. Write a brief explanation of the malfunction, even though you may have called the repair agency detailing the problem before you sent the equipment. The note of explanation will help the technician to diagnose and correct the difficulty more accurately and quickly.

When you have adequate local service, do not ship the equipment from your area. Be especially careful in transporting the microcomputer system to the repair agency: occasionally, additional damage is inflicted by a sudden stop, a sharp turn, or other traffic problems en route to the store. Tell the technician as precisely as possible what the malfunction is, how often it occurs, and so on. An intermittent problem is hard to track down, and the service department may have trouble duplicating it in the shop. Your verbal or written description will help.

Following are some additional suggestions that may make the repair or servicing of your computer system less painful and costly.

1. Join a user's group, if available, and possibly get free service. Most user's groups have engineers, technicians, or others capable of solving system problems. However, you generally get what you pay for, and if the service is free you can't expect much in the way of a warranty on the workmanship. In addition, part-time technicians may have trouble getting certain specialized parts.

2. Try to find out which service centers are the best. Get referrals from users who know. Your state department of public instruction (microcomputer division), the local microcomputer department at the state university or college, or a trusted friend can help here.

3. Get an estimate on how long the repair is likely to take. Some repair shops have facilities to provide one-day service, the normal repair will take two or three days, or it may take weeks if a special part must be ordered from the factory. In such cases it may pay to shop around to see if another repair agency has the special part in stock.

4. Check into the availability of loaners. Although this is generally not standard procedure, if you protest loudly enough you may be able to have the use of one while your system is being repaired.

5. Cultivate a friendship with the people at your local computer store. If you consistently purchase printer ribbons, diskettes, cables, diskette storage cases, and other equipment from them, chances are good that they will give you preferred-customer treatment on repairs.

6. When you pick up the repaired system, ask the service center to list in detail exactly what was done. Talk to the service manager or service technician if possible. Beware of motherboard or interface board swaps that fix your problem by substituting a used board that may have its own

problems. (Jot down serial numbers of your boards before sending the equipment in for service, then check to see if an unauthorized substitution was made.)

7. If a motherboard, interface board, or other component such as a disk drive is replaced, the warranty on the new component should match that of the original. If the component fails within the warranty period—usually ninety days or, in some cases, one year—you shouldn't have to pay for repair or replacement.

8. Have the service shop call you if the repair will exceed a certain amount. Just as with repairs to your automobile, if you feel that the estimated charge is unreasonable, take the system somewhere else.

9. When you pick up the repaired system, try it on the spot. This will take some additional time and, perhaps, cause some frustration, but the inconvenience will be worth it because it is possible that a subtle problem may not be fixed. If your original problem occurred intermittently, ask the service people if they operated the system long enough to see if the problem reappeared after the repair. You don't want to take the microcomputer system back to your school or home only to have the problem reappear the first time the system is used.

## SUMMARY

In the introduction to this chapter we discussed that teachers need to know how a microcomputer works so they can, in turn, assist students as they learn about computers. Although one can operate a computer without knowing about the mechanics involved, teachers have special concerns that are quite different from those of the typical computer user. Because they are called upon to respond to the needs of students and to provide a wide range of information in response to questions that are often spontaneous, teachers must have at their command a considerable store of knowledge. Knowing something about how a computer manages data and instructions, and how it is constructed internally, will better prepare the teacher to build upon student curiosity as it relates to these matters. Additionally, if a unit on computer literacy is undertaken, the subject of how computers work is quite appropriate; it is also very interesting to most students. We discussed the differences and similarities between the three classes of computers—mainframe, minicomputer, and microcomputer—and included some idea of basic costs of each.

The binary system that is used by all computers to process data was illustrated, including a discussion of bits, bytes, and the ASCII code. The methodology utilized in the binary code to represent different letters, numbers, and symbols was explained, including samples of several letters and numbers. All digital computers consist of some basic components, which were discussed in detail: a central processing unit that contains a control unit, an arithmetic unit, and a logic unit. The types of memory, RAM and ROM, were presented, along with a detailed discussion of why one kind is volatile (RAM) and the other nonvolatile (ROM).

We discussed the peripheral devices that can be purchased to make a complete microcomputer system. A minimum system typically consists of the microcomputer, a monitor, and a cassette or disk drive for external storage of data. To this basic system can be added a number of peripheral devices that will add capabilities and special functions deemed essential for a particular program. Peripheral devices, although adding additional costs, provide the means for bringing the total world of microcomputing into the school and individual classrooms.

In an introduction to the peripheral storage devices it was noted that cassette drive systems are losing favor because of the slow speeds at which data is accessed and that the floppy disk is the most common mass storage medium in use in the schools. Procedures for handling and utilizing the disk system were presented in considerable detail. The advantages and disadvantages of a hard disk drive (Winchester) system were outlined.

The three types of monitors—monochrome, composite color, and RGB color—were discussed and contrasted with a regular TV receiver modified for use with a microcomputer. This discussion included strengths of the monitor, such as speed of display and amount of data handled. Five tests are listed that can be applied in the evaluation of a monitor to help ensure the selection of a quality device. A brief discussion introducing the flat-panel displays (liquid crystal, plasma display, electroluminescent panel, and electrophoretic display) was presented.

The strengths and weaknesses of the two major kinds of printers—impact and nonimpact—were discussed, including samples of what the printing looks like and the capabilities of each type of printer.

The use of a modem to enable the computer to access remote data bases was described. In this chapter and chapter 6, on telecommunication, we detail how a school can utilize the services of an information utility and a Computerized Bulletin Board System (BBS) to bring the world outside the class into the school.

The alternative input devices, not meant to replace the keyboard but to supplement it, were discussed. The mouse, light pens, touch screens, graphics tablets, voice input devices, joysticks, and optical mark readers were considered from the standpoint of how they function and how they can be utilized in classroom or school computer programs.

We also included in this chapter some ideas and suggestions for the maintenance and repair of a microcomputer system. It is important not to smoke around the computer and to protect the microcomputer system from dirt and dust and the harmful effect static electricity can have on both the microcomputer system and the diskettes. Some suggestions on procedures needed to facilitate major repairs on the computer system were advanced.

# REFERENCES

Adams, D. R., et al. *Computer Information Systems: An Introduction*. Chicago, IL: South-Western Publishing Co., 1983.

Alessi, S. M., and Trollip, S. R. *Computer-based Instruction: Methods and Development*. Englewood Cliffs, NJ: Prentice-Hall, 1985.

Anderson, E. "Do You Talk to Your Apple?" *Electronic Education* (January 1984): 38.

Barden, J. E. "Deep Byte's Repair Tips." *Popular Computing* (May 1983): 56–57.

Bitter, G. G. *Computers in Today's World*. New York: John Wiley & Sons, 1984.

Buchsbaum, W. H. *Personal Computer's Handbook*. Indianapolis, IN: Howard W. Sams, 1983.

Burke, R. "Selecting Micros for Schools." *Electronic Learning* (March 1984): 18–23.

Coburn, E. *Microcomputers: Hardware, Software, and Programming*. Indianapolis: Bobbs-Merrill, 1984.

Coburn, P., et al. *Practical Guide to Computers in Education*. Menlo Park, CA: Addison Wesley Publishing Co., 1982.

Crowley, T. H. *Understanding Computers*. New York: McGraw-Hill Book Co., 1976.

Dayton, D. K. "Computer-assisted Graphics." *Instructional Innovator* (September 1981): 16–18.

Duece, M., and Schoenan, R. "Mini, Micro, and/or Mainframe?" *Electronic Learning* (May 1983): 34–35.

Harper, D. O., and Stewart, J. H. *Run: Computer Education*. Monterey, CA: Brooks-Cole Publishing Co., 1983.

Harvey, W. J. "Optical Mark Readers: What's New." *Electronic Learning* (September 1983): 108–12.

Jones, W., et al. *Computer Literacy: Programming, Problem Solving, Projects on the Apple*. Reston, VA: Reston Publishing Co., 1983.

Kolb, A. C. "Which Keyboard Should We Use?" *Classroom Computer Learning* (September 1984): 66–69.

Mandall, S. L. *Computers and Data Processing: Concepts and Applications*, 2nd ed. New York: West Publishing Co., 1982.

Morris, D. "Printers, Printers, Printers." *Educational Computing* (October 1983): 34–37.

Powers, M. J., et al. *Computer Information Systems Development: Analysis and Design*. West Chicago, IL: South-Western Publishing Co., 1984.

Radin, S., and Lee, F. *Computers in the Classroom—A Survival Guide for Teachers*. Chicago, IL: Science Research Associates, 1984.

Richman, E. *Spotlight on Computer Literacy*. New York: Random House, 1982.

Smith, R., and Spokony, M. "Your Guide to Selecting and Evaluating a Computer System." *Electronic Learning* (January 1982): 6–9.

Spencer, D. D. *The Illustrated Computer Dictionary*. 3d ed. Columbus, OH: Merrill Publishing Co., 1986.

Stallings, W. D., Jr., and Blissmer, R. H. *Computer Annual*. New York: John Wiley & Sons, 1984.

Trainor, T. N. *Computer Literacy: Concepts and Applications*. Santa Cruz, CA: Mitchell Publishing, 1984.

Vensel, G., and Schilling L. "VersaWriter: Low Cost Apple Graphics." *Electronic Education* (February 1982): 28–29.

Williams, J. M. "When His Computer Talks, He Listens." *Electronic Learning* (January 1983): 32–33.

# 3

# SELECTING
# A
# SYSTEM

## INTRODUCTION

*System* is a better term to use than is *microcomputer* when considering selection and purchase. A microcomputer can be purchased for a modest price, but not much can be done with it until various components (the peripherals) are added to form the system. So, along with the computer itself, mention will be made in this chapter of monitors, printers, disk drives, cassette recorders, modems, and various alternative input devices such as joysticks and graphics tablets. An example of a complete system is shown in figure 3.1.

The system that is finally acquired can represent a considerable investment; therefore, a cool-headed, organized approach to its selection is definitely in order. Some people get caught up in the excitement of acquiring their very first microcomputer system, and before they realize what has happened, they've spent a lot of money on equipment that might not be the best choice for the job.

If a school or district has already decided the brand of computer it wishes to acquire, or if a school already has a machine that is proving to be satisfactory, then the problem of selecting a computer is moot. But the acquisition of the proper peripherals is forever a vital concern. It is in this area that the greatest latitude is found—there are so many different styles and kinds of add-ons that making the right selection can become a bit confusing.

**FIGURE 3.1   A Microcomputer System** (Courtesy of Apple Computer, Inc.)

One way to take some of the confusion out of the selection process is to consider a number of preliminary factors before the subject of equipment even comes up. A good place to start is with applications: what will the system be used for?

## STEP I: IDENTIFY MAJOR APPLICATIONS

Listing all the things that can be accomplished with a microcomputer system will not really help with the selection process because some applications simply would not be very useful in a classroom setting. For example, a microcomputer can be programmed to do a variety of household tasks, such as controlling the heat, monitoring the use of electricity, and turning the watering system on and off at specified times during the day or week. Scientists utilize a certain kind of interface to enable their computers to run equipment that can monitor volcanoes or mudslides and do other dangerous tasks. A psychologist might use the computer as a diagnostic tool, or he might use a specially designed program to modify behaviors. A wide range of medical applications are possible, from designing a special diet for a patient to monitoring brain waves and vital signs.

Although applications such as these are interesting and useful, they do not represent the daily tasks for which computers are needed in the schools. To some extent, educators have to be generalists when it comes to using the equipment—they have to reach as many students as possible, address a diverse spectrum of needs, and be forever aware of the economics involved. So, exactly what are computers used for in the schools? Here are some typical applications.

## Programming and Authoring

When the subject of programming is mentioned, many people think only of BASIC, but this is a narrow point of view. Although BASIC is the "on-board" language of most micros, it certainly isn't the only one that should be considered. In addition to BASIC, teachers should look at authoring languages such as PILOT as an excellent option for writing lessons. PILOT offers a defined format for the authoring of text-based lessons, an excellent graphics editor (colorful illustrations can be created and combined with the text), and an exciting sound capability (you can incorporate sound with text and graphics). The newer SuperPILOT is even more versatile than the standard version and is now available for several models of computers.

Logo is a very popular language that has taken the classroom by storm. Logo is open-ended and unstructured in comparison to PILOT (although it has a specified set of rules just like any other language). The most widely used Logo feature is turtle graphics, but it is possible to do some creative and exciting things with text also; and you can even operate robots using Logo.

Now that the Educational Testing Service has elected to use Pascal for their advanced placement test in computer science, this language is suddenly in the spotlight. But elementary teachers most likely will not need to rush out and learn it—the approach will be to emphasize Pascal in the high schools.

Programming in BASIC generally requires no special disk-based programs, as do PILOT and Logo, because the language is built into most classroom computers. Thus, teachers can get involved with BASIC programming activities immediately. Simple programs are fun to write—the students enjoy the elementary-level activities, but many are not content to stop there. They continue to create increasingly more advanced programs and often surpass the teacher in their level of expertise. Some teachers also continue to expand their skills, writing a variety of tailor-made programs for use in their classes. In addition to the languages mentioned above, FORTRAN and Cobol are taught in some high schools, the former having science and math applications and the latter being useful in business and data processing classes. For more information on this subject see chapter 7 on programming.

## Computer Literacy

Definitions of computer literacy abound, but typically they stress the impact of the computer on society, as well as how the computer works. In the elementary school the students proceed through the operation of the machine using aids such as a homemade memory board with pockets to hold numerical values. The basics of binary arithmetic might be illustrated by having students stand for a binary one and sit for a zero—a lineup of eight students can thus represent many numbers.

The actual hands-on portion of a computer literacy unit would include learning to turn the machine on and off, learning to operate the disk drives (or cassette recorders), and memorizing and using commands to load a program, run it, and so on. In addition, students would learn to operate the printer and other peripheral devices such as graphics tablets, if these are available. As a result of such a unit, students should feel as comfortable with the system as possible.

Although the study of computers in relation to social issues can be carried out in the absence of equipment, familiarity with an actual computer is immensely helpful when the lesson is designed to teach a computer's makeup and function. By working with the machine, students develop a feeling not only for how information is stored, retrieved, and possibly pirated, damaged, or destroyed but also for the capabilities and limitations of the technology.

## Computer-Assisted Instruction

Many educators feel that computer-assisted instruction should be the primary application for the classroom computer. The objective is not to learn *about* the machine but rather to learn *with* it. Traditional subjects are formatted to run on the computer, and the student is taught about math, science, languages, and so on, with the machine serving as the tutor.

A number of diverse CAI formats are recognized, including tutorials, simulations, drill-and-practice lessons, and instructional games. The typical tutorial is designed to teach new material rather than to drill the students in areas that are already familiar to them. The program adapts to the needs of the student on the basis of input from an ongoing question-and-answer dialogue, presenting new information only when the old has been mastered.

Drill-and-practice programs assume that a concept or principle is known but that drill is needed to enhance the knowledge. Some authors prefer to separate the terms *drill* and *practice*, pointing out that there is a subtle difference between the two (for a discussion of these terms, see chapter 4).

Simulations attempt to replicate to the extent possible realistic situations from the physical world. This type of computer-based learning is widespread, being used by pilots, astronauts, medical personnel, and many others.

Instructional games have many formats, but all involve competition, rules, rewards, and entertainment. Many instructional games are based on the arcade format, but virtually every imaginable kind of game has now been adapted to operate on the computer. For more information on the kinds of CAI, refer to chapter 4, on instructional software.

## Graphics

Although graphics is sometimes included under programming, new hardware—in the form of graphics tablets—and software devoted exclusively to the generation of graphics have made the use of these devices much more popular than creating graphics by writing programs. Of course, you can still write programs to take advantage of the computer's built-in graphics mode, but such an approach is much more demanding than is tracing a line on a graphics tablet with your finger or a stylus. Students can use the graphics they create to illustrate relationships in math, science, social studies, and so forth. These can then be included as illustrations in research papers created on the word processor.

## Music

As with the production of graphics, the creation of music takes several forms. You can write programs in BASIC to activate the computer's sound circuitry, or you can attach various peripheral devices that enable you to be a musician without the need to be a programmer. Many commercial programs respond to input from the computer keyboard or the special music peripherals by displaying notes when certain keys are pressed, printing hard copy of a composition, playing it (often in sounds that represent an instrument of your choice), and so on. Some computers are much more capable than others in the production of music. A machine with built-in sound circuitry is the best choice if the study of music is one of the major applications.

## Computer-Managed Instruction

A typical computer-managed instruction program generates a file for each student that includes such information as classes, subjects, and performance. Scores and other data are fed into the system and stored in the files, which may be accessed with ease at any time. The important feature of a CMI system, though, is its ability to analyze data statistically and to summarize it into meaningful records for each student. These ongoing, updated records of student performance are then used for diagnosing needs and prescribing appropriate learning activities. Reports can be prepared for parents, not only to inform them about their child's progress but also to improve public relations.

Although many CMI programs are self-contained and dedicated to management functions exclusively, some CMI components are being incorporated into tutorial and drill-and-practice programs along with the learning software, enabling students to be kept updated concerning their performance on current lessons.

CMI systems have been used at the school and district levels for years but are now becoming more popular with individual teachers at the classroom level.

## Networking and Telecommunications

An instructor may find it desirable to hook several computer stations to a central one or to attach several student computers to a pair of disk drives and a printer (a good way to save money). Several microcomputers can also be linked together so that they interact as equals. These are examples of multiuser systems (often called networks).

Many hardware manufacturers can provide a ready-made networking system that will enable a school's microcomputers to communicate with one another and to access common disk drives and printers. A shared system uses one microcomputer as the control for the printer and the drives. The master micro is accessed by several classroom computers through a communications interface box. (Interconnecting several such boxes will increase the number of computers that can be included in the system.)

School microcomputers can be linked to a remote data base through the use of a modem and the telephone lines: this is termed *telecomputing*. Students involved in research requiring considerable amounts of information find this to be a useful technique: it is as if they have access to a vast library but with the advantages that the material is always up-to-date, it is easy to access, and all of the operations can be carried out right from the classroom. For a discussion of this subject see chapter 6.

## Word Processing

Word processing is one of the most useful skills a student can develop. Students write more—and enjoy it more—using the word processor than when using traditional means. From the wide selection of word processing packages available you can find a program to fit your particular need, whether it is an exploratory session at the elementary level, professional word processing in the high school, or anything in between.

A word processing program converts the computer into a special kind of typewriter. The keyboard is used in the same manner as a typewriter, but the document is saved on a disk and the monitor displays the text as it is typed into the computer. The real power of the word processor, however, is its ability to provide some special functions that make the typewriter obsolete: the user never has to erase a mistake or use messy correction fluid; the cut-and-paste routine is accomplished with a keystroke or two; and formats, once set, are saved to be used over and over. With advanced word processing programs, even typing errors are caught and corrected. The word processor is fast becoming an important aid to the teacher, particularly in courses where numbers of documents, reports, exams, and handouts are generated. For a detailed discussion of this subject, see chapter 5 on tool software.

## Special Education Applications

Although the keyboard is used in some special education applications, it is in conjunction with the alternative input devices that the computer is really beginning to assist the handicapped. For those who are virtually immobile, a device permits the user to communicate with the computer through eye movement. For those who cannot speak there are voice synthesizers. A handicapped person who is unable to operate the computer through other means can use voice input to make it function. With the constant expansion and upgrading of alternative input devices, the future looks very promising. Communication is now possible that special education teachers only dreamed about just a few short years ago.

## Classroom Management

Teachers spend a large amount of time daily in unchallenging but essential nonteaching activities that can collectively be termed *classroom management*. Among these chores are maintaining records of student attendance and performance, preparing handouts, issuing reports, and making out grades. The computer can take much of the tedium out of this kind of work; and once the system has been set up, the students themselves can assume responsibility for many of the less confidential duties, learning to operate the computer in the process.

Many teachers who are now ardent users of computers for instruction were attracted initially by their management potential. The software is probably the most important consideration where record keeping is involved, but the hardware—and particularly the printer—is also significant.

## Robots

Though not as widespread as many other applications, the use of classroom robots has caught on in some schools.

Robots are more than educational gimmicks: they can encourage and support certain kinds of learning activities. Although some robots have a deceptive, toylike appearance—they might have wheels or tracks, be brightly colored, or wear embellishments of various kinds—the feature that takes them out of the realm of mere playthings is that they are programmable—they can be directed to perform various movements and actions by a stored program that the user can create, save, and use over again.

In programming the robot the student gets involved in creative problem-solving activities. Because the robot is typically large and imbued with a kind of life of its own, students find programming activities more motivating than when the end result is simply displayed on a screen.

## STEP II: EXAMINE THE SOFTWARE

With a background of potential areas of application, it will be much easier for you to construct a set of needs or objectives to which a system can be matched. The next step is to examine the quality and determine the quantity of available software in the areas of your choice. A number of sources for this kind of information are available.

Chapter 4, on instructional software, is a good place to start: it describes the various categories of software and provides hints on what to look for in a program as well as a useful evaluation form. Also, appendix B offers an extensive list of software producers.

The various journals on educational computing are another source; these typically evaluate a selection of software packages in each issue. Most evaluations are carried out in a thorough manner and include such features as photographs of typical screen displays. A list of journals is included in appendix D.

A visit to local computer stores will provide additional information on available software. Also, schools in your district or state with an operational microcomputer facility may have helpful information. A number of state school offices now have centralized software repositories in which an ever-increasing selection of programs is stored; these provide excellent previewing opportunities. Directories of educational software provide listings, descriptions, and previews of current titles—these are among the very best sources of information if you want a broad-based survey of software.

The availability of appropriate software is an extremely important factor in selecting which of the various system configurations will best meet your specific needs.

## STEP III: EXAMINE THE HARDWARE

### The Microcomputer

The keyboard is a major item to consider when selecting a computer. Since most of the work is actually done at the keyboard, if it is not well designed and comfortable, the task will be more difficult. The amount of main memory (storage inside the computer) can also be important; the need varies with different applications. Some users find the graphics and sound capabilities to be important factors when selecting a machine. The nature of the display can be critical: how many characters can be displayed across the screen is important, particularly if word processing is being considered. Also of concern are how much and how easily the capabilities can be expanded. The kind of microprocessor and interface(s) that come built in might be of interest to some users. Finally, the type of operating system is a factor in some cases. In the following paragraphs we will examine these and other features in greater detail.

**Keyboard.** Some keyboards are separate from the computer and can be moved about freely, being attached only by a flexible cord. Among the machines using this sytem are the IBM PC and the Macintosh. Others have the keyboard integrated with the computer, providing less flexibility. The Apple IIe, Commodore 64, and TRS 80 are of this configuration, which has proved to be quite satisfactory for classroom use.

Keyboards on computers such as the IBM have special function keys that are particularly useful for word processing (see fig. 3.2). Other machines permit you to assign special functions to keys so that various operations are made faster and easier; for example, you may want to assign BASIC keywords to certain keys when programming, enabling you to enter a command without having to type it in its entirety each time.

**FIGURE 3.2    A Keyboard Showing the Function Keys**

Some keyboards include a built-in numeric pad, which is similar to a small calculator. This device is most useful if considerable work with numbers is anticipated. When this feature is not included, a separate pad, like the one shown in figure 3.3, can often be plugged into the computer as a peripheral.

Don't buy a computer before you have had a chance to give the keyboard a really good workout. As a general rule, the closer it approximates a typewriter, the better it will be for most applications.

**Memory.**  The term *memory*, you may recall, is used in reference to the space that is set aside within the computer to hold a prewritten program, such as one stored on a disk, or a program (or other information) that is input from the keyboard. Memory is measured in kilobytes (K), with one K amounting to just over 1,000 characters (numbers and letters). Thus, a 64K memory is capable of holding over 64,000 characters. This particular kind of memory, random access memory (RAM), is temporary storage—it holds programs while the computer is using them, then it is emptied out and made ready to hold different information.

Most people check into the amount of RAM a computer provides but pay little attention to the ROM (read only memory). RAM has been likened to a notebook into which information can be written. When the entry is finished, the page can be torn out and a new, blank page is made available. ROM, on the other hand, is like a book. When the computer is acquired, its ROM is already filled

**FIGURE 3.3   A Detachable Numeric Pad** (Courtesy of Apple Computer, Inc.)

with information that can't be changed. As with a book, the larger the ROM, the more information ("free" programs) it will contain. Thus, the more ROM the computer has, the more things it can do without the need for directions from the user or from disk-based programs.

**Expandability.** Expandability refers to the capability of the basic system to be adapted to perform additional tasks. Computers that are easily expanded can be upgraded as additional functions are desired. A direct-connect modem, for example, makes it possible to communicate over the telephone lines. Also, additional memory can be installed in the form of cards or cartridges. (The term *card* refers to a circuit board that contains the necessary electronics to enable the computer to do things it wasn't originally set up to do. The method of placing a card in an expansion slot is illustrated in figure 3.4).

The dealer can show you how to expand the machine, or the documentation should provide instructions. Advertisements in journals will give you an indication of the many expansion devices available. Some expansion devices sit outside the computer and serve as an interface between some peripheral and the computer. (Recall that an interface is the electronic circuitry that links an input/output device, such as a printer or disk drive, to the computer itself.) For example, a color interface can be used to generate high-resolution graphics that some

FIGURE 3.4 **Adding an Eighty-Column Card** (Courtesy of Apple Computer, Inc.)

computers are otherwise incapable of producing. Also, memory packs can hook onto the outside of certain micros to give them more memory.

**The Display.** An eighty-column display is an important feature if word processing is a major function. Although word processing is certainly possible with a forty-column display, only half of the page is seen on the screen at one time; for some users this is a problem. Many inexpensive computers display short lines and lack the capability for expansion.

**Color and Sound.** Although most computers have a built-in color capability, a few do not: check the specifications to resolve this question. Sound capabilities range all the way from the ability to emit a little beep to the actual production of music. If this feature is important, ask the dealer for a demonstration.

**The Microprocessor.** As we have discussed, the microprocessor is the brains of the system. The brand name matters little; what is important is the size of the "word" the computer works with, which is a function of the microprocessor. A computer built around an 8-bit processor can address 64K of RAM, or over 64,000 memory spaces. By adding an electronic component (a card), the capacity can be doubled to 128K. This may seem like a lot, but when you recall that a byte represents a single letter or number, the amount seems less impressive. With a 16-bit processor the size of the memory goes up astronomically. A processor of this size can address from about one million to sixteen million bytes, or, to use computer terminology, from one megabyte to sixteen megabytes. There are also 32-bit processors, which enhance the computer's capabilities even more dramatically.

The advantages that 16-bit computers offer over the 8-bit ones are greater speed, greater storage, and the ability to handle larger and more complex programs. For most educational applications these are not very important considerations because the 8-bit machines on the market have not as yet reached the limits of their capabilities. As time goes on, however, and more elaborate programs become available, the advantages of the 16-bit machines will make them even more attractive and desirable.

**The Interface.**  The RS-232C interface is an electronic device used by some computers for communicating with the outside world. Modems use this connector to permit information typed on the keyboard to be sent over telephone lines. It is the most common kind of serial interface; computers that have it are capable of linking up with compatible peripherals without the need for an extra interfacing device.

Another type of interface—*parallel* interface—is also available. While *serial* transmission refers to the transmission of the bits that make up a signal one at a time in a series of pulses, *parallel* transmission involves sending the signals eight bits (one byte) at a time, as a chunk of information.

**The Operating System.**  An operating system is a program that converts the common commands from a disk-based program or a keyboard into the specific commands needed by a peripheral to make it operate. A number of operating systems are available, the more popular ones being those for the Apple and the IBM.

MS-DOS is used with the very popular IBM microcomputers and IBM-compatible systems. Apple has its own operating systems (DOS-3.3 and the newer ProDOS) and, like the IBM, has many imitators.

More educational software is currently available for the Apple than for any other microcomputer. In order to take advantage of this, various companies have created Apple "workalikes" that can run the programs. The IBM system has also become very popular and also has many emulators. Large amounts of software are being produced to take advantage of the IBMs and their clones; fortunately, many of these programs are of an educational nature.

**Graphics.**  The ability to generate graphics is a feature of virtually all microcomputers, but some have greater capability than others. The number of available graphics modes varies with the kind of computer, but the two most common ones are the high-resolution and the low-resolution modes. In the "high-res" mode the graphics have lines and details; in the "low-res" mode the graphics are composed of squares the size of a character.

The quality of the graphics is determined in large part by the number of pixels the computer activates on the screen. The higher the number of pixels, the more detailed will be the graphics. But if the computer can generate only low-resolution (block) graphics, even the finest monitor can do nothing more than display these blocks in bright colors and sharp detail. The standard number of hues is either eight (high-res) or sixteen (low-res), but some computers can display far more than this. If graphics is an important feature to you, be certain to check it out.

**Music.** Although most computers are capable of generating sound, some come better equipped for this task than others. The number of voices (sound channels), along with the octave range, make a difference in the quality of musical output. The more capable machines allow for up to nine octaves, and some have three or four voices. A built-in speaker is also a useful enhancement.

## Peripherals

The capability of a system to meet specific needs is largely determined by the kinds of peripherals that are hooked to the computer. A basic system suited to the teaching of computer awareness might consist of nothing more than an inexpensive micro with a television set and cassette recorder for peripherals. On the other hand, a good CAI system should have a disk drive and a quality color monitor to be most effective. Word processing and certain other applications will require, in addition to a good monitor and disk drive, a printer of some kind so that a hard copy of the document can be saved. Some computers provide for the output of sound signals to an external amplifier and high-quality speakers. Such an arrangement greatly enhances the production of music. For large-class use the capability of a computer to support several large monitors, situated around the room for easy viewing, is a useful feature: it makes both the demonstration of software and word processors and the teaching of programming much more effective. Finally, computers used to generate graphics are frequently attached to peripherals such as color printers, plotters, and graphics tablets.

The next section emphasizes selecting the proper peripherals to create systems that are uniquely suited to perform a certain task. Because standard devices were discussed extensively in chapter 2, they will not be described further; we will examine certain specialized peripherals, however—such as the braille printer for the blind and keyboards for music production—in some detail.

## STEP IV: MATCH THINGS UP

Now that you have considered some potential applications and identified the characteristics of various components, you are in a position to select the system that will best fit your particular needs. In the following pages the various applications will be matched with the appropriate hardware, thus identifying a range of possible systems.

## Programming and Authoring

If the objective is to program in BASIC, almost any microcomputer will serve the purpose (fig. 3.5); you need neither a powerful machine with lots of memory nor fancy peripherals. The programs can be saved on a cassette tape (although disks

FIGURE 3.5    An Inexpensive Computer Can Be Used for Programming
Exercises

are recommended), the lengthier programs having a cassette all to themselves,
which obviates the necessity of searching through the tape to find a specific program each time it is needed. The availability of software is unimportant because
most microcomputers come with BASIC built into them (or a disk containing
BASIC comes with the machine)—BASIC is the micro's native language.

If the plan is to use an authoring language such as PILOT, however, the requirements are a bit different. To author in Apple PILOT, for example, you will
need a computer with at least 48K of memory to hold the program. Also, two
disk drives are required, one for the author disk and one for the lesson disk. If
possible, a monitor rather than a TV receiver should be used to take advantage
of the excellent graphics capabilities.

The problem is somewhat the same if the objective is to teach Pascal. Many
computers are insufficient because the language itself takes up a large amount of

internal memory. If the computer lacks sufficient memory, it can probably be expanded by adding a card or a memory pack. However, the program's availability must be considered—Pascal is not available for every micro on the market. Also, the quality of the documentation is a factor because teachers may have to learn how to use this language on their own. Although some public school personnel know how to program in Pascal and can assist their colleagues, formal inservice classes are not generally available. The increased interest in this language is reflected by the tendency of universities and colleges to offer more Pascal classes than ever before. As more teachers plan to prepare students for the Pascal-based advanced placement exams, options for learning this language are certain to increase, and the quality of the documentation will continue to be of top priority.

A computer with lots of memory is also needed to run Logo. Although small versions of this language are available, full Logo requires a machine with 64K of RAM. Some computers provide a wider range of colors for use with this language than the usual six, so a good color monitor is essential to make use of the turtle graphics capabilities.

For any programming application it is wise to have the best keyboard you can afford (although it is not as critical with this application as it is with word processing, for example). Most experts agree, though, that economizing on the keyboard will ultimately lead to dissatisfaction as the range of applications continues to expand.

## Computer Literacy

Computer literacy is an area in which the acquisition of several inexpensive computers might take precedence over the purchase of one or two more expensive ones, depending in large part upon the prevailing consensus as to what computer literacy entails. If the objective is simply to have the students load and run a few programs and perhaps write a few lines of BASIC, or to use the computer for such activities as learning about ethics in a computerized society or discussing the impact of computers on jobs, no unusual peripherals are needed. Some additional equipment, however, such as an inexpensive printer, can be most useful. For external storage, inexpensive cassette recorders are adequate, although they are much slower and less reliable than disk drives. A monitor is not needed—the computer can simply be hooked up to the school's television set—but if one is purchased, a monochrome model will be adequate (although much is lost when programs that include colorful graphic passages are run).

A bonus from acquiring a number of inexpensive computers is that students can check them out and take them home. Cheaper systems are expendable, whereas more expensive ones must be made to last as long as possible. If the cheap machines serve a useful purpose for two or three years, the school has most likely recouped its investment. Also, when one of them breaks down, it can be passed on to the electronics class to be worked on by the students. If they fix it, all the better, but if not, nothing is really lost.

## Computer-Assisted Instruction

Be sure to purchase a system that has quantities of good software available if CAI is to be the major application (regardless of the deals on hardware that are advertised). Figure 3.6 shows a small section of the thousands of CAI programs that are available. More educational programs are currently on the market for the Apple than for any other machine, but IBM, Commodore, and Radio Shack also have good selections.

As mentioned previously, disk-based programs are preferred over those on cassette (although many teachers report satisfactory results from the latter), one reason being that many more programs are available on disks than on cassettes. Also, with a bit of training, students find the disk system easier to use than its cassette-based counterpart.

Many of the best programs require a considerable amount of memory, so this becomes an important factor in the selection of a CAI system. Also, a color display is essential if the graphics capabilities of many programs are to be realized. Although a monitor will provide much higher quality resolution and color, if you must economize, simply hook the computer up to the school's color TV.

Networking is one way to stretch a school's CAI resources, hooking several computers to a centrally located printer and disk drive. To make this arrangement work, you must purchase a controller to synchronize the operation of all the components. The cost of the controller is modest when compared to the cost

**FIGURE 3.6  Some CAI Software**

of providing multiple printers and drives for a number of stations. There are other ways to network, and you may wish to check out the options to determine if any of them would be useful in your school. A word of warning, though: copyright restrictions are such that, without an agreement from the publisher, many good programs cannot legally be used in a network. So, before a school makes a commitment to networking, this problem should be thoroughly examined.

## Graphics

Most microcomputers have pretty good graphics capabilities, some far better than others. Most machines generate graphics through the use of the same integrated circuit chip that performs the other normal functions, but some machines, such as the Atari, use a separate chip for this purpose; this approach makes the generation of superior graphics possible.

As with other applications, the kind of program determines the end result. For example, a combination of graphic designs and fancy type can be produced by such programs as Fontrix and Print Shop. You can create banners, illustrations for publications, personalized stationery, or just about anything you wish with programs of this kind. The completed designs are then printed as hard copy using a dot matrix printer. An example of a graph made with Fontrix is shown in figure 3.7, and the design in figure 3.8 was created with the Print Shop program. Other graphics programs are Pixit and Blazing Paddles (both from Baudville), Poster (Scholastic Software), Delta Drawing (Spinnaker), and PC Paint (Mouse Systems).

Some programs are designed primarily to generate screen graphics that are incorporated into a computer-based lesson; others develop simulations or produce original material for photographic slides. The PILOT authoring pro-

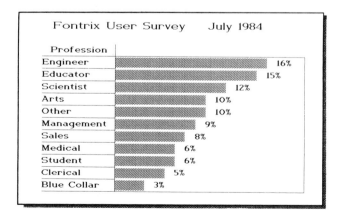

**FIGURE 3.7 A Graphic Created with the Fontrix Program** (Courtesy of Data Transforms, Inc.)

**FIGURE 3.8    A Design from Print Shop** (Courtesy of Broderbund Software)

gram, which includes a good graphics editor that lets you create graphics to illustrate a disk-based lesson, is an example of software dedicated mainly to the creation of displays for the computer screen.

In large part, the quality of screen graphics is determined by the kind of display used. An RGB monitor is preferable, but it is too expensive for most educational applications. Composite color monitors do an excellent job for a reasonable price, and the color TV receiver is next in quality. The least desirable graphic display device is the monochrome television receiver, although color does not necessarily mean quality in computer monitors: for certain graphics applications where color is of secondary importance, high-fidelity monochrome computer monitors, such as those used with the Macintosh, yield excellent results.

The number of available colors on systems with two graphics modes typically varies from eight in the high-resolution mode to sixteen in low-res, but some computers are capable of generating many more colors than this by varying the luminance of the hues. Also, a built-in character set on some machines causes various kinds of graphics characters to be printed instead of letters when the proper keys are pressed.

Various alternative input devices permit the drawing of graphics without using the keyboard for cursor movement. Graphics tablets are very convenient and quite easy to use: the KoalaPad, for example, which was described in chapter

2, permits the user to define various kinds of figures by moving a stylus or finger over its surface. Figure 3.9 shows a user selecting the draw mode from the display of options on the screen. A press of the button at the top of the pad will provide a clear screen for drawing.

Penpad, a sophisticated version of the graphics tablet, has a paper-covered surface upon which the user actually draws in ink with a special pen; the movements of the pen send electronic signals to the computer, where they are translated into a graphic display (see fig. 3.10). A unique feature of the system is that it is capable of reading text that is printed on the pad: a letter (even a relatively crude one) can be recognized and displayed as a precise character on the screen. Combinations of graphics and text can be created in a natural, direct fashion using this system.

The mouse is another friendly device that makes input simple and easy. The Macintosh uses this device to direct the cursor to the various selections shown at the edges of the screen in figure 3.11. The selected option is "pulled" into the drawing space, where it is used in the creation of the illustration.

If hard copy (graphics on paper or plastic) is desired, a printer or plotter is needed. The least expensive device for this purpose is a dot matrix printer. Al-

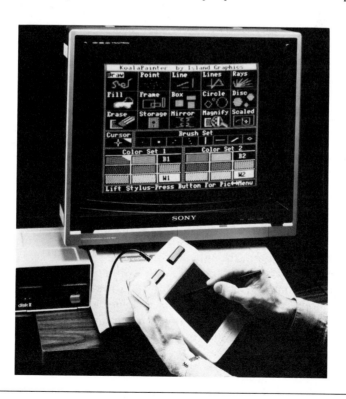

FIGURE 3.9 The KoalaPad Being Used with the KoalaPainter Graphics Program (Courtesy of Koala Technologies Corporation)

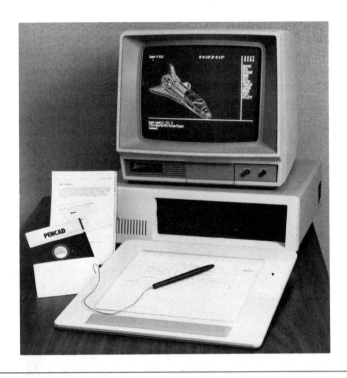

FIGURE 3.10  The Penpad System (Courtesy of Pencept, Inc.)

though monochrome printers are the most common, versions with multicolored ribbons are available for the production of colored hard-copy graphics. Many programs permit the generation of colored hard copy with the proper printer. KoalaPainter, used with the KoalaPad, is an example of such a program: colored graphics are printed on paper using a color dot matrix printer.

Inkjet printers, which produce hard copy of exceptional quality, are now reasonably priced and within the budget of most schools. Plotters, although useful, are limited to special applications and are still fairly expensive in the more versatile models; once again, though, advances in technology have caused prices to drop dramatically. The graphics produced by plotters are perhaps the best of all, due to the fact that pens are used to do the drawing.

The availability of graphics software packages is an important consideration in choosing a system. The selection for certain brands of computers is broader than for others, so a little research in this area will be worthwhile.

## Music

Some individuals enjoy the challenge of writing programs in BASIC to cause the computer to produce music, but this is time-consuming and involves learning a specialized kind of programming. If you wish to learn to create compositions using standard notation and to study traditional music theory, commercial music software will permit you to circumvent the programming and get right down to the music. Thus, the types of programs available for a given brand of computer is an important consideration.

An example of a music program with many useful features is Bank Street Music Writer. You can place notes in any position on the blank screen staff simply by moving the cursor to the selected spot. The music can then be played back and changed if desired; a printing option lets you print sheet music once the composition is finished (see fig. 3.12).

Another program that lets you create your own musical compositions is Polywriter. Its print option produces clean, professional-looking sheet music on a dot matrix printer (see fig. 3.13). Some other music programs are Early Games (Counterpoint Software), Music Construction Set (Electronic Arts), Songwriter (Scarborough), Music Shop (Broderbund), and Music Composer (Atari).

Some microcomputers are better music machines than others because they have built-in "music makers" in the form of special IC chips and therefore need no modification to create beautiful music. Others, however, do little more than put out a series of beeps with varying pitches and durations. To upgrade a computer of this type you will need to add a special circuit board.

FIGURE 3.11  A Macintosh Graphics Screen (Courtesy of Apple Computer, Inc.)

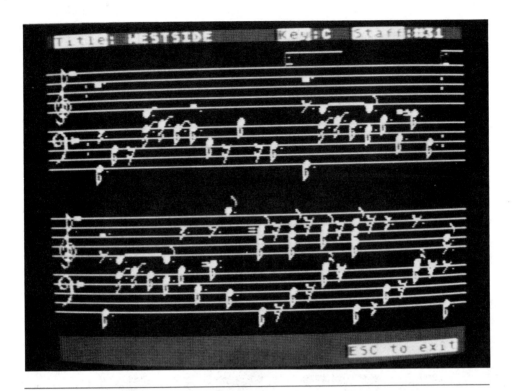

**FIGURE 3.12  A Screen Shot from Bank Street Music Writer** (©Copyright 1985, Mindscape, Inc. All rights reserved)

To create harmony you will need a computer with more than one voice. Three voices is the most common number, but a few computers (and also the plug-in circuit boards) provide more.

Another feature to consider is the number of octaves available with a given computer—this varies considerably and can range upward to eight or nine.

In addition to the computer and the software, you should consider the available add-on devices. Because the Commodore 64 has excellent music capabilities, many companies have manufactured keyboards for it. Other keyboards will work with Apples, IBMs, and some other brands. These peripherals are more nearly like musical instruments than is the standard keyboard, which resembles a typewriter. Although it is hard to imagine creating music on a typewriter, a similar keyboard is the standard input device for most music programs. By attaching a peripheral such as The Incredible Musical Keyboard from Sight and Sound Music (see fig. 3.14), you'll feel more like a musician and less like a typist.

**FIGURE 3.13** **A Printout of Sheet Music from Polywriter** (Courtesy of Passport Designs, Inc.)

## Computer-Managed Instruction

Computer-managed instruction involves collecting and manipulating data relating to student performance, then using the information to prescribe appropriate instruction. Although CMI capabilities are frequently built into many drill-and-practice and tutorial programs, a CMI program should be purchased to take full advantage of this function. Dual disk drives are useful, since a data disk is used with the program to store information about the students. A monochrome monitor is usually adequate because the display generally consists exclusively of text; some of the newer CMI packages, though, include graphics capabilities, often in color. Entry will be via the keyboard, for the most part, so a computer keyboard with a standard typewriter layout is desirable. A numeric pad makes the typing of numbers fast and convenient. For some applications you may wish to investigate alternative methods of input, such as punched cards and a card reader, or an optical scanner to save time in grading numerous tests. If the system is to be

**FIGURE 3.14** **The Incredible Musical Keyboard™** (Courtesy of Sight & Sound Music Software, Inc.)

used by a school rather than by an individual teacher, more storage will be needed; the acquisition of a hard disk drive to handle massive amounts of data may be practical.

Finally, perhaps the most important consideration is that of program quality and availability. Some CMI programs have many more useful features than others; check several of them out before making your selection.

## Networking and Telecommunications

If the objective is to tie several computers and peripherals together to form a multiuser system, you will want to investigate the available hardware designed for this purpose. Some kind of interface is usually required to handle the problems of integration and access that arise in networking, as are wires or cables to tie all the parts together.

If you wish to access a remote data base over the telephone lines, a modem and some accompanying software will be necessary. Practically all micros are capable of using a modem, and some come with one built in. Acoustic varieties are the least expensive and should serve well for school applications. You will also need a special interface (an RS-232C) that enables you to connect to the remote data base; again, some computers come with this equipment on board. A monochrome monitor is sufficient for telecommunications because the information will be in text format. Finally, a printer will be needed so that hard copy can be saved for future study; dot matrix printers work nicely for this purpose.

## Word Processing

Plan to spend some time trying out the various programs before making any decision to purchase a word processor. Some sophisticated ones, such as WordStar or WordPerfect, might be excellent if the objective is to teach word processing to high school business education majors. These would be very poor choices, though, for younger students or for older ones who merely want to learn a simple system for personal use. For these audiences programs such as Cut & Paste and The Bank Street Writer are excellent choices. For serious word processing a program that generates seventy or eighty columns is preferred (see fig. 3.15a). However, some very good programs put out as few as twenty lines; you generally have the option of increasing this number, though. A forty-line display is shown in fig. 3.15b for comparison with the more standard configuration.

Schools will find that IBM PCs have an excellent keyboard arrangement for word processing applications. There are several function keys, so it isn't necessary to type in all kinds of commands to edit text or to perform other word processing functions. However useful function keys might happen to be, though, they aren't essential for successful word processing. All that most school applications really need are a comfortable keyboard, a fairly sizable memory, and a good word processing program.

The necessary peripherals include a monochrome monitor and a printer. Although a character printer such as the daisy wheel gives the best copy, many dot matrix printers now produce good letter-quality hard copy. For most school applications an inexpensive dot matrix printer will suffice. Dual disk drives are preferred because this arrangement facilitates saving the text; however, a single drive is often suitable, particularly with simpler programs.

It has been mentioned that an adequate amount of internal memory is important to word processing. A small memory will restrict the quantity of text that can be typed in before it is necessary to save it on the disk.

## Special Education Applications

The area of special education is one in which the use of microcomputers is booming. Seemingly, innovations are coming onto the market almost every day. Many of the alternative input devices—light pens, graphics tablets, voice input units, oversized keyboards, and touch-sensitive screens—can be used for special education applications. Voice synthesizers (for those who are unable to use normal speech) can change typed input into spoken words. Switches that require a very light pressure for activation are used by the disabled to feed information to the computer. Quadriplegics are able to use devices such as this by pressing the

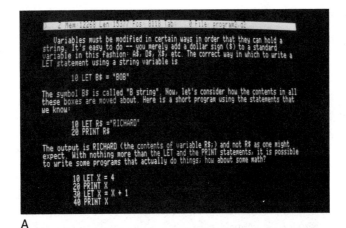

**FIGURE 3.15**  (a) An Eighty-Column Display; (b) A Forty-Column Display

switch with the cheek or chin to form phrases from characters in a display on the screen.

A variety of special peripherals has been developed to enable visually impaired and blind individuals to take advantage of various computer capabilities. Substituting VTEK's DP-10 Large Print Display Processor for the standard monitor will provide visually impaired students with characters as large as 5½ inches on a 19-inch screen (see fig. 3.16).

The Braille Display Processor translates visual output from a standard software program into braille output on a special "window" that maintains the precise screen format. The blind user can interact with any type of program, including spreadsheets, with this device. And braille printers, such as the MBOSS-1 (shown in fig. 3.17), provide the blind student with a variety of up-

**FIGURE 3.16** **DP-10 Large Print Display Processor** (Courtesy of VTEK)

to-date hard-copy materials that can be created in the classroom with a word processor.

For those who are unable to speak but can use a keyboard, equipment is available to translate typed information into spoken words. If a standard keyboard presents too great an impediment, specially designed ones can be used. The Words+ Portable Voice II, for example, provides the user with an external switch panel that serves as an expanded keyboard composed of switches varying in size from one square inch to much larger. The top surface of each switch can contain pictures, letters, words, or other appropriate symbols (fig. 3.18). Along with such adaptive devices as these, an increasing number of programs are aimed at the individual with special needs. The problem is one of selecting a computer system that not only permits the use of specific adaptive devices but also operates the software appropriate for the groups being considered. A thorough overview of the software offerings from the various producers should assist you in your selection.

## Classroom Management

The most common type of program in use for classroom management is called an "electronic gradebook." Tedious grading and record-keeping tasks are taken

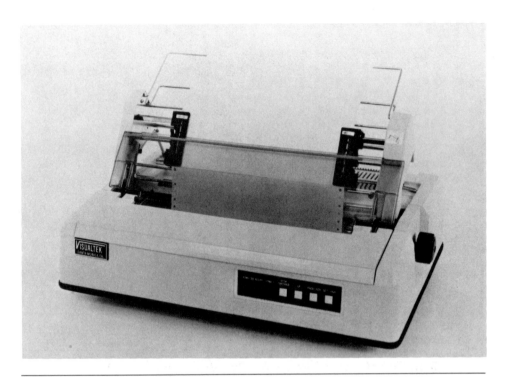

FIGURE 3.17   MBOSS-1 Braille Printer (Courtesy of VTEK)

over by the computer, for the most part, thus freeing the teacher for more stimulating activities.

A good electronic gradebook has plenty of storage for large numbers of students, classes, and subjects and for as many grades as might be given. The gradebook should also be capable of performing all the math necessary to provide the desired results, whether it is nothing more than a final grade or more complex statistics such as means, averages, and ranks. You should therefore select a program that provides a wide range of statistical functions.

Certain programs provide graphic features such as the ability to produce graphs and charts, which in most cases can be printed as hard copy. The printing of report cards, letters, progress reports, and such can also be managed by most programs. A small sample of gradebook programs includes The Graphics Gradebook (Heath), EA Gradebook (Educational Activities, Inc.), Master Grades (Midwest Software), and Classmate (Davidson and Associates); other excellent programs are also available.

Other kinds of specialized programs can perform just about any kind of classroom or school management task you can think of: financial accounting, scheduling, and attendance are among the most common. But specialized software is not required to implement a successful management plan: you can use

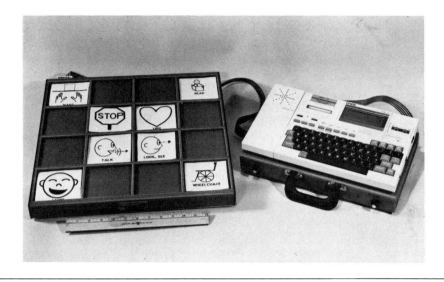

FIGURE 3.18 Words+ Portable Voice II—Expanded Keyboard Version
(Courtesy of Words+ Inc., 1125-D Stewart Court, Sunnyvale, CA 94086)

available applications programs such as word processors, spreadsheets, data base management programs, and integrated programs to do the job. Chapter 5, on tool software, explains the structure and use of these programs in detail.

The usual approach in using a spreadsheet, or "electronic ledger," is to list the names of the students in the first column, then to enter their scores in succeeding columns. Formulas can be entered to give total points, averages, or a grade for each student. You can use a similar arrangement to keep track of projects that have or have not been submitted. Whenever necessary, you can obtain a printed hard copy of the information in the spreadsheet. Some spreadsheet titles are listed in chapter 5.

Data base management packages can also be used to store categorized information about students. Using keywords that correspond to the various fields (items of information) enables you to identify students with specific characteristics and needs. This type of system is particularly useful for generating Individual Education Programs (IEPs) for special education students.

Integrated application programs combining such functions as word processing, spreadsheeting, and data base management capabilities are useful for classroom and school management applications. Educators find demanding tasks like scheduling to be much easier when they use the computer to keep track of the many variables involved.

The system required to run classroom management software need not be elaborate. A monochrome monitor is typically preferred over a color monitor because the data are displayed primarily as text. If you are considering a management package with graphic output capabilities, you will need a printer capable of producing graphics. A dot matrix printer has both text and graphic capabilities; a character printer, on the other hand, will provide excellent text but will lack the graphics capabilities.

At the school level, the system might have to be upgraded so that more storage (memory) is available. A hard disk drive could be a useful addition to the system. A printer capable of the rapid output of quality hard copy will also be needed. Again, graphics capabilities should be considered if graphs and charts are to be included in conjunction with the text.

## Robots

Because different robots do different things, setting up a list of objectives prior to purchasing one will be helpful. If you are interested simply in demonstrating certain Logo commands using something other than the traditional screen display, an inexpensive robot such as Turtle Tot will do. Various colored pens controlled by Logo commands enable the Tot to draw patterns on large sheets of paper taped to the floor.

The Scorpion, from Rhino Robots (see fig. 3.19), is a mobile robot boasting a host of special features, including a built-in microprocessor (in a sense, it car-

FIGURE 3.19   The Scorpion (Courtesy of Rhino Robots, Inc.)

ries its intelligence around with it). Topo is a larger, more expensive robot that has speech capabilities, is more humanlike in appearance, and is controlled through radio signals generated at the computer.

Other robots, more like the dedicated devices found in industry, are stationary versions that most often assume the configuration of a mechanical arm. A unit on careers, a project in the math class, or a demonstration in physics might be enhanced through the use of devices of this nature. These stationary robots, like those that move around the room, are programmable; indeed, some students have even programmed them to play chess.

An XR Educational Robot is shown in figure 3.20. This machine has features of a true robot, such as DC servo drive (a device that speeds up or slows down the movement), but it has the educational feature of open construction for observability.

Among the necessary requirements for making the computer compatible with the robot is the availability of the language the robot understands. Most robots work with Logo, although some use BASIC and a few can be programmed in FORTH. The RS-232C interface is required with some applications; the robot is linked to the computer via this interface with a long, flexible cord. Others require a radio frequency interface that enables the computer to communicate without a physical link-up such as a cord. Sophisticated robots are

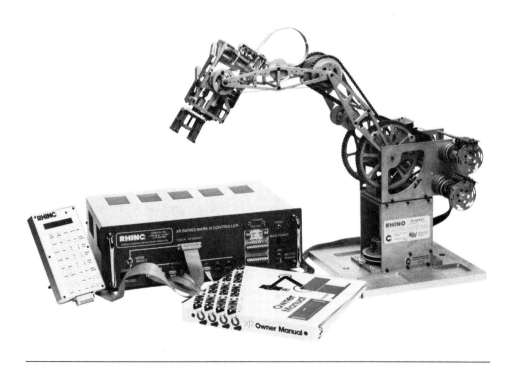

**FIGURE 3.20  The XR Educational Robot** (Courtesy of Rhino Robots, Inc.)

designed so that programs can be stored inside them, thus emancipating them from dependence on the computer.

Currently, robots will only work on certain microcomputers, so it is important to determine prior to purchasing one if it will work with your machine.

## STEP V: TRY IT YOURSELF

Plan to spend some time visiting the vendors; it can be fun as well as educational. Although it is not always feasible to assemble the precise system of choice prior to final purchase, you can check out the various components in preferred combinations whenever possible and in other configurations when necessary. For example, the printer you have chosen may not be part of the inventory of the vendor who sells your brand of computer, but you can still determine how well it performs regardless of the computer with which it is working. On the other hand, be certain that a selected peripheral—the printer for example—is compatible with the preferred micro. This holds true for all components. An RGB monitor may provide vivid color in a demonstration setting, but some popular computers won't accommodate monitors of this type.

Set aside an hour or two for each session if you can manage, gather some software and documentation, settle down at the computer, and turn it on. Try out the keyboard; see how it responds. You should check the keyboard for construction—it should feel firm and sturdy. Is the layout of any special keys logical? What about the spacing of the keys: about right, too crowded, too far apart? How about key action? Full-stroke keys are generally preferred. There should be some kind of feedback so that you know when the character has been transmitted—the way the key feels when it is pressed, for example, or the sound that is made upon key contact (if such a sound is likely to get on your nerves, find out if it can be turned on and off). Regular typewriters are mechanical and give feedback as the keys are pressed; but computer keyboards are electronic and feel very different from the mechanical ones, so some kind of contrived feedback is useful. According to some rating scales, the keyboard is ranked next in importance (along with memory size) to the cost of the computer system itself, so it is a very important item.

Load an application program such as a word processor. If you aren't sure how to proceed, ask the salesperson for help or refer to the documentation. Check the clarity of the text display and the number of characters per line. Some computers generate forty or fewer characters, which may not be adequate if word processing is to be one of the important applications.

Run a couple of instructional programs that have abundant text and graphics. Are the words legible? Is the color rich and saturated? Keep in mind that the quality of the display is in large part determined by the monitor; don't blame the computer for inferior output if the monitor is at fault. If the program being reviewed has sound, consider the tone and quality. If sound capability is important to you, ask to try a program in which sound is used extensively. Finally, if composition is of interest, ask to use one of the new programs for composing music (if one is available).

Examine the various peripherals such as joysticks, touch tablets, modems, and speech synthesizers. Your vendor may not have all of these on hand, but he should be able to show you literature to illustrate the potential of a particular brand of computer.

Try out as many functions included in the documentation as you have time for. See how easy or difficult it is to load a program, run it, and list it (if permitted). Create some information of your own and save it on the disk. Using the documentation as a guide, see what can be done with your homemade program. All of these steps are particularly useful if programming activities are to be carried out by students.

While you are there, you will want to get a feel for how helpful and supportive the vendor is going to be. Some are definitely more interested and more knowledgeable than others, and this is a very important consideration when selecting a system.

## SUMMARY

Although many educators will not have the opportunity to be involved in the selection of a microcomputer system for their school, others will find themselves on committees whose task is to make this decision. Additionally, some individuals will elect to buy their own personal system and will want to make the best choice possible.

Many less capable microcomputers have either disappeared from the market altogether or are slowly fading from the scene. Unfortunately, a few very good machines have suffered a similar fate. As a result, fewer distinctive computers are available today than was the case a short time ago. Certainly there are more brands, but many of these are workalikes that use either the IBM or Apple operating systems; thus the choice has been somewhat diminished, and the selection of a computer has therefore become a bit less frustrating.

The peripheral market, on the other hand, is bulging with an ever-expanding selection of devices that, when coupled with the computer, create a diverse array of systems calculated to serve virtually every conceivable need.

It is in putting computer systems together that the approach described in this chapter is most useful. The first step is to define the objectives—the applications for which the system will be used. Next, consider the available software and examine the hardware. Finally, match the desired applications with the available hardware and software to identify the best system.

Once the selection has been made, shopping begins. The chapter concludes with a discussion of things to do and to look for when purchasing a system. Starting with a wish list is a good idea. The extent and nature of vendor support is an important consideration, as is the quality of the documentation. Also of importance are the reputation of the company, the number of computers it has in the field, and the amount of available software.

Using criteria such as those described should enable the educator to do a better job of equipment acquisition. Having completed this chapter, you should now be well prepared to examine and perhaps select a computer system. Hopefully, your quest will be a pleasant and successful one.

## REFERENCES

Barbour, A. "Memory Expansion Boards." *Electronic Learning* (March 1986): 46–48.

Burke, R. "Selecting Micros for Schools." *Electronic Learning* (April 1984): 18–23.

Coburn, E. *Microcomputers: Hardware, Software, and Programming.* Indianapolis: Bobbs-Merrill, 1984.

Dyrli, O. "The Hardware Game: Sorting the Winners from the Losers." *Classroom Computer Learning* (April/May 1984): 59–61.

*Electronic Learning.* "EL's National Directory of Software Preview Centers Part I." *Electronic Learning* (January 1984): 59–62, 102–7.

————. "EL's National Directory of Software Preview Centers Part II." *Electronic Learning* (February 1984): 68–70, 100–112.

————. "Tracking Down the Right Computer." *Electronic Learning* (January 1984): 39–45.

Jones, W., et al. *Computer Literacy.* Reston, VA: Reston, 1983.

Leininger, S. "The No-Compromise Computer." *Popular Computing* (July 1982): 80–84.

"The 1986/87 Classroom Computer Learning Hardware Buyers' Guide." *Classroom Computer Learning* (March 1986): 25–35.

Noland, J. "Buying That First Computer." *Electronic Education* (March 1984): 19, 50.

Rubin, C., and Strehlo, K. "Why So Many Computers Look Like the IBM Standard." *Personal Computing* (March 1984): 52–65.

Smith, R., and Spokony, M. "Your Guide to Selecting and Evaluating a Computer System." *Electronic Education* (March/April 1982): 6–9.

# 4

# INSTRUCTIONAL SOFTWARE

## INTRODUCTION

Over the past few years the quality of computer-based instructional software has undergone considerable improvement. Many of the early programs were written by computer buffs who had little background in learning theory or pedagogy. As educators became familiar with programming techniques they began to create lessons that met their instructional needs but were far from being technically elegant. Today, however, an effort is being made to unify the two camps and thereby create sound lessons that are also technically well programmed.

This happy marriage has come about for a number of reasons. For one thing, some of the large textbook manufacturers are getting involved, thus bringing their considerable resources to bear on the problem. The federal government is also interested in improving the product and has implemented a number of plans with this purpose in mind. Software manufacturers have come to recognize the sales potential of good educational packages to both the home and school markets and have geared up to meet the need: estimates are that for every dollar spent to acquire computers, between five and eight are spent for software.

Some producers have put together high-powered teams of subject matter specialists, experts in learning theory, professional programmers, and instructional developers in an effort to produce the best possible programs. Comparing one of the newer programs with almost any of the older ones will illustrate that this effort is paying off.

The distinction made between *software* and *courseware* is worth mentioning here, since you will encounter these terms repeatedly. Software refers to the computer program stored on a medium such as a disk or tape. Courseware is an educational term used to refer to instructional materials consisting of computer-based lessons (or software) together with related print materials such as guides, workbooks, worksheets, appropriate maps and diagrams, teacher's manuals, and perhaps other traditional kinds of media (fig. 4.1).

## THE GENERAL PURPOSE CONCEPT

Why is software such an important item? Simply stated, it is the software that makes the computer such a versatile device.

Microcomputers are general purpose machines; that is, they are capable of performing a wide variety of functions given the appropriate programs to guide them. Dedicated computers exist because of the nature of the tasks they perform. A dedicated computer might control a system of traffic signals or be used

**FIGURE 4.1   Courseware Includes the Disk-based Program and Various Print Materials**

in a diagnostic laboratory. A more ubiquitous dedicated computer is a word processor—not a general purpose computer loaded with a word processing program but a computer made for this purpose exclusively.

General purpose systems are made to perform one task or another by changing the set of instructions (the program) the computer follows; the computer thus changes roles as readily as the user changes programs. At the conclusion of a math session, for example, a graphics program can enable students to create colorful designs or perhaps animated figures using the same machine. Furthermore, the programs, if well designed, emulate the best in instructional pedagogy. Thus it is the software, and not the computer, that is the most critical element in meeting the students' instructional needs.

## SYSTEM SOFTWARE

Before moving on to the discussion of the applications programs that permit the computer to change its character and functions, let us consider some little-known, special programs whose sole function is to manage the computer and its peripherals. These essential programs, some of which were built into the computer as special integrated circuit chips at the time it was manufactured, are referred to as *system software*. When programs are stored in the ROM, they are often referred to as *firmware*. (Many kinds of programs, including word processors and graphics programs, are available as firmware.)

One such program is the BASIC language interpreter (or compiler in some cases). Since the words used in BASIC cannot be understood directly by the CPU, which can only respond to instructions written in a binary code, an interpreter must be used to convert the higher-level programming language instructions into the lower-level machine language. Some microcomputers do not have an internally stored BASIC: these machines use a cartridge, which the user inserts into a slot, or have the language stored on a disk.

A second firmware-based program is the monitor, whose duties are to serve as the overseer of the system, monitor the movement of information to and from the keyboard and display, and relay all this to the CPU. Expert programmers are able to enter the monitor by typing in special commands; then they can find out precisely what is stored in a memory space, change the contents, and even create programs using machine language instructions if they wish.

A third kind of system software is the operating system. Among other things, this program tells the computer how to deal with an application or instructional program that is stored on a disk. The program on the disk is made up of instructions that are meant to work with the program itself, not to manage the internal housekeeping operations of the computer, which is the responsibility of the system software.

An essential part of the operating system, if disk drives are to be used, is the disk operating system (DOS). Various approaches to making the DOS available to the computer are used. At times it must be loaded from a disk before the computer can run a program (fig. 4.2). Often it is placed right on the disk along with

**FIGURE 4.2    A Disk Containing the DOS and a Manual Explaining Its Use**

the application program. The DOS instructions on the disk enable the computer
and the drives to communicate with each other and to work together. Thus, before a brand-new disk can work it must be "initialized"; the DOS commands must
be added and the surface formatted so that other kinds of programs can be
stored there (directions for this operation are included in the manual that comes
with every computer).

   Although you won't be aware of the operating system because it does its
work so unobtrusively, the converse is true of the instructional programs that
you will run. These are the applications programs that put all that information
on the screen, ask for input, give feedback, instruct you, and sometimes frustrate
you. Our principal concern in this and upcoming chapters will be for programs
of this type—those that reside outside the machine on a storage medium such as
a diskette. Programs of this nature typically are part of a package that includes
documentation and, in many cases, textual materials such as workbooks and
worksheets. This software (or courseware) makes a special purpose device of the

general purpose microcomputer. There are basically three broad categories of instructional software, each of which has a number of unique features.

## THREE MODES

Microcomputers seem to have unlimited uses in education: teachers, administrators, and students discover new applications almost daily. Students create musical works using computers. Aspiring artists replace brushes with keyboards, canvases with display screens. Using the computer as a drill master in math or languages is a common practice. And writers find the word processing functions—composing text, editing it, and printing it—both timesaving and convenient.

The many seemingly unrelated applications make more sense when they are considered within the context of some kind of classification scheme, such as that devised by Robert P. Taylor of Teachers College in New York, which uses three broad headings: the *tutor* mode, the *tool* mode, and the *tutee* mode. When the computer is used to instruct in traditional subject matter areas, it becomes a tutor; when used as an aid to performing a task, it is a tool; when it becomes the object to be studied and programmed, it is a tutee.

### The Tutor Mode

Appropriate software enables the computer to tutor the student in a broad range of subjects. The efficiency with which this is done depends upon how expertly the specific program was designed; thus, the more accomplished the instructional designer and the programmer, the better the program. Among the problems intrinsic to teaching programs is that of individualization: whereas a human teacher is able to respond to the needs of the student on the basis of observation and interaction, a programmer must anticipate potential needs and build strategies for dealing with them into the program.

The term computer-assisted instruction is commonly used to describe what takes place in the tutor mode. The broad view of CAI typically includes a number of different program formats, among which is the tutorial. Although drill-and-practice programs, simulations, and instructional games are also classified as types of CAI, confusion can be avoided if the term *tutor* is understood in the broad sense of *teacher*. Thus the teacher (or tutor) may use a tutorial approach when new concepts are being taught but may use drills to reinforce what has been learned during the tutorial sequence (fig. 4.3).

The tutor mode at its best includes diagnostic capabilities to determine the needs of the particular student, prescription functions that provide appropriate content and activities, tutorial functions to assist the student through the program, and assessment and record-keeping capabilities to manage instruction. Although increased interest is being given to other kinds of CAI programs, drill-and-practice activities continue to predominate in the classroom. This condition is bound to change, however, as other kinds of activities, such as word processing and discovery programs, gain in favor and availability.

**FIGURE 4.3    Computers Being Used in the Tutor Mode** (Courtesy of Commodore Electronics Limited)

## The Tool Mode

A tool is defined as an instrument for doing work or accomplishing a task. Once a worker becomes proficient with it, the tool then becomes an extension to be used intuitively, without the need for premeditation. To observe instances of the computer being used as a tool it is only necessary to visit a bank, a typical office, or almost any other place where information is being processed or created—including the schools.

In the tool mode the computer is not looked upon as an aid to, or surrogate for, the teacher, as it is in the tutor mode; nor is it an object to be studied, as in the tutee mode. Rather, it serves a utilitarian function in getting a job done. The particular program that is working within the computer determines the nature of the tasks that can be accomplished. When the computer becomes a tool, it assumes a variety of identities. It may become a paintbrush, enabling an artist to create colorful graphics; it may change into a magical typewriter that permits the aspiring author to manipulate words and paragraphs with the press of a key; or it may be transformed into an electronic spreadsheet capable of reflecting constantly changing data.

The widespread acceptance of tool applications such as word processing and data base management has caused schools to rethink the meaning of computer literacy. Where once this term implied programming, it is rapidly coming to mean the competent use of a variety of computerized tools (for a discussion of this application, see chapter 5).

## The Tutee Mode

For a third computer use, the roles are reversed: the machine becomes the tutee and the student becomes the tutor. The student teaches the computer by programming it (fig. 4.4). In this approach, learning about computers is seen as a discipline unique unto itself. The subject matter is the computer, rather than a more traditional subject such as English, math, or biology. Students learn first and foremost how to program, but they may also learn something about how the computer works.

Whereas using the computer as a tool can be thought of as an extension of the CAI approach, the idea of programming (the computer as subject matter) is quite a different thing. Software is the essential ingredient in both the tutor and tool modes: it converts the computer from a math to a science teacher or changes it from a special kind of typewriter into an artist's electronic canvas. But when the computer becomes the subject for study, as in the tutee mode, the software, though indispensable, is unobtrusive. The student seems to interact directly with the computer. Where formerly the essence of the machine was masked by the software with which the student interacted, now the machine obeys only those instructions that come directly from the student.

## THE KINDS OF CAI SOFTWARE

In the pages that follow, emphasis will be placed upon the varieties of instructional software; however, we have also included computer-managed instruction in this chapter because programs of this type perform many of the tasks of the human teacher (such as keeping records, grading tests, and prescribing instruction).

No standard classification scheme for educational software or courseware has yet been adopted, and some confusion exists because of this. Some authors place simulations in the larger category of instructional games; others accept drill and practice and tutorials as types of CAI programs but place all other types into some other category.

In this text, the system as outlined by P. Coburn, et al. in *Practical Guide to Computers in Education* is used with modifications. These authors classify drill and practice, tutorials, simulations, and instructional games as computer-assisted instruction, and they place applications such as word processing and telecomputing into a category they call "instructional/learning tools."

## Drill and Practice

Some authors (see Dennis and Kansky) point out that there is a distinction between a drill lesson and a practice lesson. They prefer to use the terms separately, while acknowledging the fact that both share a common purpose: "to fix concepts previously learned." Drills, according to this approach, should be used "to describe activities which seek to fix simple associations such as the names and

FIGURE 4.4   Programming: The Computer as a Tutee

symbols of the chemical elements." In contrast, a practice activity will lead to "the
smooth execution of some process or procedure." Although such a fine distinction does exist, we will follow the popular trend and lump the terms together. If
we were involved in the development of instruction and the authoring of lessons
rather than in evaluating courseware, a separation of the two activities would
definitely be in order.

The drill-and-practice program encourages the improvement of skills that
have been previously learned. For example, the design of a math-based program
is such that speed and accuracy will be enhanced through its use. Because a certain degree of familiarity with the set of concepts being stressed is required
before a student can successfully interact with most drill-and-practice CAI lessons, numerous activities typically precede and accompany the computerized
instruction.

Programs of this type are very common and, although the trend is changing, make up the bulk of CAI packages. The predominance of drill-and-practice
programs is most likely a consequence of the relative ease with which both professional and amateur programmers can turn them out. Indeed, most teacher-
authored programs are of this variety.

Most educators are quick to admit that many of the computer-based drill-
and-practice exercises could be carried out just as well and much more economically with such aids as handouts and workbooks. This situation has caused some
to feel that drill and practice is not a legitimate use for computers, the argument

being that the computer's potential far exceeds running programs of this nature, so other uses should be found that take advantage of the machine's untapped capabilities.

There are certainly compelling arguments, on the other hand, in favor of the drill-and-practice approach. Teachers commonly spend an inordinate amount of time drilling students—which the computer can handle very effectively—when they could be putting their energies into more creative activities. Much of the new drill-and-practice software is designed to take advantage of computer capabilities that were overlooked in the first round of program production.

One of the newer, well-designed programs is Basic Math Competency Skill Building from Educational Activities (fig. 4.5). It offers a range of options from rounding off numbers to generating means, medians, and modes and, as with many programs of this kind, provides more than just straight practice—useful tutorial features help students master potentially difficult principles.

Another example of a complete drill-and-practice series is Spelling Series, from MicroEd, Inc. This set of 180 lessons is designed to supplement regular class instruction at the elementary level. Students select the lesson of their choice from a menu that describes the rules or patterns taught. A list of ten words is then displayed, followed by a sequence of ten sentences with one word missing. The student then completes the sentence using the appropriate word from the list (he may recall the list whenever he can't remember the words). At the conclusion of each lesson, the student's performance is summarized and a list is displayed of words that presented problems.

Often the drill-and-practice component is built into a game format (fig. 4.6). A well-designed program of this kind will add a touch of novelty that might keep the students on task for a longer period.

## Tutorials

In the tutorial mode the computer assumes the role of the teacher who, like Plato of old, involves the students in a one-on-one dialogue that increases in complexity as the lesson progresses. Unlike drill-and-practice programs, which stress the enhancement of known facts, tutorials teach new concepts as they build on old ones. Although a few tutorials require teacher intervention, most are entirely self-contained. A typical lesson of this type begins with an assessment of the student's knowledge, followed by a set of instructions or other essential information so the lesson can proceed.

The nature of the student's response determines what the computer does next. If the response is correct, some appropriate reinforcement occurs and the program moves ahead to the next sequence. If the response is only partially satisfactory, additional information is provided and the student is again questioned. In the case of a totally incorrect response, the computer will present a review sequence before moving ahead.

Students are often confounded by the humanlike qualities of a well-designed tutorial: the computer seems to tailor its responses personally. Indeed,

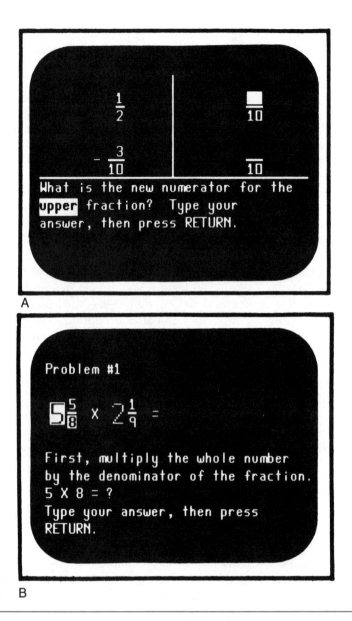

**FIGURE 4.5   Two Screen Shots from a Drill on Fractions** (Courtesy of Educational Activities, Inc.)

the machine seems to be interested in no one but the current user and directs every response to that person alone, even using what may be perceived as a kind of bedside manner—this is really one-on-one instruction at its best.

**FIGURE 4.6** Learning from a Drill-and-Practice Program That Has Gamelike Qualities (Courtesy of Commodore Electronics Limited)

Among the excellent tutorials are three from MCE, Inc. that deal with formal reasoning and logical thinking: The 4th R—Reasoning (for middle school students) is illustrated in figure 4.7; a screen shot from Reasoning: The Logical Process (for secondary students) is shown in figure 4.8; and The Lost R —Reasoning is the third program in the series. These tutorials make use of colorful graphics, provide helpful prompts and personalized feedback, and offer several levels of difficulty in each problem category.

As an example, The Lost R—Reasoning begins with a menu of three categories: True or False, How Many, and Puzzles. Selecting one of the three causes a submenu to appear that lists three levels of difficulty within the chosen category. For instance, selecting How Many brings up the following submenu listing: How Many (Easy); Some, All, or None; Sets (Hard). Here is a typical question from How Many (Easy):

```
Some squares have 4 sides
```

```
True or False
```

The answer must be false because *all* squares have four sides. A screen filled with colorful squares reinforces the concept.

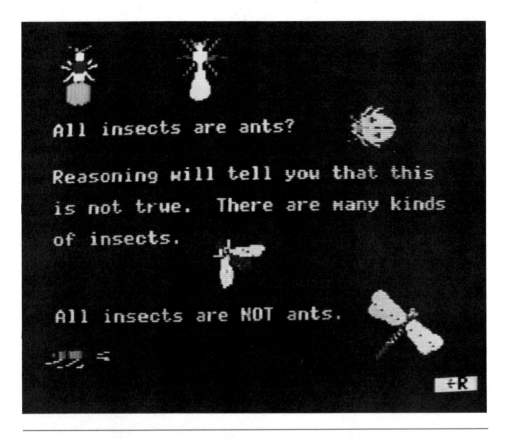

FIGURE 4.7   A Sample Screen Display from The 4th R—Reasoning (Courtesy of MCE, Inc.)

A question from Puzzles (medium difficulty) follows:

```
Ron has 6 green socks and 6 black socks. How many
must he take so he has 2 socks that match?
```

After a predetermined number of incorrect responses the following answer is given:

```
Ron needs to take 3 socks. He can get 2 black
socks and a green sock, 2 green socks and a black
sock, or 3 of one color.
```

Again, colorful graphics visually emphasize the concept that has been covered. As with tutorials in general, this program builds upon prior knowledge, becoming increasingly more complex as the lessons progress.

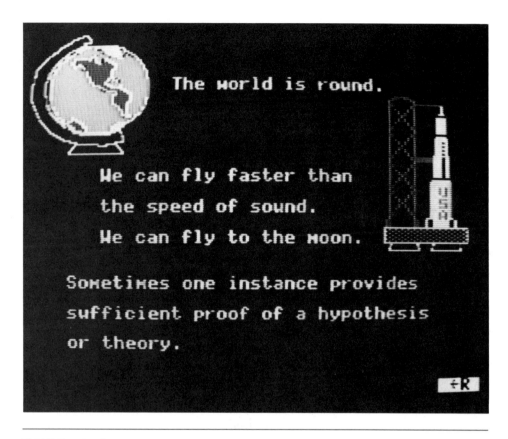

FIGURE 4.8  Reasoning: The Logical Process Is a Tutorial for Secondary and Gifted Elementary Students (Courtesy of MCE, Inc.)

## Simulations

Programs in the simulation category are designed to represent real-world events in an encapsulated form. Simulations are highly interactive and involve the student as an essential element in the "real-life" situation that is set up. Many excellent simulations are available, but the more complex ones require that a considerable amount of prior study be undertaken before they can be successfully used. For example, the program Three Mile Island is accompanied by a booklet that explains the essentials of operating a nuclear power plant; this supplemental material must be rather thoroughly understood if the computer-based lesson is to be meaningful.

A simulation is typically the central component in a broad-based lesson that includes active student input as one of the major characteristics. By varying the nature and magnitude of the input, students are able to determine what effect such variables would have on an actual system. Through the use of simulations, students can crash an airplane, go bankrupt, melt down a nuclear reactor, or run a tanker aground on a sandbar without the actual loss of a drop of oil or a human life. Conversely, they can become wealthy, balance an ecosystem, land a lunar module on the moon's surface, or bring a tanker into home port without earning a cent or getting moondust on their shoes.

Two excellent examples of flight simulators are JET and Flight Simulator II (see figs. 4.9a and b). A full-screen, 3-D, window view simulates the movement of the plane over varying terrain. Flight controls and instrument panels for visual and instrument flight are included, so that once a student feels comfortable with the controls, she can indulge in an aerial dogfight to test her flying skills.

Conducting experiments in heredity can be a long-drawn-out process due to the time it takes to produce and raise the necessary generations of experimental plants or animals. The simulation called Heredity Dog, illustrated in figure 4.10, solves this problem by rapidly producing litters of puppies from parents with different colored coats. The genetic makeup of the puppies is made to approximate that in nature through the random assignment of parental genes. By replicating an experiment students soon discover that there is a definable logic to the randomness, and expected ratios are ultimately obtained. Work sheets and other supplemental materials add to the usefulness of this program.

Simulations come in a number of formats; one with a touch of fantasy is Run for the Money, illustrated in figure 4.11. A pair of spaceships have crash-landed on the distant planet Simian due to the loss of their protective paint cover. The problem is to acquire more paint so the spacecraft can be made spaceworthy once again. Players must manufacture products that can be sold at a profit, which can then be used to purchase the special paint. In the process of trying to escape from the planet, students learn about the free enterprise system as they buy raw materials, produce an item, set prices, advertise, and compete with others who are also trying to escape.

A second simulation with a similar theme (economics) is Simpolicon, from Cross Cultural Software. This program, however, is based upon a real-world society and its problems, rather than a make-believe society. It teaches economic, political, and social concepts through realistic portrayal of the complex problems of national economic development. The players, assuming the roles of the country's leading economic-political experts, must manage the limited resources in such a manner that a stable and secure society with a well-balanced economy results. They are challenged to use their skills and knowledge to provide for the needs of the citizens through effective and efficient economic production, but they must not do this at the expense of the environment or overlook the society's needs for security. The program is so extensive that it can be used as a complete social studies course.

Simulations are valuable primarily because of the real-life problem-solving activities they present for the students. Although some games seem to be simulations, as a general rule, simulations attempt to replicate real-world situations whereas games do not. Another effective use of simulations is for experiments, such as those that would require expensive, specialized equipment in the actual setting (fig. 4.12) or that are too dangerous to be carried out in the classroom.

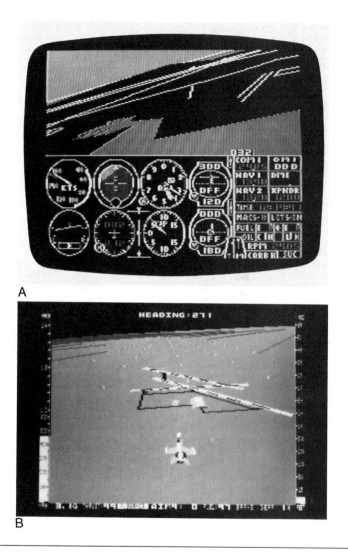

**FIGURE 4.9** (a) A Typical Screen Display from Flight Simulator II; (b) JET Simulates a Supersonic F-16 or F-18 Jet Fighter (Courtesy of SubLOGIC Corp.)

Unlike most other varieties of CAI, simulations can be adapted for group use; as a matter of fact, many educators prefer this approach. Complete lessons can be successfully built around a microcomputer simulation, possibly extending over several weeks, with suitable supplemental activities introduced at appropriate times. Most simulation packages—the Minnesota Educational Computing Consortium (MECC) simulations, for example—include extensive supplemental materials such as maps, workbooks, and manuals. With materials of this nature,

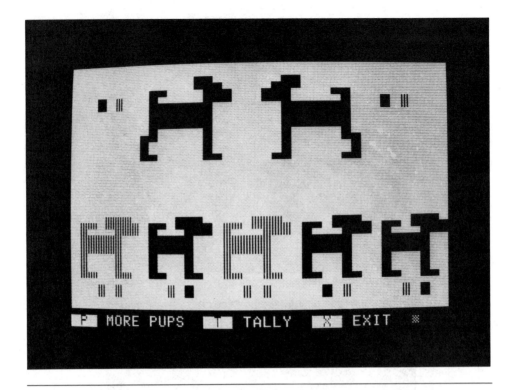

**FIGURE 4.10  A Screen Shot from Heredity Dog; Note the Various Coat Patterns of the Puppies** (Used with permission of HRM Software, Pleasantville, NY 10570)

students are able to spend considerable time between computer sessions on related activities, the end result frequently being a thorough and complete understanding of the concepts and principles involved.

## Games

Most computer-based games resemble games in general: they involve competition, and there is a winner and a loser. Some computer-based varieties pit student against student; a more common approach is to have the student play against the machine. Challenge is another feature. A challenge exists when there is a degree of uncertainty involved: if the outcome is predictable there is no challenge and therefore no reason to play. Players will soon figure out a fail-safe way to win if the program presents the material in an identical manner each time. To afford the greatest challenge, a game should be designed to randomize the sequence of presentation. Games also have rules that the players must understand and follow (fig. 4.13).

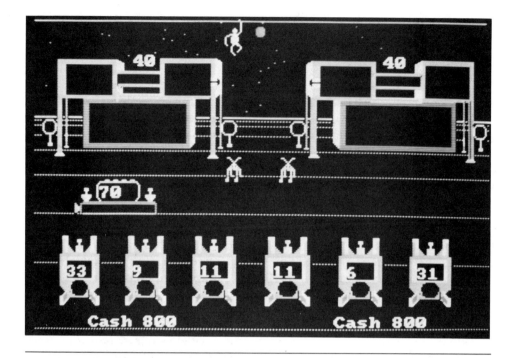

FIGURE 4.11    A Screen Shot from Run for the Money Showing the Spaceships and Scoring Features (Courtesy of The Scarborough System)

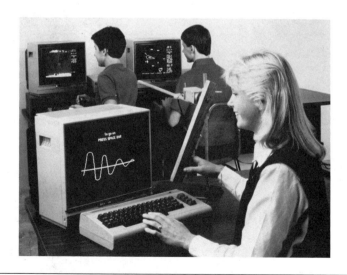

FIGURE 4.12    Computers Lend Themselves to a Variety of Simulations (Courtesy of Commodore Electronics Limited)

An innovative approach to educational game construction is to permit more than one player to cooperate in a collective effort to triumph over a series of obstacles. This is an excellent way to encourage socialization and represents a computerized equivalent of team games.

The newer collaborative games give sections of the display to different players, who must work in harmony to make their strategies effective. The opponent in this type of game is not another student but the computer. Perhaps the developers of this format are reflecting the feelings that many groups express as they band together to resist collectively what they perceive to be the sinister threat of a dehumanizing technology; then, on the other hand, they may simply be tired of seeing students involved in competition among themselves. The better games provide for different skill levels by permitting the player to select succeeding levels of difficulty until the game presents a challenge or by automatically upgrading the level of difficulty as the player improves.

Some educators use games as rewards for work well done—they can be very effective as reinforcement if used judiciously. Games can also reduce the feelings of apprehension that some individuals have toward computers (this is seldom a problem with children, however).

Some programmers have been criticized for incorporating too much violence into the games they create, whether designed for instruction or for entertainment. The violence-action format has been cited as one reason traditional video games seem to appeal more to males than to females. Fortunately, this situ-

FIGURE 4.13  **Computerized Games Are Very Popular** (Courtesy of Commodore Electronics Limited)

ation has been recognized, and as a result, considerable effort is being made to modify the philosophy underlying this type of CAI.

Many varieties of games are available as microcomputer programs. Although a large percentage cannot be classified as educational (they are primarily meant for entertainment), there is a growing list of games that have utility in the classroom. These fall into several categories, three of which are described here.

**Adventure Games.** Adventure games are intriguing, not because of any direct competition between parties, but because of the challenge that arises as a student tries different strategies in an effort to resolve a dilemma. An adventure game presents the dilemma in the form of environments and choices selected from real-world instances; in this respect, they are related to simulations (as a matter of fact, some refer to simulations as "simulation games").

Mind Castle I and Mind Castle II, illustrated in figures 4.14a and b, are adventure games that challenge a student's reasoning skills. A review in *Electronic Learning* describes the two games.

> The games take place in an ornate Victorian castle which contains a treasure in its tower. Players move from the cellar to the tower by solving a certain number of logic problems contained on each floor of the castle. The game can be played by one student, or by a group of students. The accompanying documentation contains answers to the logic problems, a floor plan of the castle, and hints on how to solve the problems.*

These programs make extensive use of graphics, which makes them visually attractive and more understandable.

**Arcade Games.** Some instructional games are patterned after the familiar arcade variety—they incorporate rocket ships, androids, laser guns, and the like, and the objective is to blast the enemy or get blasted.

Two popular instructional arcade games are Math Blaster and Word Attack (see figs. 4.15a and b). Both present the student with drills and sets of questions, then culminate with tests in the form of action-filled arcade segments. The student gets points for shooting down the word that matches a definition (Word Attack) or the correct answer to a math problem (Math Blaster). Various levels of difficulty are provided in both games, and students or teachers can add their own problems if desired.

Another exciting arcade game, Night Mission Pinball, incorporates an element of simulation (fig. 4.16). It has dazzling graphics and color, together with ten levels of play. The game remains challenging as the program adapts to the skill levels of single or multiple players, and a built-in editor permits the creation of "custom modes." Programs of this kind not only are fun to play but also encourage the development of appropriate strategies and may enhance problem-solving skills.

---

*Steven B. Isackson and Mark Donovan, "The 4th R—Reasoning, Reasoning: The Logical Process, Mind Castle I, Mind Castle II" (review), *Electronic Learning* 4 (March 1985): 5. Reprinted by permission.

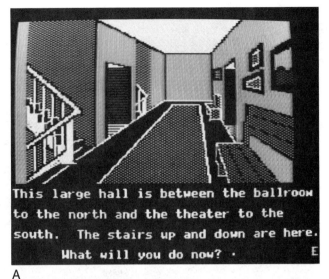

A

B

FIGURE 4.14  (a) A Screen Shot from Mind Castle Showing One of the Rooms in the Victorian Castle; (b) Problems Must be Solved to Move About in the Castle; Here Is a Typical Problem (Courtesy of MCE, Inc.)

**Logic Games.**  Logic games are often referred to as problem-solving software. The player must approach this type of game analytically—it takes more than the mastery of a simple list of rules to win at this game.

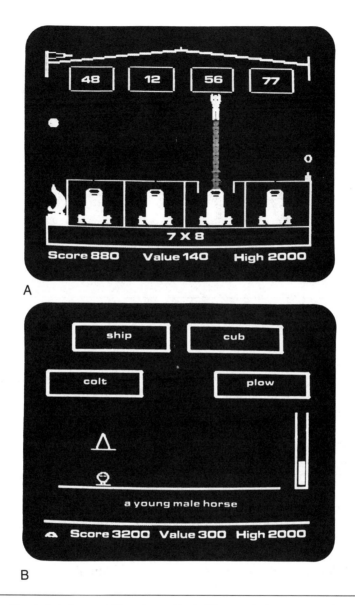

FIGURE 4.15 (a) A Screen Shot from Math Blaster; (b) A Typical Question Screen from Word Attack (Courtesy of Davidson & Associates, Inc., 3135 Kashiwa St., Torrance, CA 90505)

The Learning Company has brought out several intriguing problem-solving programs, including Moptown, Magic Spells, Gertrude's Secrets, and Rocky's Boots; and Spinnaker offers Facemaker and Story Machine. These new

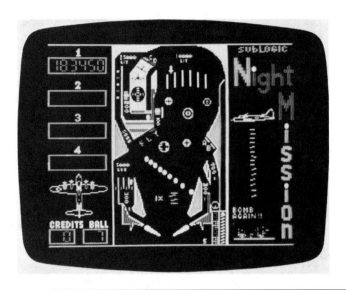

FIGURE 4.16  SubLOGIC'S Night Mission Pinball Recreates the Look and Sound
of a Real Pinball Table (Courtesy of SubLOGIC Corp.)

logic games are a considerable improvement over their predecessors. They are
designed to maximize the unique attributes of the computer and are therefore
more colorful, action-packed, and interactive than ever before.

In Arrow Dynamics (fig. 4.17) the challenge is to move an arrow from one
point on the screen to another by typing descriptive words such as "turn" to direct the arrow. Numerous levels of complexity are offered, making the program
suitable for use by students from the elementary to senior high grades. Elementary students can move the arrow directly with a series of words that constitute a
simple program. As more advanced levels are selected, various obstacles are introduced, each one causing the arrow to react in a specific way (for example, an
angled "mirror" deflects the arrow, turning it ninety degrees). As the game increases in complexity, combinations of obstacles move the arrow in diverse (but
predictable) ways; the student must thus exercise a number of problem-solving
skills to guide the arrow to its goal and win the game.

In another popular game, The Factory, students select various kinds of machines (some of which are shown in fig. 4.18) to make up the production line in a
factory. As a piece of raw material passes along the line, the machines leave their
imprints on it—drilling holes or painting patterns, for example. When the finished product emerges, the other players' task is to create machines that can duplicate that product.

Before leaving this discussion of the types of CAI, it should be noted that
most programs typically incorporate more than one variety in their design. For
example, a program might be basically a tutorial but have drill-and-practice seg-

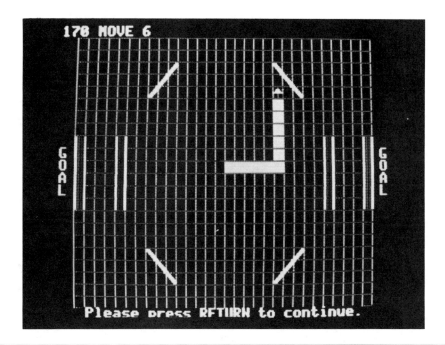

**FIGURE 4.17   A Screen Shot from Arrow Dynamics Showing the Four Angled "Mirrors" and Other Features** (Produced by Sunburst Communications, Inc. Copyright 1984)

ments interspersed throughout. Simulations frequently offer gamelike interludes, and some games are essentially simulations. Shortly you will be introduced to an evaluation form that requires an identification of the type of CAI involved. Because more than one kind can be included in a given program, you should attempt to identify the *primary* type of CAI, which may not be the exclusive one in every case; for some programs, though, you may wish to mark more than one kind of CAI.

## COMPUTER-MANAGED INSTRUCTION

Prior to the advent of the microcomputer, the large-scale management of instruction was performed by mainframes or minicomputers that were frequently located in a district office. A few systems were so designed that a centrally located computer could service schools in several states, providing them with an analysis of student performance and prescriptions for appropriate follow-up instruction. Today microcomputers are capable of performing many of the CMI functions that were formerly the domain of the mainframes. Although they cannot store the massive amounts of data that larger systems can

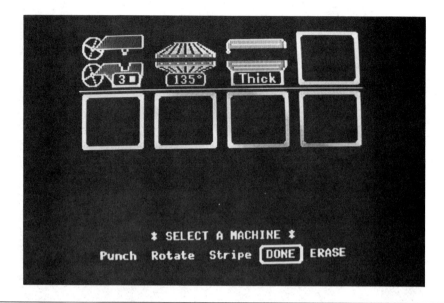

**FIGURE 4.18  The Factory Gives Students a Logical Challenge** (Produced by Sunburst Communications, Inc. Copyright 1984)

handle, the rapidly decreasing cost of hard disk systems is making microcomputer use possible for those who need more storage.

The microcomputer is capable of performing many of the management tasks related to individualized and group instruction and has become an important tool in the effort to meet the growing demands for accountability in education. The management function has become all the more important as educators have found themselves under increasingly heavy criticism from various constituencies. The emergence of the "back to basics" movement, and the concomitant call for improved documentation, has magnified the need for better ways to conduct the business of education. Computer-managed instruction can provide at least a partial response to these growing concerns.

Unlike CAI, computer-managed instruction is not used to instruct students directly; rather, it is a computer-based tool for gathering and analyzing data on student performance (record-keeping), developing student profiles (reports), and determining appropriate learning activities (prescriptions). CMI may be used in conjunction with any instructional approach; it is not limited to computer-based activities. The management function is just as useful for traditional classroom instruction with text and workbooks as it is for CAI.

An example of the use of CMI in a traditional setting is that of the Robert Frost Elementary School in Salt Lake City. In the late sixties and early seventies, the Westinghouse Plan was implemented at this school. A central computer in Iowa City managed the program, and the school itself was constructed so that the instructional activities prescribed by the computer might be carried out in special rooms designed to accommodate small groups.

Every child took tests in each area of the curriculum. The results were sent to the computer for analysis, and areas in which weaknesses were detected were identified on a printout. The computer then created a POS (plan of study), and from this, TLUs (teaching-learning units) were designed. Students were organized into small groups, each involved with a given TLU. With ongoing assessment, students moved from one lesson to the next as they mastered the materials.

Teachers and students routinely updated performance cards, which were passed through a reader that sent the scores back to Iowa City at the end of each day for analysis; by morning, computer prescriptions had been returned to the school. Although problems were occasionally encountered—when the computer was down or late in transmitting the needed information—for the most part the experiment was a success.

The Westinghouse program at Frost was phased out after a few years, due in part to budgetary constraints. During the last year or two, a lack of funding made it necessary to score all tests by hand, which placed excessive demands on the teaching corps and led to an understandable disillusionment on the part of some individuals.

CMI microcomputer packages have solved many of the problems experienced by the teachers at Frost. The microcomputer is more immediately accessible and can be used whenever the teacher has some unencumbered time. Also, results are more immediate—there is no need to wait until the following day for a report. And the information can be fed into the system in small segments and at different times (if this is the most convenient approach) rather than as a complete batch. Additionally, the costs of acquiring a microcomputer-based CMI system are much less than those involved in using a mainframe. Microcomputer-based CMI is still not as capable as the more powerful mainframes, but the technology continues to improve.

Although the keyboard remains the most widely used method for entering data, other approaches are becoming popular because of the relative slowness of keyboard entry. Card readers, for example, are a viable option if the quantity of data is great enough to warrant the expense of the equipment and the special cards. An optical scanner for scoring tests is another approach that speeds up the input process; although this device uses special sheets, the savings in time and effort might make it worthwhile.

Having students take tests directly at the computer (rather than placing answers on paper to be entered at a later time) is an option to using any method for input of accumulated data. A local university uses this approach to test for proficiency in metrics. Students interact with a computer-based tutorial until they feel they have mastered the subject; they then take the test while at the computer. The program maintains a running score, provides for a predetermined number of tries at a question, and displays a final total, along with information on how well the student performed and whether or not he passed the exam.

The complexity of CMI programs varies widely. Some have too few functions; others are overly complicated, even for many school (as opposed to classroom) applications. They range from the simplest programs, which are merely electronic gradebooks that store grades and perhaps generate means and standard deviations, to more capable ones that prescribe appropriate activities based on student performance, permit the retrieval of selected information, and provide reports in a number of different formats.

The current trend is to include a CMI component in CAI programs, enabling constant monitoring of the student's progress throughout the lesson. Testing is thus ongoing, feedback instantaneous—there is never any doubt about the student's performance. CMI components are included in many of the newer drill-and-practice programs and much tutorial courseware.

## SOFTWARE EVALUATION

At some point you may find it necessary and desirable to evaluate a selection of instructional programs. Where do you begin? How should you proceed? What are the criteria that are used? These questions will be addressed in the following sections.

The business of evaluating computer-based teaching materials appears to be new and different, but in actual practice it is not very far removed from evaluating materials of other mediums. However, there are a few dimensions that are unique to the computer and its attendant software and must therefore be taken into account in an effective evaluation.

As you evaluate software there are certain steps you should take to ensure that nothing escapes your critical judgment. Make it a habit to start from the beginning every time the program is run. Much of the current software goes through exactly the same sequence with each use, which is not really the best design. The only way to tell if different problems are randomly generated on each run is to reboot each time (turn the machine off and start from scratch). This involves a bit more effort and time, but it is the best way to check things out.

Plan to change roles each time you use the program. The first time through you can be the teacher: do everything correctly, and look at things from the instructor's perspective. Next, take the role of the bright, serious student who desires to have an enlightening experience with the computer. Check to see if the program is friendly: it should be easy to run, the vocabulary should be appropriate for the particular learner group, and the instructions should be clear. Answer the questions as correctly as possible, but try different versions of the correct answer to see how the program responds: some programs output such phrases as "that's wrong" if an answer is misspelled, but a good program will be able to handle such an error in a better way. Also, examine the nature of the reinforcement: a program that says "greeeeat, that's right" every time a correct answer is given will not maintain student enthusiasm for very long. On the other hand, the feedback for wrong answers is often even more deadening: "That's wrong, stupid" will certainly not encourage a student who is having problems. Finally, try it as a "heathen"—do your best to make it crash. Enter any far-out answer that comes to mind. If the program can't handle input such as this, it probably isn't worth considering any further. Some programs simply crash if the answer is inappropriate, and you can be sure that sooner or later a student will type in a wrong answer.

## SOFTWARE PREVIEW

Before proceeding with the evaluation exercise, we should mention the problems involved in acquiring programs for preview and evaluation. At times software publishers are unwilling to make programs available for fear of unauthorized copying. Other publishers will send partial programs to give the user a sense of the content. Still others freely distribute their materials on a timed return basis if no purchase is made.

A number of software producers have attempted to provide a reasonable substitute for the open-preview option, realizing full well their dilemma: if they send out the software, they will sometimes make a sale but they risk having their materials pirated; on the other hand, if they don't send out the software, they will most likely lose the sale, since educators are reluctant to buy a program sight unseen. Some of the options being implemented include sending company representatives to the schools for demonstrations (a costly process); setting up preview facilities at retail outlets; and making programs available to teachers at district and state resource centers.

Preview packages are provided by some manufacturers for a reduced price. The disk actually contains the entire program, but a portion of it is locked and cannot be run without introducing a special code to unlock it. If the prospective buyer determines that the program meets her needs on the basis of the portion available for preview, the manufacturer provides the code to unlock the rest of it for an additional fee. If, on the other hand, the program is deemed unsuitable on the basis of the sample, the transaction is ended—there is no additional charge, but the price of the preview is not refunded.

Some companies will exchange one title for another under certain circumstances. Many will permit a customer to try the software out for thirty days, after which time, if it proves to be unsuitable, it can be returned and the order will be cancelled. An increasing number of companies send the materials out under a guaranty (generally ninety days); if the program is unsound, it can be returned, with an explanation, for a refund.

These practices, though becoming more common, are not without problems for the producers. Even though the disk might be copy protected, there is always the danger that a copying program will be used to break the lock. A practice that is sometimes engaged in by previewers is that of using the program intensively, then simply sending it back to the company. Provisions are sometimes made to keep track of this kind of misuse, however: a record of the number of times the program has been used is automatically recorded on the disk, and if it seems inordinately high, the producer will probably think twice before sending out another preview program to the offending teacher or school.

## Some Options

Innovative approaches to the software preview problem are beginning to appear now that producers are aware of the extent of consumer resistance to the restrictive policies of the past. The "software sampler"—sample programs on disks bound into various periodicals—is one plan that holds promise. Microsoft, one of the largest producers of software in the world, included a sample of their new word processing program in a recent issue of *PC World*. Other periodicals are following suit, but the current orientation is strictly toward business rather than education.

Another interesting innovation is the software rental plan, used by a small number of companies. Software can be rented at a reasonable cost (20 to 25 percent of the manufacturer's suggested retail price) for a period of one week: if purchase is desired, the total rental fee then applies to the purchase price.

This is an attractive plan, to be sure, but not necessarily to the manufacturers, who point out that a rentee might simply copy a program (most of which aren't locked) and then return it to the rental company—a cheap way to get an expensive piece of software. Several manufacturers have already sued certain rental companies, and it remains to be seen how the litigation will turn out. Most educators will agree, however, that this is a unique idea that could—if the problems are worked out—go a long way toward resolving the software review dilemma.

If a decision is made to acquire a particular program even though previewing is not possible for one reason or another, there are still things a prospective buyer can do to get some idea of what the program is like. A good first step is to contact another educator who is familiar with the courseware in question. A look at what reviewers have to say can also be helpful: such journals as *Personal Software, Classroom Computer Learning,* and *Electronic Learning* offer in-depth reviews on a number of different packages in each issue, including pictures of typical screen displays so the physical features of the program can be better appreciated. There are also organizations specializing in reviews that offer extensive information on various selected titles in such publications as the EPIE reports (Educational Products Information Exchange), the microSIFT reviews from NWREL (Northwest Regional Evaluation Laboratory), *Software Reports* from Allenback Industries, and *Software Reports* from Trade Service Publications. Lists of additional journals and other sources of software reviews are included in appendixes C, D, and E.

Certain producers are well known because of ongoing advertising in top-flight journals or because of numerous positive reviews in various publications—this is a good indication of the general credibility of the firm. Also, good programs become highly visible through the plaudits they receive from satisfied users. Another consideration is the manner in which producers typically develop their materials: if a field-testing program is in place, for example, you can feel confident that the materials will be of better quality than if they have never been tested. Although there are some unreliable software producers, a fairly large core of reputable companies has evolved that offers the educator a consistently good product supported by ethical and fair backup policies.

If you should desire to preview a specific program and it is not available at the time, you can get a feel for the general quality of the line of courseware by previewing other products from the producer of the preferred program. If all efforts to obtain a preview have failed and the program is not available locally, it may become necessary to resort to the mails. The products and service of mail-order vendors should prove satisfactory if the company advertises month after month in the journals: certain vendor names have become virtual household words because of this continuous exposure.

Before purchasing mail-order software it is advisable to read through the advertisement thoroughly so the terms of the sale are clear. If the terms seem vague, write to the vendor explaining your concerns; if questions still exist, the obvious solution is simply to bypass that particular vendor.

As a final caveat, remember that software publishers don't offer warranties beyond some rather general ones. If a statistical package is advertised as being capable of running a two-way analysis of variance, for example, and it will do this, there isn't much the buyer can do if it appears to be lacking in user friendly characteristics or decent documentation.

## DOCUMENTATION

The nature of the documentation is one of the more important considerations in any decision to purchase software. Although this aspect of program evaluation is mentioned later, it merits additional attention. The following discussion will be helpful as you consider this important software feature.

### A Description

Fortunately, documentation is improving. There was a time not too long ago when the instructional package consisted solely of the disk (often a cassette tape), a licensing agreement, and a plastic wrapper. Nowadays a variety of well-conceived printed materials—the documentation—typically accompanies the disk. The documentation's functions are to teach you in the most direct manner how to use the program and to inform you of its characteristics (fig. 4.19); once this has been accomplished, it should serve as an ongoing reference.

Some courseware, such as that from MECC (Minnesota Educational Computer Consortium) and Control Data Corporation (PLATO), also includes workbooks and other related materials that students use directly as part of a total lesson; these materials are often accompanied by teacher workbooks. Although educators commonly refer to all of this printed material (and to similar materials that might be included in the computer program itself) as documentation, to purists the term is used to describe only those materials that relate to the operation of the program and to its characteristics; curriculum materials constitute yet another category and are thus not considered part of the documentation.

FIGURE 4.19    Documentation Gives Instructions on Using a Program

## Development

Although much current documentation is not yet as good as it might be, it is so greatly improved over the earlier versions that comparisons are difficult to make. There are several reasons for the poor quality of early documentation (and some that is current). The early material (sparse as it was) was often written by the technical people who created the programs. After the exhilarating challenge of conceiving, writing, and debugging a program, compiling a written set of directions in lay language was an exercise for which few had any enthusiasm. Thus, the manuals were written as an afterthought; they were typically poorly planned and illustrated, frequently incomplete, and couched in confusing technical terms (at least for the user). Today the trend is to hire people who have a background in writing and to bring in illustrators and designers to dress things up and clarify concepts through graphics. In some cases producers go to considerable trouble to develop a profile of the typical user; documentation is then created systematically with this person's needs in mind. This is a more pragmatic approach than the one used by those who hold that writing documentation is more of an art than a science.

Regardless of the philosophy involved, the finished product is now more polished than was formerly the case (see fig. 4.20). Some of the documentation still in use with older programs looks as if it had been turned out on Gutenberg's original hardware. The new materials are visually appealing—they emulate much of the commercial packaging in their attention to design and aesthetics. But external appearance is far from being the only improvement.

Printed documentation need not be so comprehensive if the program itself has some of this information built into it (often in the form of a tutorial). The popular word processing program The Bank Street Writer has an outstanding tutorial as part of the program; Rocky's Boots is another example of this approach, and there are many more. In addition, help options are available in many programs: in response to a typed command (such as an *H* or a *?*, for example), material will appear on the screen to help you solve your current problem. Although building documentation into a program is gaining in favor, there are those who maintain that there simply is no substitute for well-written printed documentation, citing the ease with which a manual can be used—it can even be taken home if necessary, and it requires no electronics. Of course, many would

FIGURE 4.20  Documentation Is an Important Part of the Software Package

argue that the computer itself should be available for checkout, but the lack of machines makes this idea unfeasible in most cases. The ideal situation is probably one that combines the best features of both the disk-based and printed formats.

## Importance

When software is being considered for purchase, the quality of the documentation must surely be an important factor. Documentation is the main source of information about a program. With complicated applications such as word processing, the quality of support materials is extremely critical; even simple drill-and-practice lessons require at least a minimal amount of explanatory material. A recent incident in a local school illustrates the frustration that often results when instructions are not available. Both the students and the teacher complained of a math program that wouldn't run. When the program was loaded from the disk, a logo appeared, but that was all. There was neither a cursor nor any other indication of what the user should do. Finally, a teacher with some background in computer use volunteered to take a look. She found that the user had to type in the words "run math program" in order to get things to work. The only way a student could ever figure that out is by looking at the documentation —but there was no mention whatsoever in the meager manual of the steps necessary to run the program. Fortunately, as we have emphasized before, documentation quality is generally improving.

## Evaluating Documentation

As you set out to purchase software, be certain to put the documentation to the test. Take time to read through the manual to determine how understandable it is; if it is overflowing with computerese, beware. The documentation should include the names of those who designed and wrote the program. The producer or company that distributes the program, along with addresses and telephone numbers, should appear somewhere in the materials. Dates are also useful—they give the previewer an indication of how current the materials are. The brand of computer and the particular model for which the program was designed must also be part of the documentation; the brand name alone often isn't sufficient because of the tendency of most companies to create new lines of machines that are incompatible with the older models. Also, the DOS might be different from one program to the next, even when the computer brand is the same. Apple's older DOS, the 3.2 version, used a formatting system that differs from the newer 3.3 DOS. Thus, a program in one format won't work with a system that is set up for the other.

The description of the program is perhaps the most useful part of the documentation. It should be rather complete, including a statement of the objectives, the grade levels covered, what the user can expect to see as the program runs, and other such considerations. In addition, information should be provided on how to get the program up and running, how to call up a help screen, ways to get out of the program before it terminates, and how to use cursor movement keys (for word processing and graphics programs).

The kind of output the user should expect when the program is running might also be described if it is of an unusual nature: illustrations of typical screen displays are often useful. If supplemental materials (such as workbooks) are included as part of the total package, they should be mentioned. Data pertaining to any field testing that was part of program validation procedures may also be of interest to potential users, so this should be included. Documentation is a most important factor when considering software for purchase—it is worth a second look.

## THE SOFTWARE EVALUATION FORM

Guidelines for the evaluation of courseware have been developed by a number of organizations including the Northwest Regional Evaluation Laboratory (NWREL), the Educational Products Information Exchange (EPIE), and the Minnesota Educational Computer Consortium (MECC). NWREL provides a useful evaluation form and an evaluator's guide through its MicroSIFT clearinghouse. EPIE/Consumers Union also publishes an evaluation form that is widely used, and TESS (The Educational Software Selector) is also a useful tool. In addition to providing excellent CAI programs to the schools, MECC has been engaged in courseware evaluation for many years. They, like the other organizations mentioned, have developed an evaluation model that is quite useful for educators. Additional versions of evaluation forms can be obtained from school districts, textbooks, and periodicals oriented toward instructional computing. A selection of forms is shown in figure 4.21.

The form presented in this text (fig. 4.22) is a composite one that has evolved over time. It has proved useful in various versions to hundreds of students in our classes and numerous educators. Some individuals, however, will prefer to create one to fit their own needs. In any case, this form can be valuable, not only to the one who evaluates the courseware, but also to others who desire a quick overview. Obviously, total consensus is seldom possible in any kind of evaluation—what is useful to one individual may not have the slightest utility for another. On the other hand, usefulness and quality are not synonymous—a poor program is poor whether or not it can be used in a particular setting. It is thus possible to determine, on the basis of the information on the evaluation form relating to overall quality, if a preview will be worthwhile.

When evaluating any kind of instructional medium it is useful to have a list of things to consider; the evaluation form arranges these in a logical format. However, the brevity of the typical evaluation form makes it advisable that some kind of supporting material be provided to define the meaning of the terms more completely. The following explanations, therefore, relate to items on the form and are presented in order (please note that self-explanatory items are not included).

FIGURE 4.21   Evaluation Forms Are Available in a Number of Different Formats

*Program title.* The program title is generally displayed prominently on the documentation as well as on the support materials such as workbooks and teacher guides. It will also appear in a smaller format on the disk's label. Some sample titles are "Money! Money!" (Hartley), "Metric System Tutor" (Cygnus Software), and "Science: Human Body" (BrainBank).

*Version.* Software producers normally update their programs, thus creating several versions of the same program. Determining which version you have is not always a simple task. For some programs the version will be clearly indicated in the documentation; at other times it will show up in the title screen when the program is booted. However, in some instances there is no convenient way to determine the version, in which case you may wish to write "unknown" in the space provided on the form. Versions often assume strange identities: they might be represented as a date ("9.19.83," for example), or the DOS version might be used ("DOS 3.3").

*Producer.* You should be able to locate the producer's name in the documentation or on the title screen when the program is run. Typical producer's names are Apple Computer, Inc., Hartley's Courseware, BrainBank!, Cygnus Software, Edusoft, and Sirius Software.

*Cost.* Cost is often difficult to discover—the documentation virtually never includes the price of the package, and it isn't indicated in the program either. Don't leave the space blank if you can't determine the cost: once again, write "unknown" or put in a question mark. People who refer to the evaluation later might think blank spaces indicate a slip on the part of the evaluator; at least a question mark eliminates this possibility. On the other hand, if invoices or software lists such as those from MECC are available, you will be able to come up with a price for the program (evaluations in journals also list prices). Although this criterion may not seem important, it often is. Most courseware packages are rather modest in price, but occasionally an expensive one appears: a price tag of $250 is likely to discourage a teacher who would otherwise waste her time previewing an unaffordable program.

*Copyright date.* A program's copyright date, which typically appears on the title page of the documentation, can be most helpful: although some older programs are fine, many not only are outdated from the standpoint of content but also may be low in quality.

*Required hardware.* If the program will run on the equipment at hand, the available hardware is obviously adequate. But once again, the documentation should provide the brand and model of the appropriate computer; often included are the size of the memory and the number of drives required. For example, one documentation booklet says: "This courseware requires a 48K Apple II+ or IIe or a Franklin Ace 1000 with one disk drive." Not all documentation is this helpful, so it may be necessary simply to list the name of the machine that will run the program, as suggested above.

In addition to the computer, required peripherals (joysticks, game paddles, and so on) should be listed, as well as the preferred type of monitor (a color monitor to make some programs more attractive or effective, for example, or a monochrome display for word processing).

*Required software.* The type of operating system can be listed under required software if the information is available (though often it isn't). Apple uses DOS 3.3 as a rule, but occasionally DOS 3.2 crops up; to run a program in the older format requires some special steps, so identifying the system is useful.

Some reviewers also list the version of BASIC in which the program was written (Integer BASIC, for example) in this space. If none of this seems to apply, however, you may simply want to draw a line through the space.

*Backup policy.* You will frequently be unable to determine what a particular producer's backup policy is; write "unknown" in the blank in such cases. You should be fully aware of the implications of copying, even for backup purposes; see the discussions at the conclusion of this chapter and in chapter 9.

*I. Program Characteristics*

*1. Subject matter area.* Typical subject matter areas are math, English, art, biology, music, and social studies. Specific topics are metrics, algebra, and binary

**FIGURE 4.22   Example of a Typical Software Evaluation Form**

---

SOFTWARE EVALUATION FORM

Program title _____ Version _____

Producer _____ Cost _____ Copyright date _____

Required hardware _____ Required software _____
      (Include mirocomputer brand, memory, other)

Storage medium: _____ 3″ disk _____ 5″ disk _____ 8″ disk _____ cassette tape _____ cartridge

Name of reviewer _____ Date _____

Address or school _____

Backup policy _____

I. PROGRAM CHARACTERISTICS

1. Subject matter area _____ Specific topic _____

2. Grade level(s)     Pre   K   1   2   3   4   5   6   7   8   9   10   11   12   Adult   College

3. Objectives: Clearly stated? _____ Yes _____ No   If stated, list them. If not stated, describe what
you perceive them to be: _____
_____

4. Is documentation provided? _____ Yes _____ No   If provided, describe briefly: _____
_____

5. What prerequisite skills should the student have? _____

6. Appropriate number of users: _____ individual _____ pairs _____ small group _____ entire class

7. Nature of the program (check as many as apply)

      _____ Drill and practice      _____ Demonstration
      _____ Game      _____ Problem solving
      _____ Simulation      _____ Tool (i.e., word processing, graphics)
      _____ Testing      _____ Computer-managed instruction
      _____ Tutorial      _____ Other (specify)

II. DESCRIPTION: In your own words, describe the program. Tell what it is about, how it is
structured, etc.

---

## III. CONTENT

Key: Y = Yes    ? = Not Sure    N = No    NA = Not Applicable

Y  ?  N  NA  1.  The content of the program is accurate.
Y  ?  N  NA  2.  The content is appropriate for the objectives.
Y  ?  N  NA  3.  The content is consistent with expectations of school, district.
Y  ?  N  NA  4.  The level of sophistication is appropriate.
Y  ?  N  NA  5.  The content is free of bias.

## IV. RUNNING THE PROGRAM

Y  ?  N  NA   1.  The instructions are clear and easy to understand.
Y  ?  N  NA   2.  The screen display is well designed.
Y  ?  N  NA   3.  The program is free of bugs.
Y  ?  N  NA   4.  The material is well organized and presented effectively.
Y  ?  N  NA   5.  Various ability levels are provided for.
Y  ?  N  NA   6.  Graphics and sound are used to enhance the program rather than as embellishments.
Y  ?  N  NA   7.  The student engages in ongoing interaction with the computer.
Y  ?  N  NA   8.  Feedback, both negative and positive, is effective and not demeaning.
Y  ?  N  NA   9.  The student is assisted through the program with appropriate cues and prompts.
Y  ?  N  NA  10.  Pacing and sequencing can be controlled.
Y  ?  N  NA  11.  Instructions can be skipped if desired.
Y  ?  N  NA  12.  Instructions and help screens can be accessed at any time.
Y  ?  N  NA  13.  A tutorial or sample program is provided.
Y  ?  N  NA  14.  The program will tolerate inappropriate input without malfunctioning.
Y  ?  N  NA  15.  The program represents an appropriate use of the computer.
Y  ?  N  NA  16.  The program achieves the stated objectives.

## V. MAJOR STRENGTHS AND WEAKNESSES

Identify the major strengths of this program.



Identify the major weaknesses of this program.



## VI. RECOMMENDATION (check one only)

_____ Excellent program; recommend purchase
_____ Good program; consider purchase
_____ Fair program; might wait
_____ Poor program; would not purchase

arithmetic in the subject matter area of math, or verbs, nouns, spelling, and capitalization in the area of English.

2. *Grade level.* If grade level is not indicated in the documentation, make an educated guess. The term "pre" is used in the evaluation form to indicate preschool, and "adult" refers to noncollege adult students. Note that more than one grade level may be marked if appropriate.

3. *Objectives.* Although objectives sometimes appear in the program, they often will be included in the printed materials. If the objectives are not specified, simply note what you feel they should be (you may have to wait until you have finished your evaluation to do this).

4. *Is documentation provided?* Refer to the documentation section earlier in this chapter for an in-depth discussion of the subject.

5. *What prerequisite skills should the student have?* Determining necessary prerequisites may call for a guess, but this will not be difficult once you get into the program. Students frequently encounter problems because the programmer assumed they would possess certain prior skills. The question to ask is, "What skills do I need to work with this lesson successfully?" (for example, does a grammar program assume that you know the parts of speech?).

6. *Appropriate number of users.* Good documentation will indicate the number of users the program is designed for, but an educated guess will suffice if such information is lacking. Do you see the program as being useful for only one person or possibly two at a computer? Might it be used with a small group? Or a large one?

7. *Nature of the program.* For a description of the different varieties of software (tutorials, drill and practice, simulations, and games) see the section earlier in this chapter. As you attempt to identify the nature of a particular program, note that it might incorporate more than just one type.

## II. Description

In your own words—short and to the point—tell what the program is about, how it is structured, and whatever else you feel is necessary to describe it.

## III. Content

Examine the key at the beginning of this section on the evaluation form before you proceed; circle only one symbol for each item.

1. *The content of the program is accurate.* Is the material free from factual errors? Are spelling and grammar correct?

2. *The content is appropriate for the objectives.* Consider what the software will be used for and ask if it will accomplish the task. Also consider the setting in which it will be used; if other quiet activities are taking place in the same room, for example, sound generated as part of the program might be disruptive. In addition, determine how much time a student will require to derive some benefit—a lengthy program might take more time than is normally available. (Some programs of this type, however, permit you to store the results, so the program can be continued at a later time.)

*3. The content is consistent with expectations of school districts.* Many school districts have curriculum guides that are meant to serve as outlines for a particular unit of study. If the program seems to diverge too radically from the prescribed guidelines, it might not be suitable. (If you are uncertain about this one, circle the ? or the NA.)

*4. The level of sophistication is appropriate.* Examine the vocabulary level—at times it might be too difficult or too easy for the intended audience. Input is another consideration: young children can type in single letters on the keyboard, but they will have trouble if too much typing is required. A lesson designed to be used by learning-disabled students should have special characteristics tailored to meet their special needs. Simple, childlike graphics might offend an older student, but an animated character accompanied by a tune might be effective reinforcement for a younger one.

*5. The content is free of bias.* Biases—such as stereotyping or representing racial groups inappropriately—might be reflected in the way the language is used or in the actual words used.

*IV. Running the Program*

*1. The instructions are clear and easy to understand.* Words common to everyday discourse should be used in the language of the program rather than computerese. Such phrases as "input error," "reenter," and "illegal quantity" can be frustrating to the user; it is better to substitute phrases such as "please type your answer again," "the number is too large," or "try a different word."

*2. The screen display is well designed.* The quality of the text display is of great importance. Many schools use television receivers for the display, and fine resolution of the characters cannot be taken for granted. Even when a monitor is available, clarity will suffer if the design is not good. Text should be uncrowded, and the format should be consistent throughout the program. Each *frame,* or individual screen display, should contain a complete idea. Rather than presenting a math problem in a fragmented way over several frames, for example, the program should break the problem into logical steps and present them one per frame.

Often the screen goes blank when a program is being loaded from a disk. Students frequently believe that something is wrong with the system and begin to punch keys. Some kind of display should therefore be on the screen during this period to reassure the user that nothing is wrong. (Some programs use phrases such as "Loading Metric Tutor" or "Gassing up.")

*3. The program is free of bugs.* Programs should not crash, (that is, stop dead) if the wrong keys are pressed. It is wise to input some incorrect responses when evaluating courseware to see how the computer reacts.

*4. The material is well organized and presented effectively.* The material should be presented in small segments; the sequencing should be logical and should reflect a consistent pattern of progression. Definitions should be given when appropriate, and examples are useful.

*5. Various ability levels are provided for.* The user should be able to select from various levels of difficulty to accommodate her ability. The number of questions presented should also be flexible. Computer-based games that are too easy or too difficult are not very popular with students—if the computer wins every time, it is intimidating; if the human invariably wins, there is no challenge.

*6. Graphics and sound are used to enhance the program rather than as embellishments.* In the fifties and sixties researchers proved that embellishing films and filmstrips with colorful, purely decorative graphics did not improve the educational value of the medium and, in fact, often diminished it. These findings are as viable today for microcomputers as they were years ago for films. Embellishments frequently do nothing more than detract from important content.

Many highly embellished programs receive positive ratings because they are so colorful and attractive. An in-depth analysis, however, frequently reveals a dressed-up drill-and-practice program of questionable instructional value: don't be fooled into rating a program high when in fact it may be relatively worthless.

Sound can be used to enhance a program, but it should be employed judiciously. One program uses sound much like a Bronx cheer when a mistake is made—needless to say, kids hate it. If sound is used as a prompt, it should precede the display of textual material rather than occur at the same time.

*7. The student engages in ongoing interaction with the computer.* Interaction is among the more important attributes of CAI; the program should take advantage of this feature. If the user merely sits as a passive viewer, a textbook might do the job as effectively. (Note that simply pressing the space bar does not constitute interaction.)

*8. Feedback, both negative and positive, is effective and not demeaning.* From research on learning we know that feedback is most useful when it informs the learner of an incorrect response. This should not be done in a demeaning manner, of course, but rather should use helpful and instructive language. The feedback should immediately follow the response and should give whatever information is needed to clarify the problem. If a string of correct responses has brought about numerous positive comments, reinforcement should become less frequent; it is better to use positive feedback sparingly than to overdo it.

The reinforcement for an incorrect response is more rewarding than it is for a correct one in a few programs. One in particular makes sounds and displays colorful graphics for a wrong answer but simply moves on to the next question if the response is correct.

An incorrect response should not elicit insulting feedback. A curt "wrong" is not as good as something like "close, but not quite." Also, the prompt "try again" is not particularly useful if the student simply does not know how to work a problem. After a certain number of incorrect responses, helpful information should appear so the student can move on.

*9. The student is assisted through the program with appropriate cues and prompts.* Some programs include tutorial-like screens and sample programs to help the user. In a math program a cue such as "that number is too small" may be helpful initially. An approach used in a grammar program is to give the definition for a part of speech when the student gives an incorrect response; for example, if the student is asked to respond with a verb and types in something else, the computer responds with "remember, a verb shows action, try again."

*10. Pacing and sequencing can be controlled.* Students often complain that they are tied into a program and can't jump around; they must start at the beginning and work straight through to the end. Some programs are modularized, enabling the student to move backward or forward to any module desired. Menus, directions, problems to be worked, and other displays should be left on the screen long enough for the user to attend to them and respond as needed. Using a prompt such as "press space bar to continue" is helpful.

Some programs have an extensive set of directions that scrolls up the screen. Although this technique is commonly used to list credits for a motion picture or TV program, it is generally a poor practice in CAI.

*11. Instructions can be skipped if desired.* Many programs force the user to pass through a sequence of instructions with each use—this becomes very boring after a few times. A better approach is for the computer to ask, "Do you want instructions? Type Yes or No."

*12. Instructions and help screens can be accessed at any time.* Menus, submenus, and other information screens should be available whenever needed to help guide the user through a program. Students thus will never be left dangling: if they get lost or confused, an appropriate display is only a keypunch away.

If a student reaches an impasse while working through a lesson, he should be able to get help immediately. Many programs offer help screens containing essential information, such as constant values in a math program or conversions in a tutorial on metrics. A graphics program might list the number keys and the colors they represent, along with the cursor moves and special key functions. A program on map reading may display the map when prompted to do so.

*13. A tutorial or sample program is provided.* Some programs have tutorials right on the disk. For example, the Bank Street Writer word processor, from Broderbund, has a tutorial on the back side of the program disk. After using the tutorial students can proceed to the word processor with confidence. Map Reading, from Micro Power and Light, uses examples to familiarize the user with the proper way to read maps. The user has the option to pass up some or all of the examples if she feels competent to move ahead without them.

*14. The program will tolerate inappropriate input without malfunctioning.* A common format used when designing courseware is multiple choice, with the choice restricted to a set of letters or numbers. At times, however, it is useful to have the input consist of words; a problem arises, though, if the answer is correct but the spelling is not. Some programs are designed to tolerate errors in spelling up to a point: if one error is allowed, for example, then "Warshington" would be accepted (with an *r*).

Routines to redirect the user after an incorrect response can be quite useful. For example, one program consists of multiple-choice questions with the selections numbered from 1 to 4. Lacking directions, some students type in the word rather than the numeral, and the response is immediate: "That is not correct." But those who make this mistake are given no indication of why the response is incorrect. To remedy this situation the programmer should anticipate the problem and provide for it with a message such as "Please type in the number 1, 2, 3, or 4."

*15. The program represents an appropriate use of the computer.* As you evaluate the program, ask yourself if the objectives might be met as effectively through some method other than CAI. Be sure to consider the logistics involved: although a teacher working one-on-one with a student might be as effective as the computer-based tutorial, or even more so, in large classes only minimal individualized instruction is possible. Programs that might be considered inappropriate use of computers are some of the simple drill-and-practice programs.

*16. The program achieves the stated objectives.* The inclusion of objectives in either the printed documentation or the program (or both) can be most helpful in determining the usefulness of the program. Sometimes, however, objectives are stated but not dealt with in the program: listing a set of objectives does not necessarily mean that they are realized in full or even in part through the use of the materials. To deal with this problem, preview the program yourself, keeping the objectives in mind. Where the objectives are not stated, or even alluded to, you can prepare a set after preview (although this is not the best approach, it is often the only alternative).

### V. Major Strengths and Weaknesses

After you have run the program, you should have a good feel for its strong and weak points; list the most important in each category. A major strength, for example, is "good graphics and text displays"; "unable to break out of the program" is an example of a weakness.

### VI. Recommendations

To indicate your recommendation, simply place a mark in the blank opposite the rating you feel to be most appropriate.

## Now That It's Over

Using an evaluation form can be a challenging experience the first time through —the process seems overly complicated, perhaps even needlessly so. But after the form has been used once or twice, applying it to subsequent evaluations becomes almost routine.

As mentioned previously, the form is useful in two respects: first, it furnishes the reviewer with a logical and thorough evaluation procedure, and second, it provides information to others with an interest in a particular courseware title, either for purchase for a school or for checkout from the resource center for use in the classroom.

The completed evaluation forms should be shared with others. Many schools, districts, and state organizations have established courseware libraries or preview centers to house these and other computer-related materials. People who use the facilities and the courseware are urged to complete a standardized evaluation form—available at the centers—for each preview; this practice has led to the establishment of libraries of evaluations. Educators are using the collections widely and find the evaluations to be highly informative and a time-saving substitute for the actual preview.

## PUBLIC DOMAIN SOFTWARE

Most of the programs discussed in this chapter are commercial ones. To acquire a good library of software of this type, a school must be willing and able to expend a considerable amount of money. But what of those schools that, for one reason or another, cannot justify such expenditures? Must they simply go without? Fortunately, there are free or inexpensive programs widely available: the public domain software. The quality of this type of material ranges from extremely good to terrible (as you might expect)—the problem is one of finding it and sorting out the good from the bad.

Many of the programs have been written by professional programmers in their spare time and have simply been passed around. Others are the products of teachers who, not knowing how to market them (some are not marketable) or not caring to, have shared them with other educators. Programs that have been in circulation for a time frequently benefit from the alterations made by users; although not always the case, it is generally legal to alter these programs in any way.

Locating public domain software is often a kind of treasure hunt at which you may come up empty-handed. Various users groups (see appendix F) are noted for the free software they pass around among their members; these individuals are known to the local vendors, who can usually give interested parties information on how to contact them.

Chapter 6, on networking and telecommunications, has information on how to access the electronic bulletin boards that are spread across the country. This is an excellent source for free software—you acquire it electronically using the telephone lines and a modem. In addition, various publications list public domain software. For example, hundreds of free programs for the IBM PC, ranging from business applications to games, are listed in a software guide from the PC Software Interest Group.

Perhaps the most useful source for educators is SOFTSWAP, a mail-order service that offers over two hundred public domain programs of an educational nature. Individuals who wish to copy any of these need only visit the center (located in San Mateo, California) with a blank disk—the programs are free. If you prefer to use the mail, you can purchase any set of programs for a given computer, subject, and grade level on a single disk for ten dollars. Most programs have been donated by teacher-programmers; all have been evaluated, edited, and modified by volunteers so that standards are maintained.

## SOFTWARE PIRACY

We will conclude this chapter with a discussion of a problem of increasing magnitude: the illegal copying or pirating of software by students and teachers alike.

Although programs such as those in the SOFTSWAP library can be copied outright, no such provisions exist for commercial programs. Although a few producers state in the documentation that their program can be copied, this is not the common case; most warn that copying is an infringement of the copyright law and admonish the user not to do it. What is very clear, however, is that the law permits the purchaser of a program to have a single backup copy on hand in case an accident occurs that renders the software unusable. The trouble is that the copying doesn't stop at this: many educators are engaged in wholesale copying, creating dozens of duplicates from a single original.

Why be so concerned about this kind of activity? After all, shouldn't teachers be permitted to provide students with the tools they need to learn effectively? Although this is the rationale behind most software copying, it cannot be defended. Pirating copyrighted programs is clearly illegal, and producers can sue for damages if they are inclined to do so.

The seemingly innocent activity of copying a few disks has widespread ramifications. For one thing, an ethical issue is involved. Teachers are setting a bad example for students if they engage in piracy or permit it to go on in their classes. The other side of the problem is a financial one. There are reports of small, struggling software companies going broke because of financial losses that may be due in part to illegal copying. Though it is difficult to substantiate claims of this kind, there can be no doubt that producers in general lose large amounts of money through lost sales that are directly related to pirating.

According to a survey conducted by *Electronic Learning,* 54 percent of the respondents indicated that educators feel free to copy disks for use with more than one computer. In other words, more than half of the educators responding to the survey felt that pirating was justified.

What can be done about this state of affairs? Recognizing that this is a problem of serious proportions that must be attended to, both software producers and educators are getting involved in the effort to find a solution. Some producers now offer a site license plan that gives the school permission to make multiple copies of a program or to load the program into multiple computers through other means. Another plan is to provide multiple copies of a program at a discount price. Schools can stress the legal implications of software piracy. They can begin to clamp down on violators by taking them to task. After all, it isn't just the teacher who is liable; the district itself could be in line for a lawsuit.

Finally, cooperative efforts between school districts and software producers are beginning to appear. It is in the best interest of both parties that the problem be resolved, and the philosophy of working together to reach a common goal is beginning to show results. For a further discussion of software piracy refer to chapter 9.

## SUMMARY

This chapter examined the kinds of instructional programs—drill and practice, tutorials, simulations, and games—and gave examples of each; in addition, it discussed computer-managed instruction.

When used as a tutor, the computer assumes many of the duties traditionally performed (though sometimes reluctantly) by the human teacher. Computers can provide the student indefinitely with a variety of individualized drill-and-practice lessons without losing patience. Tutorials start with a concept that is unfamiliar to the student and, through interactive input and output, guide him through to mastery. Simulations provide a realistic situation with which the student interacts; her decisions result in consequences, but none have the potentially disastrous impact of a real-world decision. Through simulations a student can engage in experimentation and make mistakes without the expenditure of anything more than a little time: he can fly and crash an airplane, melt down an atomic reactor, or cause a business to go bankrupt, and then try it again—nothing is lost, much is gained.

Instructional games provide a learning experience within the context of rules, competition, winning, and losing. Games are also used for reinforcement when this is appropriate. And computer-managed instruction enables the teacher to maintain records, score tests, diagnose needs, and prescribe instruction in a very efficient and effective manner.

A systematic approach to the evaluation of instructional software was outlined in this chapter, including a useful evaluation form. Finally, some implications of software piracy were discussed, and suggestions were offered for dealing with the problem.

## REFERENCES

Alessi, S., and Trollip, S. *Computer-based Instruction: Methods and Development.* Englewood Cliffs, NJ: Prentice-Hall, 1985.

Bitter, G., and Camuse, R. *Using a Microcomputer in the Classroom.* Reston, VA: Reston, 1984.

Coburn, E. *Microcomputers: Hardware, Software, and Programming.* Indianapolis: Bobbs-Merrill, 1984.

Coburn, P., Kelman, P., Roberts, N., Snyder, T., Watt, D., and Weiner, C. *Practical Guide to Computers in Education.* Reading, MA: Addison-Wesley, 1982.

Cohen, V. "Criteria for the Evaluation of Microcomputer Courseware." *Educational Technology* (January 1983): 9–14.

Collopy, D. "Software Documentation: Reading a Package by Its Cover." *Personal Computing* (February 1983): 134–44.

Dennis, J., and Kansky, R. *Instructional Computing: An Action Guide for Teachers.* Dallas: Scott, Foresman, 1984.

Dunathan, A. "What Is a Game?" *Audiovisual Instruction* (May 1978): 14–15.

"EL's National Directory of Software Preview Centers Part I." *Electronic Learning* (January 1984): 59–62, 102–7.

"EL's National Directory of Software Preview Centers Part II." *Electronic Learning* (February 1984): 68–70, 100–112.

Fisher, G. "Where to Find Good Reviews of Educational Software." *Electronic Learning* (October 1983): 86–87.

Kayser, R., and King, G. "Seven Steps to Buying Better Software." *Electronic Education* (March 1984): 14, 56.

McAlpin, A. "'Software Copying Growing Problem' Readers Say." *Electronic Education* (September 1984): 20–21.

Neumann, R. "How to Find Good Software." *Electronic Learning* (October 1982): 40–41.

Riordon, T. "How to Select Software You Can Trust." *Classroom Computer News* (March 1983): 56–61.

Vockell, E., and Rivers, R. *Instructional Computing for Today's Teachers.* New York: Macmillan, 1984.

Walker, D., and Hess, R. *Instructional Software Principles and Perspectives for Design and Use.* Belmont, CA: Wadsworth, 1984.

Watt, D. "Games Designed for Learning." *Popular Computing* (July 1983): 65–67.

# 5

# TOOL
# SOFTWARE

## INTRODUCTION

The use of computers in the schools, aside from CAI applications, is gradually changing from an emphasis on programming to an orientation that might be described as occupational. The reasons for this trend are many, but one important factor appears to be the realization that though few children will grow up to become programmers, a large percentage of them will use the computer as a tool to assist them in their work.

One computerized tool is the word processor, which will be featured in this chapter, along with spreadsheets and data base management programs; these are the most common of the tool software programs. Although others might be included, such as statistical packages, administrative and record-keeping programs, and graphics and music programs, lack of space prevents discussing them here.

## SPREADSHEETS

The computer-based spreadsheet is an electronic representation of the extensive record-keeping, planning, and projecting activities that were formerly carried out laboriously with pencil, paper, and a calculator. When the electronic spreadsheet is displayed upon the screen, it appears as two axes, one across the top of the screen, the other down the side (see fig. 5.1). The rows (horizontal) and columns (vertical) that are formed can represent any kind of data desired—the user makes this determination. Wherever a row and a column intersect, a *cell* is formed that accepts information typed in by the user. In most programs the columns are labeled with letters, and the rows with numbers; thus, a cell is identified with a letter/number combination called a coordinate—D2, for example (column D, row 2). The information is stored in a manner that replicates the matrix on the screen; the content of any cell is therefore accessible according to the predetermined, coded pattern. Although various programs offer different numbers of rows and columns in the format, there are typically ample cells to accommodate the data.

Because of its size, the total spreadsheet cannot be viewed on the screen at one time—it is necessary to scroll both horizontally and vertically as the work progresses. Two different types of information can be entered into a spreadsheet: words (called labels) and numbers and formulas (called values). Figure 5.2a shows an example of how the labels on a spreadsheet might be organized. (The one shown here is MagiCalc, although other spreadsheets use a similar format.) Values can be entered into the appropriate cells to complete the spreadsheet, as shown in figure 5.2b. In the illustration, columns B through F contain values in the form of dollar amounts. Changing a single figure alters all related values. For example, if the cost of freight were to be increased, the profit would change to reflect the added overhead.

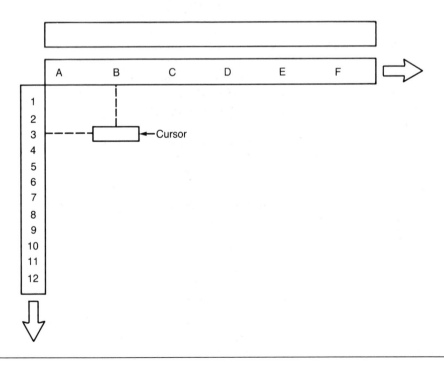

FIGURE 5.1   A Typical Spreadsheet Arrangement with the Cursor at Cell B3

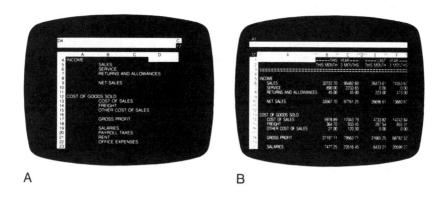

**FIGURE 5.2 (a) Headings and Subheadings in a Spreadsheet; (b) A Spreadsheet Showing Labels and Values** (Courtesy of Artsci, Inc.)

Note that this spreadsheet was designed for the express purpose of determining costs and profit. In another case you might wish to use the inflation rates from various years to see what effect they would have on the long-term value of the dollar. It is interesting to learn, for example, that ten years hence $148 would be required to equal the purchasing power of $100 today if the inflation rate over the ten-year period remains a constant 4 percent.

A spreadsheet must be designed to perform a certain function. You can't simply sit down at the keyboard and enter anything that comes to mind; the program obeys the desires of the user only if the necessary formulas and information are properly organized. Starting from scratch to design a spreadsheet for every application is not necessary, however. The alternative is to use a template—a spreadsheet designed for a given application that includes all the formulas, labels, and so on to perform a certain job. If the format fits your particular need, you can proceed to enter the data immediately. Templates are available in a number of standard formats, some of which are useful for classroom or school record-keeping applications.

An important capability of most modern spreadsheets is the generation of sophisticated graphics. Data can be displayed or printed out as graphics, typically in color, rather than as text and numerical data. Also, spreadsheets can be extremely useful as analytical tools and are frequently used in applications that are not commonly thought of as business oriented. Examples of this type of application are the prediction of enrollments in a district's elementary schools and the preparation of reports for college physics courses. The spreadsheet is an extremely flexible tool, with applications limited only by the imagination of the user.

## SPREADSHEETS IN THE CLASSROOM

Many spreadsheet programs are far too expensive for use in the schools; VisiCalc, however—the original electronic spreadsheet program, which served as the model for all the others—is available in some schools. It is fairly easy to master, although, like most other spreadsheets, it has some very powerful commands that require an effort to learn; most of these, however, are not really essential for normal classroom activities (though they would be useful, and even necessary, in a secondary business education class, for example).

Many other spreadsheets, some relatively inexpensive, are suitable for use in the schools. AceCalc (the educational version of MagiCalc) is an example of a low-priced, capable spreadsheet that includes excellent documentation and a tutorial. PractiCalc is a highly regarded program for Apple, IBM, and Commodore computers, among others. KidCalc is a simplified, easy-to-use spreadsheet for students in the upper elementary grades. And SuperCalc 3 is an education-oriented tool selling for less than twenty-five dollars—a price that any school can afford.

Once the program has been loaded into the computer and is up and running, the student may proceed to enter data by moving the cursor to the specific cell and typing the information. Various kinds of information can be entered; traditional business uses include keeping inventories, devising budgets, and maintaining records. But one of the most useful and exciting applications is in the realm of speculation, the what-if scenario. Spreadsheets enable users to construct a complete set of interrelated information that can represent a profile of an aspect of a business or other enterprise. The real strength of the electronic spreadsheet is in its what-if capabilities: changing the value of any cell automatically causes related values to be modified.

The first exercise need not be very complicated; it can be as simple as counting the kinds of birds observed and then entering this data into the computer. Figure 5.3 illustrates an elementary exercise that makes use of several spreadsheet functions. Column A contains labels in the form of the names of bird species. Columns B, C, and D hold values in the form of species counted on three different field trips. Typing a formula causes the spreadsheet to com-

|    | A        | B     | C     | D   | E       |
|----|----------|-------|-------|-----|---------|
| 1  | SPECIES  | MARCH | APRIL | MAY | AVERAGE |
| 2  | Robins   | 5     | 6     | 2   | 4.33    |
| 3  | Sparrows | 12    | 5     | 9   | 8.66    |
| 4  | Juncos   | 3     | 5     | 4   | 4.00    |
| 5  | Flickers | 1     | 3     | 2   | 2.00    |
| 6  | Other    | 6     | 5     | 6   | 5.66    |
| 7  |          |       |       |     |         |
| 8  |          |       |       |     |         |
| 9  |          |       |       |     |         |
| 10 |          |       |       |     |         |

FIGURE 5.3  A Spreadsheet Exercise

pute the average, which is then displayed in column E. The formula used in this case is $+B2 + C2 + D2 / 3$ for the robins (because they are on line two), $+B3 + C3 + D3 / 3$ for the sparrows (line three), and so on. Because there are three quantities involved (numbers for March, April, and May), we divide by three to obtain the average number of each species observed. Changing a value (perhaps from a 5 to a 6 for robins observed in March) immediately causes the spreadsheet to recalculate the average related to that species.

When students feel comfortable using simple programs like this one, more complex activities can be attempted. Spreadsheets are particularly useful in the social studies area. They make possible a kind of educated prediction that could only be labeled pure speculation using older methods. The kinds of information that can be managed by a spreadsheet are virtually without number; any sort of table can be constructed. What if, for example, nations should suddenly renounce war? The implications are much more far-reaching than one would expect. How many microcomputers could be purchased for the schools using the money earmarked for the construction of ballistic missiles? If the price of computers was going down at a constant rate while the price of the missiles was rising at a different rate, how many more computers could be purchased each year? On the other hand, how many new jobs would have to be created to accommodate those who worked in war-related industries and are now unemployed? Other problems might involve situations such as the relationship of changing world populations to food production or energy resources to current and projected consumption.

An obvious application of this type of program is in business education. After the students have become familiar with how the program works, begin by having them create a grocery shopping spreadsheet. The prices of the various commodities can be changed to reflect the different prices among supermarkets. As a price is changed, the overall cost is reflected in the total, and the totals from the markets involved are also compared. More complex applications might involve setting up the budget for a simple business. The various basic costs, such as labor and materials, are entered; selected figures can then be manipulated as desired. If the cost of labor increases, the effect on the cost of the product is indicated. The amount that can be charged for the product so it will remain competitive and still produce a profit can also be determined.

Another possible exercise might send students to the stock market reports to choose a selection of stocks for an imaginary portfolio. Each day, figures can be changed on the spreadsheet, and, at a given point in time, the stocks can be cashed in. If a number of students are involved in this activity it becomes a kind of game, with potential winners and losers. Students can progress as far with spreadsheets as their ingenuity and interest will take them, and the learning that occurs from this kind of program will have practical value long after the classroom exercises have ended.

Spreadsheets are not designed for student use only, though. Many teachers use them to maintain their class records. Student names can be listed in the first column, for example, and grades placed in successive columns. A formula will calculate the student average over a series of tests, then grades can be derived from the averages, and all this can be printed out as needed.

## DATA BASE MANAGEMENT PROGRAMS

A computerized data base can be likened to a traditional file cabinet or card file containing information arranged in a hierarchical scheme, as shown in figure 5.4. The cabinet is analogous to the *data base,* in which are *files* that may be likened to a folder containing related sheets or cards; each of these is called a *record* and contains information about one item (an artist or a bird, for example). Each piece of information on a record—such as the name of the artist, his birthdate, or his style of painting—is termed a *field* (fig. 5.5.)

Data base management programs are convenient supplements to the library; they can provide students with large amounts of information, and, better still, students can create their own data bases on any subject of interest. Teachers find that students are stimulated to do research on various subjects in order to compile the information that will ultimately become the data base. Another popular and widespread application of data bases in the library is as the card catalog.

Some data base management programs display a menu on the screen that lists options from which the user can choose. Other programs use printed documentation to supply this information.

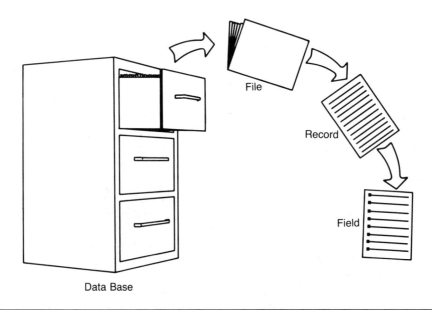

File

Record

Field

Data Base

**FIGURE 5.4  Data Bases Are Like File Cabinets in the Way They Are Organized**

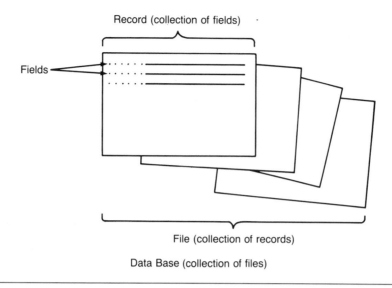

Record (collection of fields)

Fields

File (collection of records)

Data Base (collection of files)

FIGURE 5.5   How the Elements of a Data Base Are Related

## Forms

After you have loaded the program into the computer, you will be called upon to create a *form.* This operation is analogous to typing headings onto a card that will become the standard master for a series of similar cards. To do this using an electronic data base, you move the cursor to the desired positions and type in the names of the fields (the headings on a card). Sufficient space must be allowed in each field to accommodate the information to be entered. The blank form is then saved on a disk and may be recalled and filled in as desired. Information can be placed on each form adjacent to the appropriate headings, as in figure 5.6. The completed forms are then saved as a series of records, which make up a file. Some programs permit only one file to be stored per disk.

## Searching

Neither filing cabinets filled with printed materials nor computerized data bases containing electronic records are of much value if you can't find what you want in a reasonable amount of time. Both systems are arranged and accessed in rather standard ways. With a traditional file cabinet, however, a person frequently must search laboriously through all the files to locate an incidental bit of information. An electronic data base, on the other hand, permits you to specify a wide range of sort keys that can be used to find what you are looking for instantly. Data bases typically provide the user with several search options. One of these is a match that conforms precisely—the keyword (the word typed in) and the word in the record are identical. Another option allows a certain latitude by permitting the user to type a word, along with some simple code, that tells the computer to find any records containing that particular word in a designated field: the word *tree*, for example (along with the code peculiar to the program being used), might locate *family tree* and *maple tree.*

Many programs permit you to be very explicit in what you wish to find. For example, you might want to locate French artists, but only those who painted in the impressionist style—this is an example of a two-level search (artist and style). A three-level search might include the addition of a specific year of birth, which would further delimit the search. Only the more powerful data base programs permit searches on multiple levels.

## Sorting

The sorting feature permits you to enter the data base and rearrange the records in some specified manner. For example, information might be more useful if arranged in alphabetical order, or according to date or zip code. In the case of a data base on artists, you might want to sort records according to painting style. The most common ways to sort are by alphabetical or numerical order; thus the abstract expressionists would come before the surrealists. Multiple sorts arrange information according to more than one criterion. The keyword used in the sort described above—*style,* for example—is a major sort key. But some data bases can sort according to several criteria simultaneously. If the sort key *artist* were used along with *style,* this would be an example of a minor sort key. The result of this multiple sort would be the alphabetization of the artists within each style category. Depending upon the nature of the data base, you might wish to use several minor sort keys.

## DATA BASE MANAGEMENT PROGRAMS IN THE CLASSROOM

Students can be introduced to the concept of data bases by using the analogy of the filing cabinet. Once the concept is clear, the students must make some collective decisions: what the primary subject in their data base will be, what kind of information pertaining to that subject is desired, and how detailed the information will be.

When the format has been selected, the students go to various information sources such as the library, encyclopedias, or perhaps their parents to obtain material for the data base. Once they have gathered adequate information, they are ready for the computer. Several current data base programs are simple enough even for gradeschool children, once they have mastered a few fundamentals. After a short explanatory session to create forms and format records, the students can enter data to complete the records. Because few elementary students are proficient at typing, this process can be very slow. A typing tutorial can be useful at this point, but only if ample time is available for practice. When the records are complete, the data base is ready for use. Printed reports of the information obtained can be generated using the printing option built into the data base program.

Planning Sheet

Name(20 max.) [Presidents_____]

| Field Name (12 max.) | # of input spaces (23 max.) | Numbers only (Y/N) |
|---|---|---|
| Field 1 [President___] | [23] | [N] |
| Field 2 [President_#_] | [02] | [Y] |
| Field 3 [Party_____] | [23] | [N] |
| Field 4 [Years_served] | [02] | [Y] |
| Field 5 [Vice-Pres.__] | [23] | [N] |
| Field 6 [Birth_state_] | [23] | [N] |
| Field 7 [Occupation__] | [23] | [N] |
| Field 8 [Year_died___] | [04] | [Y] |
| Field 9 [Other_facts_] | (56 max.) [56] | [N] |

FIGURE 5.6  A Planning Sheet for Designing a Computerized Form for a Data Base on the U.S. Presidents (Courtesy of TIES)

Data bases are particularly useful in social studies classes because they make instantly available a quantity of data, which can be updated constantly. They permit comparisons between related variables such as gross national product, population, land area, per capita income, or whatever else might be included in the data base. Students become actively involved with information storage and retrieval and with organizational logic. They also have the opportunity to work together on projects that often become rather complex and extended.

Data bases are also useful in areas other than social studies. Any subject in which research is important, information must be accessed rapidly, organization is stressed, or innovation is desired can be taught more effectively with this helpful tool.

Software producers are beginning to recognize the need for capable, inexpensive data base management programs for use in the home and school. Several notable offerings are now on the market, including Secret Filer, from Scholastic Software, suitable for use by elementary students; Notebook Filer, from DCH Educational Software, good for the elementary grades but also satisfactory for the junior high level; Create-A-Base, from TIES, designed primarily for use by the middle school audience, with an excellent tutorial to teach students to use the program; and Scholastic PFS:File, a highly capable program from Software Publishing Corporation with features that appeal to junior and senior high students as well as teachers.

The data bases discussed in this section are local, housed and used within a particular school. Remote data bases, which are frequently extremely large and accessed via a modem and the telephone lines, will be discussed in the next chapter.

## WORD PROCESSORS

Whether you are processing food, minerals, information, or words, two common things are involved: the procedure, or succession of operations, and the product, or the result of those operations. The succession of operations in the processing of words consists of entering the text, correcting errors by deleting and inserting characters, and modifying the material by manipulating words, paragraphs, and entire blocks of text. Other operations include setting formatting features, saving files, and printing the final document. The result of skilled word processing is a neatly formatted, highly legible, error-free document whose electronic counterpart, encoded on a disk, provides instant access to the original information whenever it is needed.

The relative ease with which the succession of operations is carried out and the quality of the resulting product have led to a burgeoning market for word processors. To date, the greatest impact has been in the business sector, but the technology is rapidly gaining favor in many other areas where people work with the written language. Because one of the more important functions of the schools is teaching students to express themselves through writing, we would expect that they would be well along in the implementation of word processing practices. After a slow start, this now appears to be the case: word processing activities are gradually gaining favor in a broad range of subject matter areas. There are, however, certain difficulties inherent in the use of these programs, the primary one being that of economics. A few computers are available to greater numbers of students if they are used primarily to run drill-and-practice and tutorial courseware. Students working with a word processing program, however, are likely to tie the equipment up for hours. Allocating identical or extended blocks of time to each user does not solve the problem, either—ideas might just begin to jell as time runs out.

One important use of word processors in education is to improve writing skills. On the whole, results tend to be positive regardless of the specific approach, and it isn't just the top performers who are benefitting—individuals with a variety of abilities find that the word processor makes writing much less diffi-cult, and even enjoyable.

The Writing Workshop, from Milliken, is an example of a writing program built around a word processor. It consists of "four rooms in a house," one of which is the Milliken Word Processor itself; the others are the three modules of the workshop. Each room contains a "desk" from which the student selects op-tions to be performed in a specific room (see fig. 5.7a). Selecting FILE CABI-NET from the desk options, for example, provides the submenu shown in figure 5.7b. The options are described in noncomputer terms for easy comprehension.

A second use of word processors is vocational, where training reflects the demands of the business sector. Students adept at word processing will be better able to move into the modern electronic office than will those who lack this ex-pertise. Support for the acquisition of systems for use in business classes has been widespread, in part because goals are clearly defined. Although support in other subject matter areas is currently not as great, the positive experiences now being reported by those involved in computer-assisted writing projects should encour-age implementation of word processing programs in a broad range of subjects.

## How the Word Processor Works

A word processor consists of the software (generally on a diskette, although a few are in cassette or cartridge form) and the appropriate hardware to take advan-tage of the program's capabilities. A critical part of the package is the documen-tation, which describes in detail how the various key combinations are used to activate the different functions. The Bank Street Writer (fig. 5.8) includes a tuto-rial as part of the program, so the printed materials need not be as extensive as is typically the case. Some of the more powerful word processors, such as Word-Perfect, have rather formidable documentation; but even the more modest pro-grams that are appropriate for general school use (such as those covered in ap-pendix H) require a thorough set of directions to guide the user while the technicalities are being mastered and to serve as a reference when problems arise.

Getting started involves following the same steps common to other types of stored programs: insert the disk and wait for the program to load. Once the pro-gram is in the memory, you can generally remove the word processing disk—the program remains in memory until the computer is turned off or commands are given to clear it out. Although one disk drive is adequate for many of the word processing programs used in the classroom, some of the more powerful pro-grams must remain in the drive during use and thus require two disk drives—one to hold the word processing disk and the other to hold the data disk. After the program has loaded, some instructions will appear on the screen. Respond-ing to these puts you in the insert mode, where the text is typed in and the docu-ment composed.

The process of typing the text does not differ much from using a standard typewriter, but instead of appearing as print on paper, the text shows up on the

**FIGURE 5.7** (a) The Milliken Word Processor (MWP) Main Menu; (b) A Submenu from the MWP (Reprinted by permission of Milliken Publishing Company, St. Louis, MO)

display screen as light letters on a dark background (or occasionally dark letters on a white background, as in the Macintosh, for example). The arrangement of characters, spaces, and even mistakes corresponds exactly to what is typed in. Some word processing programs display fewer than the normal seventy to eighty characters per line. The basic version of Magic Slate, for example, displays very large letters, in a twenty-column format, that appeal to children (see fig. 5.9).

**FIGURE 5.8** **The Bank Street Writer Prompt Line in Text Entry Mode** (Courtesy of Broderbund Software)

The uniqueness of the word processing approach becomes apparent as the revision of the material proceeds. Correcting a typo or two is simple to do with a typewriter, particularly if the machine provides correction features; but changing a word or more, or inserting an entirely new passage, necessitates retyping whole sections of the document. Inserting additional text is no problem with a word processor—as the insertion is made, the text simply moves ahead to make room for it. Editing the text is one of the principal functions of a word processing program, along with print formatting, saving, loading, and printing.

## Text Editing

Text editing includes such operations as text entry, correcting typing errors by deleting and inserting characters, and modifying the material by deleting and replacing words, paragraphs, and entire blocks of text. Most programs are designed so the text can be edited as it is typed in. Often glaring errors are corrected as the composition progresses, and major modifications are made and minor errors corrected the second time through.

Some brands of microcomputers are equipped with special keys for underlining, boldfacing, and other operations. These are termed *function keys,* and

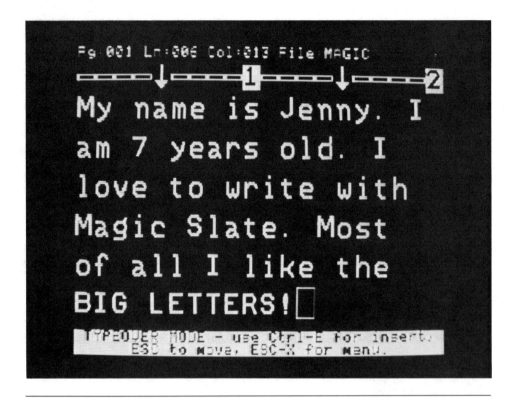

FIGURE 5.9   A Screen Display from Magic Slate Showing the Twenty-Column,
**Large Letter Format** (Produced by Sunburst Communications, Inc. Copyright
1984.)

each performs several functions that would normally involve the use of a combination of keys on the standard keyboard. The IBM PC, for example, has ten such
keys. Some micros have what are called user-definable keys, which permit the
user to assign different functions to selected keys. For example, you may wish to
assign to a key the function of displaying a particular menu. Most school computers, however, lack special keys and typically use a combination of the control and
letter keys to accomplish these tasks. With different keystrokes you can move forward and backward in the document as little as a character or as much as a page
at a time. Most programs also permit you to jump from the beginning to the end,
or the end to the beginning, of the document with a simple press of a key or two.

     As the cursor is moved up or down through the document, the lines scroll
rapidly off the bottom or top of the screen. You will have several lines to work on
at any one time; these vary in appearance according to the kind of program and
computer system being used. The most satisfactory arrangement is to have a
screen display that represents the full page layout as it will appear on the final
printed sheet. A printed page is typically from seventy to eighty characters in

width, but many computers are not able to display this number all at one time. Different programs adapt to this problem in different ways. Some break the eighty-character line into two forty-character ones and display one above the other; others scroll the line horizontally across the screen so the text disappears off the left side as you type.

Once you have found an error, move the cursor to that point and replace the character or word by either typing the correct information over it or deleting the unwanted material and then inserting the replacement. Some programs permit you to adjust the delete function so that anything from a character up to a full paragraph or more can be deleted at a stroke. A buffer is a useful feature: it saves the deleted text (up to a certain number of characters) so it can be recalled and used in another section of the document.

Moving entire sections, or blocks, of text as a unit can be very useful. To do this, you define the beginning and end of the block and then save it, to be reinserted at a different location in the document. Many programs permit a block of text to be moved directly from one place to another within the computer's memory; others require that the block (especially a large one) be defined and then saved on a disk for later insertion.

The search and replace feature is useful if you wish to find occurrences of a word in a document of any length. The search function, when used alone, positions the cursor at the first occurrence of the specified word; the computer then awaits further orders (continue the search or abort). If the search is continued through the entire document, the cursor comes to rest at each succeeding occurrence of the word. More commonly, the search and replace functions are used together, as illustrated in figure 5.10. The text editor searches through the file until the first occurrence of the specified word is found; at this point, a press of a key inserts the replacement word. This process continues until every occurrence of the old word has been found and replaced with the new word or the search has been terminated. Automatic search and replace performs these functions without intervention. In most programs the search and replace function can be used not only for words but for anything from a single character to an entire sentence.

Some programs permit you to create your own glossary of frequently used words or phrases, each of which is assigned a different key. A control key and a defining character are used to insert the word or phrase into the text where desired; thus you do not have to type the same material over and over again, saving considerable time and effort.

## Formatting

Formatting includes (among other things) setting margin widths, selecting the spacing between lines, choosing the number of lines per page, and sometimes changing the typefaces. Some word processors display formatting and other options as icons (small pictures) on the screen. MacWrite, a display of which is shown in figure 5.11, is an example of a program using this approach.

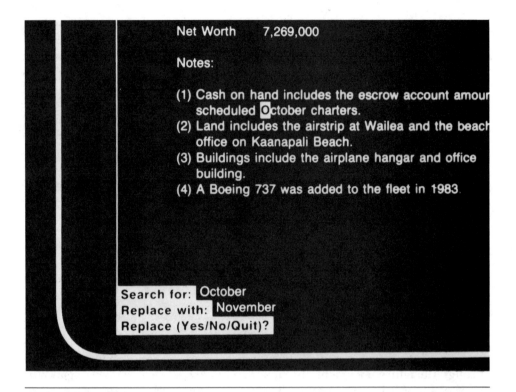

**FIGURE 5.10   Using the Search and Replace Feature of PFS:Write** (Courtesy of Software Publishing Corporation)

Two standard methods for setting the format of a document—menu-based and text-embedded—are typically provided. The first of these involves typing in changes to a basic set of commands that are displayed as a menu. For example, you may wish to have wider margins than the preset (default) format displayed in the menu. Merely type the code letters for the right and left margins followed by the new margin widths; the margin parameters in the menu display will change to reflect the modification, and the margins printed will be the width specified. The second method permits you to type formatting instructions as part of the manuscript. They may look peculiar on the screen because they appear as coded letters and numbers right in with the text, but only the results of the commands, not the text-embedded commands themselves, appear in the final printed copy.

Formatting considerations are important because they determine how the finished, printed document will look. Whereas text-embedded instructions must be entered as the document evolves, menu-based instructions need only be defined just prior to activating the printer; thus the format can be determined almost as an afterthought. On the other hand, if the system permits a full eighty-

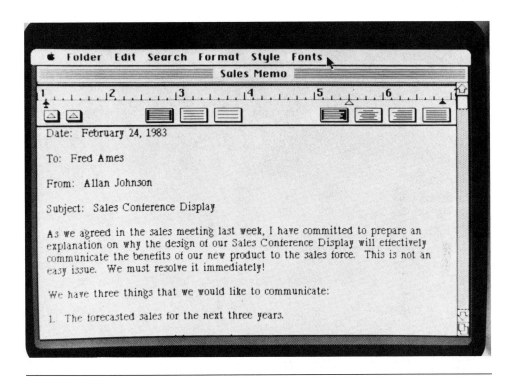

**FIGURE 5.11   The MacWrite Word Processor: Functions Are Selected from the Uppermost Line, and the Ruler Aids in Setting Tabs and Margins** (Courtesy of Apple Computer, Inc.)

column screen display, you can select the format options before starting to type and can then see the page on the screen exactly as the final printed copy will appear. Formatting options vary slightly from one program to the next, but some features are common to all. A discussion of three of the primary options follows.

**Margins.**   Some programs (such as PFS:Write) display the margin and other data on a ruler along the bottom or top of the screen (see fig. 5.12). Others permit you to call up the format values menu whenever a quick check is desired. Incidentally, most word processors have a feature called word wrap, which works like an automatic carriage return and prevents you from having to worry about margins as you type: instead of breaking a word when it runs into a margin, the word processor simply shifts the full word down to the beginning of the next line.

**Printed Lines and Line Intervals.**   The number of lines of text on each page and the width of the space between each line of type (referred to as leading) can be specified with the option that deals with printed lines and line intervals.

**Justification.**   Generally, printed material—whether from a typewriter or a computer—is left-justified. You can change this in several ways, however, if a dif-

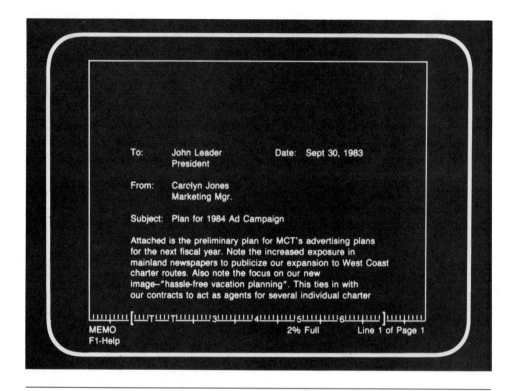

**FIGURE 5.12   PFS:Write Has a Useful Data Line at the Bottom of the Display**
(Courtesy of Software Publishing Corporation)

ferent layout is desired. Probably the most common option is fill-justify, which the computer achieves by inserting spaces between words to spread the lines out so they are flush with the right margin as well as the left. This sometimes creates sizeable breaks between words; thus, the effect is not quite as pleasing as when the spaces are equal throughout the line. A fill-justified page does, however, have a nicely balanced feel about it. A third alternative is to justify the lines on the right. Figure 5.13 shows examples of the three different options.

## Saving and Using Files

A file is a unit of information stored under a specific name. For example, if you have typed a form letter that may be used again, by giving the letter a name and saving it on a disk or tape you have created a file. It is wise to save the document being composed every ten or fifteen minutes to avoid accidents. Since information such as text, programs, graphics, and anything else currently being composed is stored in the volatile RAM, in the event of a power loss, the information will be erased. Disks and tapes, however, are permanent storage mediums—the

```
IN THIS EXAMPLE, THE RIGHT JUSTIFY (RJ) OPTION HAS
   BEEN CHOSEN. THIS IS PERHAPS THE LEAST COMMON OF
THE VARIOUS FORMATS, HOWEVER, THERE ARE TIMES WHEN
                             IT CAN BE USEFUL.
```

A

```
THIS IS AN EXAMPLE OF A PARAGRAPH THAT WAS PRINTED
USING THE LEFT JUSTIFY (LJ) OPTION. THIS IS THE
PRESET (DEFAULT VALUE) FORMAT OF MOST WORD
PROCESSORS.
```

B

```
THIS  SAMPLE  SHOWS  HOW  SETTING  THE  FILL JUSTIFY
OPTION  CAUSES  BOTH THE LEFT AND THE RIGHT MARGINS
TO  BE  ALIGNED.  NOTE  THE UNEQUAL SPACING BETWEEN
THE  WORDS.  THIS  IS  A  COMMON PROBLEM WHEN THE FJ
OPTION IS USED.
```

C

**FIGURE 5.13** (a) An Example of Right-justified Text; (b) an Example of Left-justified Text; (c) an Example of Fill-justified Text

material saved on them remains intact regardless of what happens to the computer. Plan to save short segments under the same file name to avoid having a number of separate files of varying lengths. Each time the same name is used, the file on the disk is replaced with the current contents in memory. When the document is finished and is saved for the last time, there will be one complete file on the disk under that name. Make a habit of backing up every file with a second copy, and keep the copy in a separate place so if one is damaged the other will be intact.

There are times when it might be desirable to make changes in the program. To do this, access the file by loading it from the disk into the computer. Additions, deletions, corrections, or other changes can easily be made; the modified document is then saved onto the disk. The backup copy must also be updated to reflect the change. This might seem like a great deal of extra work, but if you should lose a disk containing an updated program and discover that the backup contains the unaltered version, you will not be pleased at the oversight.

Long documents might be made up of two or more files. When the computer's memory is full, save the information on a disk or tape, clear out the memory, and start a new file with a new name. The disk will hold considerably more information than will the RAM; thus if you save one complete file after another under the same name, you will be unable to load this massive file from the disk into RAM. When the time comes to print hard copy, the document must be loaded into RAM, where it can be accessed by the computer and sent to the printer: if the file is too large for the memory, it cannot be printed out.

Some programs permit you to see how much memory has been used and how much remains, thus providing a guideline for ending a file at a suitable point (say, at the end of a paragraph). AppleWriter, for example, uses a data line display across the top of the screen: as the characters are typed in, the available memory count (about 30,000 characters to start with) diminishes, so you are always aware of precisely how long the document is and how much memory remains.

If more than a few files are created, it is a good idea to assign them names that are descriptive of the content. For example, the names "soft1," "soft2," and "soft3" were used for the three files that made up this book's software chapter. Writers often get caught up in the creative excitement of the moment and give a file the first name they think of; later, the strange names that appear in the screen catalog (the list of files on the disk) may not make much sense.

Some word processing programs permit you to save as a file the set of format values that you designed specifically for use with a particular document. When the computer is turned off for the day, you know that the values are safely stored on a disk for use during the next session at the keyboard.

## Printing

The ultimate reason for using the word processor is to obtain high-quality printed copy; the printer, therefore, is an essential component in the word processing system. The various kinds of printers are discussed, along with other peripheral devices, in chapter 2.

During the processes of text entry and editing, the printer sits quietly; once the document has been composed and corrected, saved on a disk or tape, and formatted, however, the printer goes to work. Some printers have features that must be physically selected and adjusted on the printer itself. For example, a printer might offer options such as pitch and line that permit you to alter the copy's final appearance. If such adjustments are needed, they are performed before the actual printing begins.

The program will provide a command to activate the printer; once the process has started, very little human intervention is needed unless single pages of paper rather than fanfold (continuous, attached sheets) are being used.

## WORD PROCESSORS IN THE CLASSROOM

Younger students need programs that are simple to use but still retain critical functions. Many programs, excellent for other purposes, are too complex for general educational applications, typically offering a wider selection of formatting options and editing functions than necessary for classroom use. Moreover, the more powerful the program, the more difficult it will be to learn.

With complex word processors, much of the user's energy and creativity are expended in learning to use the program. Those who intend to do a considerable amount of writing will realize a payoff once the program has been mastered and using it becomes automatic, but few youngsters have either the time or the desire to struggle with complex programs. As their frustration level mounts, their initial interest rapidly diminishes; and if their interest in writing was low before their exposure to the word processor, it is even lower after a disappointing experience.

Simple programs enable students to concentrate on the task of writing almost at the outset. They are assisted by such things as menus, simplified commands, well-written documentation, help screens, and built-in tutorials. Most find it necessary to refer to the manuals only infrequently after their initial exposure. And most of the new software is more than adequate for the needs of students as well as for those of the occasional adult user. The new, friendly programs are certainly not toys: they are highly versatile tools that include virtually all of the features of the more powerful programs, but in a somewhat restricted format.

Using the computer as a writing tool is not without problems. Anything that interferes with the thought processes involved in writing or other creative activities is bound to influence the quality of the end product. Until the word processing program is mastered, the computer is an obtrusive impediment to the free-flowing expression of ideas. Fortunately, this problem has been overcome in large part by the introduction of simplified word processing programs. The ease with which many of these can be used has made possible the introduction of this type of technology into educational settings where it was not practical before.

Perhaps the major obstacle to writing is the drudgery of editing one draft after another. Through the use of the word processor this deterrent is removed, to a large extent. When the fear of making mistakes is overcome, ideas tend to flow more freely. Students feel much less inhibited and are encouraged to concentrate on the more creative aspects of writing when it becomes apparent that mistakes can be corrected easily.

Although playing with a program to discover how it works is often the best approach, there may be times when a more structured strategy is desired. The Moby Dick exercise (see appendix H), which includes a number of typical mistakes to be corrected, represents an effective way to introduce students to word processing. This exercise was created with the younger student in mind (it is based on Bank Street Writer), but older students just beginning word processing will enjoy it also. The exercise can be modified so it can be used with other word processing programs, if desired. It is generally placed on a disk, mistakes and all, to be loaded into the computer as the session begins. The student has a printed copy of the manuscript and a line-by-line description of the commands to use and the steps to follow in correcting the errors. Note that the original document is retained as a file on the disk to be reused whenever needed; the corrected material exists only in the computer's memory and will be erased (or saved or printed) when the session is over.

Older students may find that they are able to master more advanced word processing programs, such as AppleWriter or PFS:Write, and high school business education students might prefer sophisticated programs such as WordPerfect or WordStar. Whatever the level, however, once the word processing program has been mastered, the computer becomes an extension of the student and the creative work can begin.

Students do not necessarily have to work in isolation when engaged in word processing—small group activities are practical and appropriate. A group can write collaborative stories and manage the editing activities by taking turns at the keyboard; the final draft can then be saved on a disk in preparation for printing onto paper. Word processing activities become more meaningful if actual projects—research papers, notices, school newspapers, or anthologies of student compositions, for example—are produced.

The production of a school newspaper is a particularly useful activity because of the diverse functions involved. Not only must the text be composed and edited, but blocks of text must be defined, moved about, and inserted in the appropriate places to fill the various columns. Formatting becomes a challenge as young editors figure out how to create a traditional newspaper layout. Although few inexpensive word processors will generate different varieties of type, students can design their own headlines and subheadings with transfer letters. They might also use special graphics programs such as Print Shop and Fontrix to create fancy letters. Spaces can be included in the layout to accommodate student-produced line drawings. The end result of an activity such as this is an interesting collection of reports on a variety of subjects in an error-free and attractive format.

Almost any project that involves writing can be undertaken on a word processor. The basic material for a lesson—words to be used in the creation of a poem, a limerick with the lines mixed up, a half-finished anecdote, a list of words to be alphabetized, a letter outline to be personalized by each student, or such—can be placed on a disk to be loaded by the student.

Word processing is not restricted to student use exclusively, of course—some innovative teachers have adapted it to their own needs. For example, several English teachers have devised an interesting approach to correcting student themes. They have their students compose on the word processor and then save the compositions on individual disks—one disk per student. The teachers check the themes on the computer, inserting information on needed corrections and changes, then resave the material, including the suggested refinements, back onto the disk. Students can edit their work, making corrections where noted, and then print the final draft if desired. Thus, unlike the traditional approach—where the teacher red-pencils the final product—corrections are suggested and carried out in the formative stage of composition. Students feel much better about their work and the product itself is obviously of higher quality. One problem with this approach, however, is that if the themes are of any length, they require substantial effort for the teacher to edit them.

Experience indicates that students love to use the word processor. Although it has not been clearly proven that their writing improves as a consequence of this, studies do reveal that students write longer documents and revise more extensively with word processors. The fact that documents tend to improve qualitatively in proportion to the number of revisions leads to speculation that word processing will indeed have a positive effect on the quality of student writing.

## INTEGRATED APPLICATIONS PROGRAMS

Integrated applications programs make possible the transfer of data from one application to another. For example, information from a data base can be quickly transferred to a word processor, where it can be modified, then transferred back to the data base; or information can be moved into a spreadsheet, calculations made, and the results stored in a data base.

Some integrated programs enable the user to print out data in a graphic form—such as bar, column, or circle graphs—rather than as tables. This feature was mentioned earlier in conjunction with spreadsheets. Once the information has been compiled, a command directs the computer to print it out in the form of a graphic, which is then used as the basis for an overhead transparency, a slide, or an illustration in a report or other publication.

Lotus 1-2-3, which emphasizes the spreadsheeting function, is among the better-known programs of this type. It requires considerable computer memory and will only run on the more powerful school machines such as the IBM. The PFS series consists of separate applications programs that are integrated through sharing a common command structure. Jazz is one of the highly capable inte-

**FIGURE 5.14  Appleworks Is among the More Popular Integrated Applications Programs** (Courtesy of Apple Computer, Inc.)

grated programs for the Macintosh; it makes extensive use of screen icons and the mouse. Appleworks (see fig. 5.14) was designed with schools and homes in mind and will operate on the Apple IIe and IIc. Like many integrated programs, this one is designed around the popular desktop-environment concept in which the screen display mimics what takes place in the workspace of the traditional desktop. For example, a graphic display of a folder is shown when files are being used to enable you to identify with a familiar item: the manila folder in which information is stored. You can "stack" one file on top of another and still see all the titles, just as with an actual stack of staggered folders. Information can be pulled from the folders, examined, modified, thrown away, or saved as desired.

Because programs of this type are so capable and convenient, the use of integrated applications programs is sure to increase in the years ahead.

## SUMMARY

Schools are beginning to recognize the value of using the computer as a tool. With the introduction of excellent tool programs, activities such as word processing and spreadsheeting are becoming more common in the classroom. Students who have opportunities to use computers in this manner will gain a degree of confidence and skill that will make them better able to adapt to the requirements of the modern workplace. Indeed, not only do such skills have vocational utility, but they are also useful as the student moves on to college or, for that matter, engages in home management.

Spreadsheets permit students to see the results of what-if situations through the manipulation of interrelated variables. Predictions and suppositions are analyzed, and the results made available, to an extent that was previously impossible.

Data base management programs encourage the students to practice organizational skills and to get involved in research as they create their own files of information. Programs such as these permit the rapid retrieval of information at a critical moment; enthusiasm for an activity is not diminished by the time lag that is so common with more traditional kinds of data retrieval.

Word processing is popular in English and journalism classes but is also gaining favor in other areas involving composition. Students create the school paper using word processors; notices are made letter-perfect with this tool, and students who were virtual nonwriters have been encouraged to express themselves as never before through the use of the word processor.

Mention was made in the introduction to this chapter of the many other tool applications available to the educator. You are encouraged to look into such applications as graphics generation, music composition, statistical analysis, and others that may be of interest and value—the nature and magnitude of tool programs make them a most useful addition to any software collection.

# REFERENCES

Boudrot, T. "The Magical Typewriter: A Step-by-step Guide for Choosing and Using a Word Processing Program." *Electronic Learning* (February 1983): 84–87.

Bradley, V. "Improving Students' Writing with Microcomputers." *Language Arts* (October 1982): 732–43.

DiGiammarino, F. "Text Editing." *Classroom Computer News* (November/December 1981): 32–33.

Herrmann, A. "Using the Computer as Writing Teacher: The Heart of the Great Debates." *Proceedings of the Annual Summer Conference. The Computer: Extension of the Human Mind II.* Eugene, OR: University of Oregon, 1983.

Holder, W. "Software Tools for Writers." *Byte Magazine* (July 1982): 138–63.

Papert, S. *Mindstorms: Children, Computers, and Powerful Ideas.* New York: Basic Books, 1980.

Schwartz, L. "Teaching Writing in the Age of the Word Processor and Personal Computers." *Educational Technology* (June 1983): 33–35.

Watt, D. "Tools for Writing." *Popular Computing* (January 1984): 75–78.

――――. "Word Processors and Writing." *Popular Computing* (June 1982): 124–26.

Watt, M. "Bank Street Writer, the Word Processor for Kids That's Powerful Enough for Adults." *Popular Computing* (August 1983): 190–94.

# 6

---

# TELECOMMUNICATION

## INTRODUCTION

In many schools across the United States, teachers are starting to make use of the microcomputer in many specialized ways, such as for English and creative writing. In the past, teachers have provided students with traditional stimuli (pictures cut from magazines, plots of television programs, vacation and holiday themes, and so on) for writing papers, themes, or letters. An emerging area of emphasis, however, is the use of the microcomputer linked to an electronic bulletin board system (BBS). Many teachers now access these BBSs by classroom microcomputer to provide students with reasons to communicate with students in other parts of the country. The students are required to compose letters, announcements, reports, or geographical or weather data, for example, during the regular class period; they then send this information to an electronic "pen pal" in the evening utilizing the telephone lines, a modem, and the classroom microcomputer and eagerly return to school the next day to see what messages await them.

The use of the BBS is but one of the exciting applications of the microcomputer in the classroom. The emerging area of telecommunication can provide a new type of instructional environment. Consider the advantages of linking two or more computers to impart knowledge usually available primarily in the classroom. Experts can be reached at reasonable rates and the data they impart stored on diskettes for later use; handicapped persons can be educated at home; continuing education can be arranged to accommodate working students' schedules; and campus locations can be used to initiate instruction, with branch campuses or school districts as remote sites.

Besides the BBSs, information utilities like CompuServe, Dow Jones, the Source, and Educational Resources Information Center (ERIC) are proliferating. To open up the new world now available to your display screen, you will need to add some accessories and peripherals to your microcomputer system. You will also need to be aware of some concerns and problems to make full use of your microcomputer's telecommunication capabilities. This chapter will discuss these peripherals, accessories, and concerns in detail.

### Telecommunication: A Definition

Telecommunication is long-distance communication made possible by using a signal like those used in radios and television. The broad scope of telecommunications encompasses transmission of voice, messages (such as telegrams), facsimiles (pictures), and data. Telecommunications can be broken into two distinct areas, teleprocessing and data communication. Teleprocessing, derived from a combination of the terms telecommunicating and data processing, is the processing of data at a distance. Data communication is concerned with the moving of data between terminals and a computer, or even between computers.

Demands for computer information systems (CIS) services have grown continuously since the introduction of the first computers, with the resulting need to conquer distances. Computer users who could talk to distant points by telephone reasoned that computers should be able to communicate with each other by sending data over distances without waiting for the mail or other services dependent on overland transportation and physical delivery. Demands became particularly acute in organizations with geographically dispersed operations like large corporations with many branch offices.

### MODEM

Although the idea seems simple—combine the two separate electronic technologies, telecommunication and computing—it is not as easy as simply picking up a telephone. Currently, most telephone lines handle analog signals, such as that of the human voice, transmitted as constantly varying voltages over a pair of wires. Computers, on the other hand, are digital devices, with everything they do in binary form. To use telephone lines for data transmission between two or more computers, the digital signals must be changed into analog signals to be sent over the wires (modulation), then reconverted to digital signals at the receiving end (demodulation). This translation is performed by a modem (for modulator/demodulator) (see fig. 6.1). When you are sending data, the modem changes the stream of digital information from the computer into tones (one

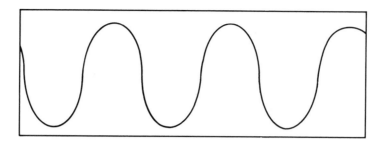

FIGURE 6.1   Analog (Smooth) Signal

tone for 1, another for 0) and sends them out over the telephone lines. At the receiving end, another modem does the opposite, translating the tones back into digital data. For the system to be complete you must have a sending terminal or computer, a modem, an analog signal along a transmission line, a modem, and the receiving computer (see fig. 6.2).

To be technically correct a modem is only the circuitry that converts digital data to analog tones and back; but because of widespread use, modem has become a generic term for the device that connects the computer and phone, no matter what other devices are added to the system for data transmission.

Two types of modems are available for use with microcomputers: acoustic couplers and direct-connect modems. An acoustic coupler, the oldest and most common type of modem, consists of a box (containing a miniature loudspeaker and microphone) with rubber cups into which is placed the handset of any standard telephone. There is no direct electrical connection with the telephone line; the computer and telephone are coupled acoustically (that is, by sound). The modem's circuitry converts the digital signals into analog tones; the microphone then picks up the tones from the earpiece and sends them out via the tiny loudspeaker next to the telephone mouthpiece. The modem transforms the choppy digital signals into smooth tones that can be sent over the telephone line (see fig. 6.3).

The low cost of acoustic couplers—between fifty and two hundred dollars—is possible because they are not connected directly to the telephone line

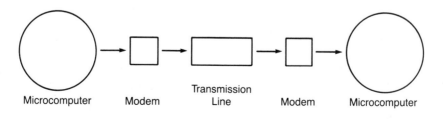

FIGURE 6.2   Utilization of a Modem in Data Transmission

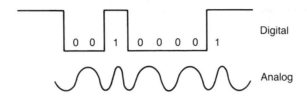

FIGURE 6.3    Comparison of Digital and Analog Signal

and therefore do not need the special circuitry required to make an electrical connection to the nationwide telephone system. They are also very easy and convenient to use—just place the handset into the cups. The acoustic coupler is rugged and convenient when traveling, particularly when you do not have access to a telephone jack (needed for a direct-connect modem).

Although they have some advantages over direct-connect modems, acoustic couplers have one large and critical disadvantage: the need for an extra microphone and loudspeaker greatly increases the chances for distortion, noise, and error in data transmission. The use of carbon granules in the microphone of the telephone handset is one area of concern. The phone works fine with normal voice transmission; with the high-speed transmission of tones needed for microcomputer use, however, the carbon granules begin to pack together, causing distortion. After a time, garbage will begin to appear on the monitor screen. Regular use of the acoustic coupler requires that you rap the handset on a hard surface to loosen the granules, preferably at the beginning of each telecommunication session. If the compacting of the granules becomes a serious problem, you can purchase (for a nominal cost) a special microphone to replace the element in the handset.

When using an acoustic coupler, dial the number on the telephone, wait for the high-pitched tone that indicates the computer on the other end of the line is connected, then put the handset into the cradle of the modem, making sure that it is cradled correctly and securely. If the handset is not completely encased by the rubber cups of the modem, there is a greater possibility of environmental noise filtering into the line, and the microphone transmission may not be clear or correctly heard.

Because of their several advantages, direct-connect modems are preferable to acoustic couplers. Instead of using cups with a microphone and loudspeaker, a direct-connect modem plugs directly into a standard modular telephone jack; it thus attaches directly to the telephone line and is hard-wired to an RS-232c port (the circuit that allows the microcomputer to send information over the telephone lines) on the microcomputer, which is built into most personal computers. The complete system, then, is composed of the microcomputer, the direct-connect modem, a telephone, and the telephone lines (see fig. 6.4). A direct-connect modem is much more error-free than the acoustic coupler because no

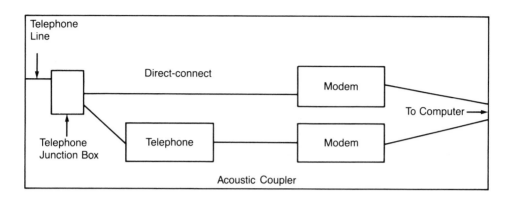

**FIGURE 6.4  Modem Hookup**

extraneous noise is introduced. Feeding and receiving tones directly to and from the phone lines is more efficient than using an acoustic coupler.

Another advantage is that direct-connect modems usually take up less space than acoustic couplers; they can sit under the telephone or may even be small enough to be placed right inside the microcomputer. The direct-connect modems, however, cost a bit more than the acoustic couplers (from $250 to $450), due to the fact that they are electrically connected to the telephone system and thus require more complicated circuitry.

Both types of modems are certified by the Federal Communications Commission (FCC) and can be connected to the existing telephone line. Although the telephone company is very selective about what is connected to the nationwide telephone network, you should not be concerned about connecting your microcomputer to the telephone system via an FCC registered modem—you are legally entitled to do so.

The direct-connect modem is easy to use: upon loading the software that comes with this device, a directory of things to do is usually displayed. The prompts direct you to type in the telephone number of the data base to be accessed as well as the kind of computer being used, the ID number, and your password. Additional menus permit you to select from a wide range of subjects. The many free data bases do not require membership or monthly fees, and you do not need ID numbers or passwords to use them.

Most modems designed for use with a microcomputer have two different transmission modes: answer and originate. You will probably use the originate mode most, especially if your main use is hooking up to information utilities (CompuServe, for example) and electronic bulletin boards (both discussed later in this chapter). When you place the call, the modem must be set in the originate position.

If a friend wants to send something from his computer to yours, you would set your modem to the answer mode. It is necessary for one modem to be set to answer and the other to originate because the frequency of the tones is different in the two modes. The difference is built in, so the system knows which microcomputer is sending and which is receiving the data. You can even purchase a modem with an auto-answer capability. In auto-answer the modem senses the ringing signal on the telephone line and automatically connects itself to the line, so messages can be received automatically, even when you are not present.

## Data Communications Speeds

The speed at which data are sent is a concern you must address when setting up your telecommunicating system. Data communications speed is measured in bits per second (bps), which is more commonly referred to as *baud* or *baud rate*. Data are sent over telephone lines in serial fashion (one bit at a time); baud rate is a measure of the total number of bits that pass a given point in a second. The most common speed used with microcomputers is 300 baud, or 300 bits per second.

You may wonder why data can't be transmitted faster, since a computer that reacts in milliseconds could surely handle data faster than 300 baud. Unfortunately, several limiting factors necessitate the slower rate. The United States has by far the finest and most reliable telephone system in the world; however, it, too (as with other systems in the world), is subject to noise, clicks, echoes, pops, and other interference that can garble and distort a communication signal. Thus data must be sent at a comparatively slow rate, so each tone can be long enough for the modem to recognize it in case of interference.

The major reason for the slower rate of transmission, however, is bandwidth. A basic law of electronics or physics is that the faster you send information, the more room it takes up in the electromagnetic spectrum, or, in other words, the broader must be the bandwidth to accommodate the fluctuations in the magnetic cycles. To give you an idea of the limitations imposed by the telephone lines, let's compare the hearing range of the human ear and the range of the telephone network. Most human ears are capable of hearing tones in the range of 20 to 20,000 hertz (cycles per second). The nationwide telephone network, however, consists of voice-grade lines, designed for the range of tones emitted in normal conversation—a range of only 30 to 3,000 hertz. All telephone lines in your home, office, or school can thus handle tones only in this narrow bandwidth. The reliability of data tones transmitted over voice-grade lines is limited.

With most acoustic couplers you are limited to the 300-baud rate because the system's extra microphone and loudspeaker make it necessary to slow down the rate of transmission so the signals can be heard and interpreted correctly. A direct-connect modem, however, permits the faster exchange of data using voice-grade lines. A standard telephone line can send data at 1,200 baud in one direction at a time. Because a direct-connect modem does not have the extra devices in the system, it can accommodate the increased rate quite adequately. To make use of more rapid data transmission you must be sure that both your direct-connect modem and that of the receiving computer are capable of handling the 1,200-baud rate.

## TERMINAL SOFTWARE

Once you have chosen a modem and learned how to use it, there is one more essential you will need to hook up to a telecomputing service: terminal software (sometimes called communications software). Terminal software is a program that disconnects some of the internal circuitry of your microcomputer and makes it a terminal of the computer to which you will hook up via the telephone lines. Because most modems use the RS-232c connector on the microcomputer, you will need a means to receive the data and send it out that port. Even if you utilize an acoustic coupler, the terminal software will still be needed to enable the microcomputer to act as a terminal for the telecommunication process.

A wide choice of terminal software is available, ranging from very basic and inexpensive to sophisticated and costly. Most terminal software costs less than $75, but sophisticated packages selling for up to $300 can dial the phone number and even log on to a system automatically. Some microcomputer operating systems already have terminal packages built into the hardware (CP/M and Radio Shack's TRS DOS, for example), so you would not need to purchase additional terminal software. Be sure to check the manual to see if your microcomputer has this feature.

If you are good at advanced programming (BASIC, Pascal, COBOL, or FORTRAN, for example), you can write a terminal program yourself. Most modem manufacturing companies offer advanced owner's manuals that detail exactly how this is done.

The basic (and least expensive) terminal software allows data to be sent out as you type on the keyboard and information to be received and displayed on the monitor. Although this basic communication software is adequate, most users want additional features, such as software that allows a printer to provide hard copy, for later study, of what is being shown on the monitor.

Some sophisticated (and expensive—up to $250) terminal software packages enable you to use the computer's microprocessor, memory, and floppy disk drive. These packages may be worth the price in the long run (provided you use them on a regular basis) because of the convenience they offer and the savings on long-distance telephone charges. Programs of this type allow you to save the data on a disk for later editing or analysis and to send a file of stored data. Some will even let you store telephone numbers and log-on sequences for a particular data base. You can also purchase an answering feature: the computer can automatically sense a dial tone, answer the phone, log on, and provide some special prerecorded responses (some packages can also turn on a printer and provide you with hard copy).

## INFORMATION UTILITIES

Now that you have purchased a modem and checked all systems, you are ready to enter the world of telecommunication. However, after you have all the equipment together, you still need an account number and a password to log on to the big systems (these are not needed for the electronic bulletin boards, as we will explain later). Fees for hooking up to and using telecomputing services can vary widely. In addition to the hourly use charge, most major services charge a first-time hookup fee. We will now discuss the major services, including fees, where they are located, how to secure data, the services they provide, and some basic log-on techniques.

## CompuServe

CompuServe is one of the world's largest suppliers of timesharing services to the business community. Through this system a company, school district, or university of any size can hook up to CompuServe's mainframe computers, via the regular telephone lines, and use mainframe power to do accounting, payroll, inventory, and many other tasks. The bulk of this activity takes place during the normal working hours of 8 A.M. to 5 P.M. In the past, these mainframe computers stood virtually idle during off-peak hours (5 P.M. to 6 A.M.), using huge amounts of electricity (they must be kept constantly running). To cut down on overhead expenses and to turn this idle time into money, CompuServe started offering computer access to microcomputer users during these slow times. This new service, named MicroNet, offers specialized services such as program swapping, advanced programming, and some reference service.

CompuServe uses a menu-driven system. A menu consists of a list of numbered choices from which you select and type in the number to access your choice. These menus are nested, which means that when the general area is accessed, another list of numbered choices is provided to further narrow the field you are exploring. You could be presented with as many as five numbered lists to finalize your choice.

CompuServe has many services designed to attract users with a wide variety of interests. Some of the highlights of their services follow.

- *Newspapers* covers ten large national newspapers, including the *Los Angeles Times, Chicago Tribune, Washington Post, New York Times*, and *San Francisco Examiner*. The entire text of the newspaper is available the same day the paper is run locally. You can also access the Associated Press newswire.
- *Finance* presents reports and services aimed at those interested in stocks, bonds, and commodities. This service includes the *Comprehensive Business Service* and *Standard and Poor's News Service,* a good lead into the "penny stocks."
- *Entertainment* includes a number of computer games, movie reviews and highlights, current information on videotape and videodisk hardware and software, and the CB Simulation. The CB Simulation allows you to communicate with other users logged on to the CompuServe system; it attracts a wide and varied group of people and can be interesting and stimulating to a microcomputer user—an electronic pen pal.

- *Communications* offers electronic mail, a service where you can leave messages for other CompuServe users; and a national bulletin board, where you can advertise items or services and scan public messages left by others. One of the outstanding features of this service is that if there is any mail waiting for you, a message to this effect appears on the monitor when you log on.

- *CompuServe users' information* is the clearinghouse for any information about CompuServe, telling what is new, what is available, and how much it will cost the user.

- *Special services* contains a great deal of special interest material, such as safety and product information for pilots, Tandy Leather, *Atari Newsletter,* the *Micro Advisor,* and federal reports.

- *Home information* offers such interest items as *Better Homes and Gardens* publications, U.S. government publications, and *Popular Science* publications dealing with energy topics or new products.

- *MicroNet,* CompuServe's original personal computer user's service, is a completely separate part of the data base, designed primarily for those who have intermediate-to-advanced knowledge of software and programming. MicroNet provides access to technical data on the DEC (Digital Equipment Corporation) computers, including technical and service manuals.

## The Source

The Source is one of the oldest of the information services, providing an information and communications service geared toward home and business use but also applicable to classroom use for information retrieval, computer literacy, and word processing. Source subscribers can monitor the schedule of current legislative activities in Congress, check the latest changes in airline schedules, and send electronic mail to other subscribers.

The United Press International service on the Source is one of the best and most easily accessed of the news services. It offers a keyword scheme for accessing specific information. News stories are categorized, using keywords widely used by educators, news reporters, and newscasters, when they are entered into UPI's mainframe computer system, which feeds into the Source. To get news from UPI offerings on the Source, you specify one of UPI's broad categories, a range of dates, and the keywords you want to find (for example, Australia, Peru, government, or judiciary). The UPI keyword is further refined (Lima, commerce, July 1985) until the desired information can be accessed.

The Source includes such areas as those described in the discussion on CompuServe: UPI service, finance, entertainment (including "chat," which allows you to communicate with users logged on to the Source), communications, Source user information, home information, and so on.

## Delphi

A recent newcomer to the information market, Delphi is a part of the General Videotex Corporation. The services from Delphi are similar to both Compu-Serve and the Source, but at this time they are not yet as extensive or broad in their coverage. However, additional services and capabilities are being added to this data base daily.

## Dialog

For years major corporations in the United States have earned additional income by sharing research and scientific information produced during research and development as well as by manufacturing and marketing phases of their business. This information is routinely filed in the memories of the corporate mainframe computers. Governmental agencies, universities, and colleges also produce research and scientific data that are stored in large mainframe computer memory. Data banks buy this information, put it in their own computers, and then resell it to other corporations, large research institutions, colleges, and universities.

Dialog Information Services buys reports, statistics, and doctoral dissertations from 140 different corporations, universities, and governmental agencies. Dialog has been used by librarians for over a decade to conduct on-line searches for information as well as to order documents from the data bases. The large Dialog data base includes the Educational Resources Information Center (ERIC, discussed below) and INSPEC, which is a physics, computers, and electronics data base. The smaller data bases available include the Exceptional Child Education Resource (ECER) for special educators and National Foundations (NF) for funding sources used in research and development.

ERIC (located in Washington, D.C. 20208) is designed to provide access to the findings of educational research. This nationwide information network is composed of clearinghouses across the country that abstract, index, and disseminate information about many different topics in the field of education. Many university and college libraries and large district media centers use this service to provide research data for student use. This information generally comes to the research institution in the form of microfiche copy rather than word-processed hard copy.

Dialog was originally developed to index and store the hundreds of thousands of documents generated by the space program in the 1960s. It now offers an index of billions of citations and abstracts on every imaginable subject and is the largest research-based data file in the world. Although Dialog's services are used primarily by professionals at libraries and universities, it is responding to the home market expansion by bringing on-line a low-cost service designed for users of microcomputers.

When using the Dialog service, a subscriber dials a toll-free number and locks on. The sign-up fee is $100, which gives the subscriber the lock-on code. The on-line services can run as high as $300 an hour, a fee that most businesses and universities can afford but that discourages most microcomputer users. The value of the service, although costly, lies in the great number and high quality of the research reports and citations available. For a person engaged in research, a twenty-minute link-up can produce over one hundred citations on most topics.

The clearinghouses listed in appendix G can provide valuable data on all aspects of the microcomputer as it applies to public school computer use in libraries, classrooms, and laboratories.

## Dow Jones News and Quotes Reporter

The Dow Jones News and Quotes Reporter service is an information utility with a much more limited scope than those mentioned above: it offers stock quotes and news from the *Wall Street Journal* and *Barrons* about particular stocks and business sectors. The service is easy to use and the data base is arranged in a highly simplified manner. A code of six or fewer letters is typed in to access the stock or business sector about which you want quotes or news. The information program running in the microcomputer converts this code into a request for information and relays it to the Dow Jones mainframe computer, which returns pages of information in the form of a monitor display. Some pages are menu pages that give two-letter codes and two-line headlines for specific news stories or stock quotes; other nonmenu pages display quotes and news stories.

## Getting Started

There are several ways to join a national network. You can call one directly on its toll-free number. Or, when you buy a modem or communications software, some networks provide trial kits—available at many microcomputer stores—which give you free hours on the system. You can also purchase a national network's comprehensive manual detailing all services offered, including menus, commands, and log-on procedures, by calling the network's customer service number. Study this manual and the guidebook that comes with the kit carefully and map out procedures on paper before attempting to log on to the system. Remember that the national networks can cost from six to fifty dollars per hour, depending on the type of service and time of day; thus your free hours could be used up wandering through menus but never reaching the data you desire to access.

If you live in a major city, you can often access a national network through a local telephone number, thus cutting down the monthly charges. If you live in a smaller city, the phone bill can be kept down by dialing a local packet-switching number. A packet-switching service, such as Telenet or Tymnet (see appendix G for address and phone numbers), receives computer information, then transmits it directly, via satellite communications, to and from the national network's headquarters. Neither Delphi nor the Source charge extra for the use of Telenet or Tymnet, but CompuServe adds a two-dollar-per-hour surcharge; the additional charge, however, will probably still be much less than the cost of a long-distance phone call.

One of the most difficult features of using a national network may be ending the telecommunication session. Be sure you learn the sign-off methods precisely before starting, or you could be trapped on the network with the phone bill continuing to climb. Simply hanging up the phone is often not sufficient: it could take a network ten to fifteen minutes to realize that the line is disconnected and not in use. Unfortunately, a charge will be made for all this time, so it is important that you know how to log off the network.

An important command to study thoroughly before you log on to the network is the help function, because it may differ from one network to another. All help commands provide essentially the same assistance—a menu that can lead you to much more specific directions for getting around the system. If you get hopelessly lost, you should sign off properly, then redial the network and start over again. Remember—human help can be obtained by dialing the network's customer service number.

## COMPUTERIZED BULLETIN BOARDS

The discussion thus far has revolved around commercial, pay-for-access information utilities. But there are actually over fifteen hundred computerized bulletin board systems (BBSs) available for home and school that provide free access. Virtually all the BBSs run on single-user microcomputers. They have been set up by individuals, computer clubs, and commercial outlets (computer stores and centers). Ward Christensen and Randy Suess, two members of the Chicago Area Computer Hobbyist Exchange (CACHE), started the first bulletin board in Chicago in 1978. Their board, BBS #1, is still in operation today and can be reached via modem at (312) 545-8086.

The BBSs do not offer the same broad range of data bases and services provided by the commercial utilities. For most systems the only data base is the current bulletin board of messages, posted by other callers. You can generally get a summary of the current messages as well as read and write messages of your own. Most messages are available to anyone, but some systems let you protect a message with a special password: this approach permits you to leave a private message for someone, provided both parties have agreed upon a password.

Because the BBSs are run on a microcomputer using floppy disk drives, they have limited disk storage for messages. The average capacity is about two hundred active messages, each limited to sixteen or fewer lines (roughly a maximum of one thousand characters per message).

Each BBS establishes its own audience after a short time in operation. The TRS 80–based systems attract TRS 80 enthusiasts and carry the latest news reports, messages, and information about TRS 80 hardware and software. Similarly, the Apple BBSs attract Apple users, IBM systems attract IBM users, and so on. Other BBSs focus on particular topics, clubs, products, or even functions; there is a genealogy BBS in Virginia, a BBS for engineers in Kansas, and one for car buffs in Michigan. There are even BBSs that cover very specialized areas: a number of elderly people were growing Japanese bonsai and discovered a BBS that dealt only with these miniature trees. Several BBSs operated by television stations offer a wide range of topics as well as news and message centers.

## Some Handy Tips

When trying your first BBS, it is best to select one close to your home, simply because of the initial trial-and-error period necessary to get to know how to make use of the service. When dialing a board that operates twenty-four hours a day, call during the late evening or on weekends when the phone rates are lowest. Remember that BBSs operate from one individual microcomputer and are connected to a single telephone line, which limits them to receiving one call at a time. This can be both a pleasure and a frustration: when connected you have exclusive use of the line, but you might also experience a long wait when trying to log on.

When dialing a computerized bulletin board the following steps, cautions, and suggestions can help.

1. Be sure that the phone is correctly connected to the modem and the modem to the computer (double-check the connections). Make certain that everything is turned on and set correctly and that the terminal software is ready to operate.
2. Carefully dial the number of the BBS you have selected. After two rings, a continuous, high-pitched tone should be heard. This is normal—the sound of telecomputing.
3. If the modem permits you to dial directly from the computer keyboard, proceed to step 4; if, however, you have used the telephone dial, perform one of two functions, depending on the make and model of the modem: (a) flip the switch on the modem to either "data" or "terminal" and then hang up the telephone handset, or (b) unplug the cord from the back of the telephone and plug it directly into the modem.
4. The microcomputer will now be connected to the other computer and the word "connect" will usually appear on the monitor screen. It is now up to you to initiate the conversation by holding down the CONTROL key and pressing the C key or by pressing RETURN, ENTER, or BREAK. In many cases you will need to press the RETURN or ENTER key twice.
5. A message will appear welcoming you to that particular BBS. You will then generally be asked to type in your name (or handle) and a password, for future use.
6. You will now be able to make use of what the board has to offer. Most BBSs have a menu of options from which to select. To do this you will need to know some systems commands. These vary from one BBS to another and will be listed when you log on. It is advisable to write them down. Some of the most common are: S (scan messages); R (retrieve or read messages); E or L (enter or leave messages); O (other BBS num-

bers); H or ? (help—a useful one to remember); and Q, B, or G (quit, bye, or goodbye).

7. Enter the letter of the desired function and press the ENTER or RE-TURN key. As you explore using the board commands, you will discover that some boards are a waste of time and money; some, on the other hand, will be useful, interesting, and worthwhile. Saving the menu information from the boards you call regularly on a disk or on paper for future reference will save you time and money in the long run.

Computerized bulletin boards operate in nearly every state, requiring only a local telephone call to exchange messages. Many users have found that some national BBSs supply valuable information that supplements the local data.

The value to you of the electronic bulletin board system in terms of cost, time, and effort expended will depend on your interest in exchanging information with other computer users. Apart from being enjoyable, a computerized bulletin board adds a human element to the hardware and software processes of the microcomputer. A BBS can be an electronic pen pal as your students send and receive messages across the country. The thoughts of individuals throughout the United States can be summoned to appear on the screen. Daily communications can come to your classroom from the "real" world outside. Special subjects can be explored with experts in other areas of the land. These capabilities introduce a whole new dimension to the chalkboard world of the school.

## LOCAL NETWORKS

Your school has installed ten microcomputers in the computer laboratory. They are in use every hour of the day, five days a week, but a few things could be improved—the software situation, for one thing. Not only are there insufficient programs, but dispensing and collecting the available programs is getting to be a huge burden. Additionally, students are not as careful with the software as they might be—some packages have even disappeared. You have previewed some excellent software packages, but the cost of purchasing ten programs of each title is more than the budget can handle and most software producers are not yet willing to provide a very good discount for the purchase of multiple copies.

Another problem is that of peripherals. You need letter-quality printers for the language arts program, but the cost is beyond the budget. A direct-connect modem and its software would also be useful. The list continues. Perhaps a local school network is the answer.

A local network is a collection of wires and electronics that connect a group of microcomputers in one location over distances that may range from as many as several thousand feet to as few as twenty-five feet. Each network is composed of at least three parts: the microcomputer and peripherals (such as disk drives, printers, modems, and graphics tablets), the interface boards or units, and the various communications cables or wires (discussed below) that transform the hardware into a network.

It has been estimated that about 40 percent of the schools in the United States that have been working with microcomputers for three years or longer have installed local network systems.* A typical school network connects a set of classroom microcomputers to a host (the teacher's microcomputer) and to one or more floppy disk drives or a hard (Winchester) disk drive, one or two printers, and other peripheral devices. By local network we mean one that is confined to one or several classrooms in the same building.

## Cables

Local area networks differ from the telephone networks we have previously discussed in that data is transmitted digitally over twisted-pair wire or coaxial cable at speeds that can range from one million to ten million bits per second. The new fiber-optic cables may play an important role in local area networks in the future because they have the capability of transmitting hundreds of millions of bits per second.

Twisted-pair wire is the simplest and least expensive medium to use in the local network; however, there is a danger that the wires will pick up extraneous environmental noises that may not be filtered out at the receiving computer. The most widely used transmission medium for local network systems is coaxial cable, such as that used in cable television connections. Coaxial cables are capable of much higher data transmission rates than twisted-pair wires but are more expensive (about twice the cost). However, since the cable consists of a wire surrounded by a flexible metal shielding, it does not pick up extraneous environmental noises. Coaxial cable also reduces the number of connecting wires to each component in the system to only two or three. This configuration does mean that data must be transmitted in serial form—one bit after another—rather than the parallel transmission normally used by microcomputers.

## Network Software

In addition to the regular CAI software, most networks require special software —commonly referred to as protocol software—to manage the network. Some packages offer the teacher a number of interesting capabilities. They allow the teacher flexibility in down-loading (moving the data from the teacher's microcomputer to the memory of the individual microcomputers on the network) curriculum programs (CAI) to the students' microcomputers: teachers can send one program to the whole class or a different program to each student. Some protocol software enables the teacher to communicate with individual students by sending to their monitors on-line messages typed from the central microcomputer keyboard. Some systems even permit the teacher to broadcast what she or any particular student is doing to all the students' microcomputers without dis-

---

*Kathryn F. Lamb, "Early Writing Utilizing Computer Networks," unpublished Master of Education thesis, University of Utah, 1985.

turbing their current work. And some software programs provide a peek function, which enables the teacher to view, on her host screen, what individual students are doing on their screens.

One of the current limitations of all local networks used for CAI, CMI, programming in languages other than BASIC, and word processing lies in the area of applications software. No copy-protected programs can be used on a shared basis; as this category includes most of the popular applications packages, new network users are very often unpleasantly surprised when they cannot boot their favorite software package and send it around the network. Some packages that can be used on a network have even posed some problems because they were not designed for multiuser environments. Another limitation of some networks is the inability of the host computer to access files or save files from another computer in the network. This problem makes any disk-interactive program useless in networked situations.

It is important once again to emphasize that copyright laws prohibit the copying of diskettes as well as using software intended for single microcomputer use in a multicomputer environment. Some microcomputer software producers allow their programs to be used on multicomputer or hard disk networks but assess the software's list price for each of the computers in the network (that is, if there are ten machines networked to a hard disk drive, they charge for ten copies of the program).

Most network users have had to choose from the limited number of usable package programs or to develop their own customized software. Many network hardware manufacturers, however, are also providing software packages for use on their networks (consult appendix G for a listing of some of these companies). Many educators believe that as networking becomes more popular, software developers will produce more and more applications packages specifically designed for multiuser environments.

## Parting Shot

Should your school invest in a local network for a particular curricular situation? If added computer capabilities are needed immediately to carry on the microcomputer literacy program, for example, the question becomes a viable one. Should you purchase additional microcomputers, printers, and disk drives, or should you network? Among the factors that will affect your decision are the concern of multiple copies of software packages (more readily available than multiuser packages), the fact that a printer can be utilized more effectively in a network than having two or three that stand idle a good part of the day, and the problems of student handling and care of the diskettes.

The answer is most likely to be found in a careful analysis of the total costs and benefits involved. If time and money can be saved by sharing resources, you should go ahead with plans for networking; if networking costs for a given situation outweigh the benefits, however, networking should be postponed. As your applications increase in complexity and the number of microcomputers and peripherals in the school grows, you may find networking an option worth considering for next year's budget planning. Whatever you do, plan wisely, know what options are available, and know which networking system is the best (not what you can afford) for your curricular needs.

## CLASSROOM APPLICATIONS

Because all areas of this country have access to telephone lines, telecomputing is possible in every classroom in America. Once you have obtained a modem and the necessary software and have arranged for a modest budget to cover the monthly telephone charges and initial hookup to utilities information networks, you are ready to hook your classroom microcomputers to the world.

One way to start is to send your students to the library to research the local and national electronic bulletin boards. The students should locate telephone numbers and area codes and find out as much about the BBSs as possible from current periodicals, monographs, bulletins, newsletters, and textbooks. Sources and bibliography included in this chapter and appendix G provide valuable information.

An interesting and useful classroom project is to construct a traditional bulletin board, using a map of the United States as a background. As BBSs are located they can be pinpointed on the bulletin board, thereby providing students with a national map that shows the extent of the availability of the BBSs. As the phone numbers of local BBSs are discovered, set aside a period of the school day to place a call, having as many students as possible present when the call is made. If networking capabilities are available in your classroom, connect all microcomputers to the BBS. (If a BBS is not available in your city, select one within a one- or two-hundred mile radius for the first try.)

If the BBS provides a good message service, have the students write some messages, staying within the limits suggested in this chapter; then have several students send their messages. A microcomputer pen pal network can be established—students can request that users of the BBS reply to the messages they send. Each day will provide a new and exciting exchange of information with other microcomputer users.

At some point you will locate specialized BBSs that will provide information on specific subjects, such as microcomputer use, health habits, areas of the United States, and genealogical research. There are bulletin board systems for use in discussing and researching virtually all classroom subjects. With a modem you are also ready to make use of a utility such as CompuServe or the Source. Although more expensive to access than the BBSs, these services can provide excitement and specific information that will make the microcomputer literacy program the highlight of the student's school day. Establish a regular after-school routine of accessing one of the utilities. Couple the modem to the classroom printer so students will have messages and information waiting for them when they come to school each morning. The data supplied can be used in all study areas of the curriculum.

As students make use of a BBS or utility, have them keep a log of the messages, times they used the service, difficulties they might have encountered, unusual occurrences, and so on. After a month or two, these logged anecdotes can be compiled into a newsletter or newspaper to be circulated throughout the school. This will call attention to the microcomputer program and provide some interesting experiences to write about, adding realism and excitement to the language arts or writing program in the school. Be sure to send a copy of the newsletter or paper to the PTA or any local business that helped sponsor the telecomputing: keeping them informed of the program will encourage these individuals and organizations to continue their support. Also invite them to see the telecomputing in action and, as part of the demonstration, let your benefactors enjoy sending a message or two.

If you find that the school's budget does not provide funds for telecomputing, ask the PTA president for some help: if you are enthusiastic about the value of the programs, you can generally secure help from this organization. You might also try a civic club or business in your town. Detail the value to the program that can come from networking and telecomputing; you may be pleasantly surprised at the amount of support that can be garnered from local sources.

## SUMMARY

Telecomputing is one of the fastest-growing segments of the microcomputer field. Every month new BBSs are added to those already available. The utilities continue to add new services and capabilities to their data bases. Prices for these services have stabilized and in some cases have been reduced as the number of users has increased.

Many schools and school districts are using networks rather than expanding individual microcomputer systems. They are finding that the total costs involved in establishing a network and linking their microcomputers together are less and the system is more functional and easier to manage than are several individual microcomputers in a classroom or school.

In this chapter we discussed the components and services needed for your school to take advantage of the telecomputing capabilities of the utilities and BBSs, plus some suggestions for setting up a network for the school. We discussed the differences between an acoustic coupler and a direct-connect modem, along with the strengths and weaknesses of each.

We provided an in-depth discussion of several of the most popular utilities —the services they provide, their costs, and how to access the data bases—as well as of the BBSs, including the use of the modem for access.

Before you begin telecommunication activities, you should make a careful analysis of the needs of your microcomputer CAI and literacy programs so your school will reap maximum benefits. The material in this chapter should provide you with the information needed to conduct the necessary analysis and to make intelligent decisions regarding a telecommunications program.

# REFERENCES

Adams, D. R., et al. *Computer Information Systems: An Introduction.* Palo Alto, CA: South-Western Publishing Co., 1983.

Bitter, G. C. *Computers in Today's World.* New York: John Wiley & Sons, 1984.

Bryons, C. "May the Source Be with You. *Time* (October 26, 1981): 63.

Coburn, P., et al. *Practical Guide to Computers in Education.* Menlo Park, CA: Addison-Wesley Publishing Co., 1982.

Gannes, S. "New Medium for Messages." *Discovery* (May 1984): 80–82.

Green, J. O. "Straight Talk about Local Networks." *Classroom Computer Learning* (September 1984): 72–77.

Licklider, T. R. "Calling Information: Telecomputing with Personal Computers." *Creative Computing* (April 1981): 78–84.

Mendell, S. L. *Computers and Data Processing.* St. Paul, MN: West Publishing Co., 1982.

Spencer, D. D. *Illustrated Computer Dictionary,* 3d ed. Columbus, OH: Merrill Publishing Co., 1986.

Stallings, W. D., Jr., and Blissmer, R. H. *Computing Annual.* New York: John Wiley & Sons, 1984.

# 7

# PROGRAMMING
# AND
# AUTHORING

## INTRODUCTION

In this chapter we will examine two methods for creating programs. The first, and more common, approach is to use one of the many programming languages (such as BASIC or Pascal) to write a program tailor-made for a certain task; the second is to use an authoring language (such as PILOT or SuperPILOT) to write a lesson for instructional purposes. Programming and authoring languages are available in different versions. Tutorials, guides, and other helpful support materials are included with the disk-based programs (fig. 7.1).

Among the several differences between programming and authoring languages, a significant one is the greater versatility the former enjoys over the latter. There are over two hundred different programming languages, each designed with a different capability in mind; but none is as tightly specific as an authoring language. FORTRAN, for example, was designed to solve a broad range of complex scientific and mathematical problems on mainframe computers. This useful language has been adapted to run on many of today's microcomputers, as have other languages not originally designed to do so.

Pascal is becoming increasingly popular and has been chosen by the College Entrance Examination Board for the Advanced Placement test in computer science because it has features that make it a good all-around language to know and use. BASIC was developed as a tool to teach programming to students, but it has been expanded in capability and has become the most common language for microcomputers. Logo was created as an open-ended, problem-solving tool simple enough for a small child to use yet possessing features sophisticated enough to challenge secondary students. BASIC and Logo are the most common languages in use in the schools and will therefore be stressed here.

Because programming languages are so versatile, they are also more demanding to use than is an authoring language. For each unique task the programmer designs a unique program, using a limited set of instructions and a tightly defined syntax to create a tool dedicated to the performance of the specific task. On the other hand, an authoring language is limited to the creation of lessons and requires no traditional programming skills. PILOT (Programmed Inquiry, Learning, or Teaching) is the primary authoring language in use in the schools. The menus and submenus that appear throughout the program permit

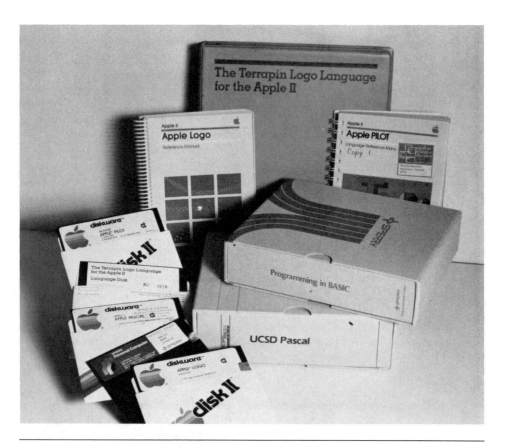

FIGURE 7.1  Programming and Authoring Packages

the user to select from options such as composing text, creating graphics, or generating music. Help screens can be called up when needed to display information such as cursor moves (for creating graphics), special key functions, or the code for the colors. Although emphasis is on programming languages in this chapter, PILOT will be discussed.

A modification of the authoring language is the authoring system, which is even more tightly structured than the language. The teacher types responses to questions concerning the subject, the nature of student responses to questions, and so on into a matrix or format; the system then assembles the completed lesson and it is ready for use.

Programmers have not always had access to the convenient languages now available. In the early days of computing, programming was a much more demanding task than it is currently. Programmers had to instruct the computer using only binary code. Since the computer could deal directly with the early programs, this served to speed up the processing of information, but there were disadvantages: the binary approach not only required great skill but also was a tedious process that was prone to error. A primitive programming method was with toggle switches: pushing the switch in one direction fed a binary 1 into the machine, pressing it in the other resulted in a 0; various combinations of 0s and 1s made up the instructions in the program. It is easy to see how such a system would lead to operator fatigue.

High-level languages were developed so the programmer could communicate with the machine at a more human level. In this kind of language English words are used, many of which are self-explanatory. A single high-level command or statement might accomplish the same results as an entire series of machine language "words," and the process is much simpler (fig. 7.2). The high-level commands must still be broken down into the binary machine code for the computer to understand them, but this is accomplished automatically through the use of special, built-in programs called compilers or interpreters. The development of such high-level languages as BASIC has made learning how to program much easier than before, and many people, including teachers, have developed this skill to some degree.

How important is it that teachers be able to write programs? Obviously, it is not necessary to be a programmer in order to operate a microcomputer. We have already seen that a commercial program on a disk is easy to use—anyone can take advantage of the professional programmer's skills by simply purchasing one of the hundreds of widely available software selections and running it. The teacher's role is such, however, that some familiarity with programming can be useful if she is to function effectively in the computer-age classroom. The degree to which a teacher may or may not become involved in programming or related activities depends upon various factors. You may recall that among the several applications identified in chapter 3 were the teaching of programming and computer awareness. To manage the first of these a knowledge of programming is essential; for the second, this skill might also be useful if programming is seen as an important component. Additionally, to succeed in integrating programming

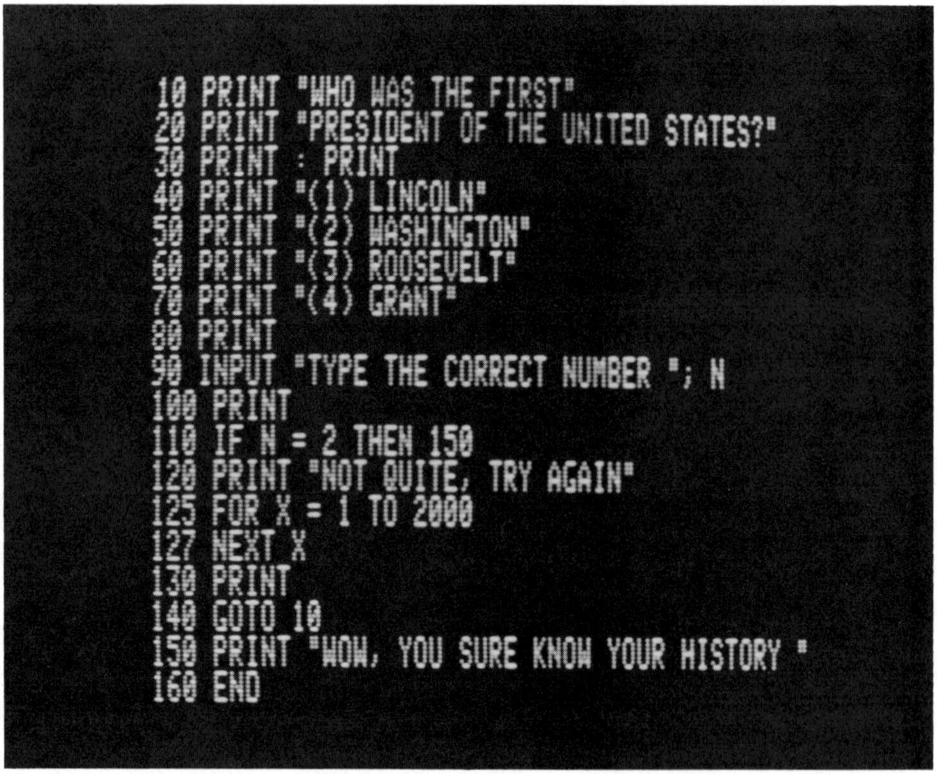

```
10 PRINT "WHO WAS THE FIRST"
20 PRINT "PRESIDENT OF THE UNITED STATES?"
30 PRINT : PRINT
40 PRINT "(1) LINCOLN"
50 PRINT "(2) WASHINGTON"
60 PRINT "(3) ROOSEVELT"
70 PRINT "(4) GRANT"
80 PRINT
90 INPUT "TYPE THE CORRECT NUMBER "; N
100 PRINT
110 IF N = 2 THEN 150
120 PRINT "NOT QUITE, TRY AGAIN"
125 FOR X = 1 TO 2000
127 NEXT X
130 PRINT
140 GOTO 10
150 PRINT "WOW, YOU SURE KNOW YOUR HISTORY "
160 END
```

FIGURE 7.2  The Computer Is Programmed by Typing a Sequence of
Instructions Made up of Special Words

into traditional subject matter activities the teacher must possess some knowledge of programming.

Admittedly, not many teachers develop the skills required to write topflight instructional programs, and those who possess the expertise are often hard-pressed to find the time for such an undertaking. Consequently, few teacher-authored programs approach the quality of the better commercial selections. Generally, unless the objective is to teach programming as a subject to those interested in computer science, it is not necessary for the teacher to be a professional-level programmer to work effectively with the overall school population.

Many teachers see programming not as an end in itself but as just another way to communicate with the computer, to appreciate its capabilities, and to understand better how it works. Thus, some programming is practiced as one of a number of strategies for introducing students to computers. Those who criticize this approach suggest that no programming at all is better than learning bad

habits from an inexpert teacher. It is likely that any such bad habits will be readily modified, however, when and if the student moves on to a specialized programming class.

Innovative teachers with programming skills are combining some programming with more traditional activities to lend a new dimension to their
classes. For example, one junior high school art teacher has developed an
exercise as part of a unit on commercial art in which students create simple
computer-generated graphics using the school's Ataris. This approach has
proved to be much more successful than the traditional one, in which examples
of computer graphics were displayed and the process for creating them discussed. In another school a fourth grade teacher has students create artistic covers for their essays using nothing more than the PRINT statement (PRINT and
other special instruction words that direct the computer are discussed later in
this chapter). A graph on paper, arranged in the manner of the computer
display, is used for the initial planning. The successive lines of computer instructions are then developed from the drawn design and typed on the keyboard in
the form of PRINT statements followed by the necessary spaces and asterisks
(or other symbols). When printed as hard copy the result is a personalized cover
(see fig. 7.3).

One teacher developed a simple spelling program using the computer's IF-
THEN capabilities. The program was designed so students could update the vocabulary list as desired by substituting new words. For the program to work
properly the words had to be spelled correctly; thus the activity of inserting each

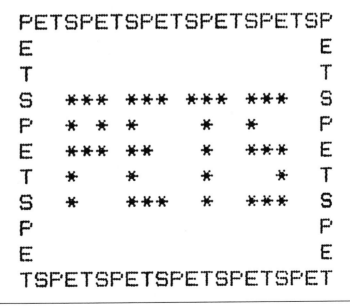

FIGURE 7.3   A Simple BASIC Program Was Used to Create This Cover Design

new word involved considerable vocabulary learning in itself. As a further example, an article by Nancy Kuechle describes how she and her students use a few selected BASIC keywords (PRINT, INPUT, GOTO, and IF-THEN) to create interactive adventure stories. As a story unfolds a situation arises in which the student must make a decision; on the basis of the decision one or another path is taken, which can lead to another decision, and so on. And finally, for an excellent activity involving programming and math, you may wish to refer to an article by Gerald Elgarten entitled "Programming Perimeters"; it includes a handy worksheet that can be most useful for translating the concept of finding perimeters into a finished program in BASIC.

Despite the successes enjoyed by many teachers, the controversy over whether or not to involve the general student population in programming activities continues. One of the more common arguments against requiring programming is that most students won't need it as a vocational tool once they are out of school, so in-school time should be used in more productive ways—becoming more skilled in math and language areas, for example. As computers become more user friendly, so the argument goes, programming skills will be necessary only for those who make computers their profession. (The term *user friendly*, you will recall, is used to describe the extent to which a computer and its programs adapt to the way people do things; conversely, an unfriendly system is one in which the user is forced to adapt to the idiosyncrasies of the machine.) Although a large number of jobs require employees to work with computers, the nature of these machines is such that few people even think of them as computers. The clerk who passes the groceries over the bar code reader is not really concerned about the technology involved, nor is the teller in the bank who types in the details of a deposit and gives out the deposit slip.

The rationale for the inclusion of programming in computer literacy courses is that it enables students to find out for themselves if they have an interest in this activity. Those who advocate this approach would use a parallel argument for including just about any subject, with the possible exception of the basics, in the curriculum. Others who support the teaching of programming maintain that the main benefit of the exercises involved is the enhancement of the ability to think and reason logically. Arthur Luehrmann, an eloquent spokesman for the "pro-programmers," says that to enable the computer to carry out its tasks, the student must first think through all the steps involved in precise detail. He points out that "all of the intellectual merit of a computer course derives from this simple statement of fact: to write a successful computer program, one must understand the problem and its solution." This exercise in precise thinking is perceived as a highly desirable learning experience.

Seymour Papert, who was instrumental in developing Logo, defends the teaching of programming throughout his book *Mindstorms*. He states:

> In many schools today, the phrase "computer-aided instruction" means making the computer teach the child. One might say the *computer is being used to program the child.* In my vision, the *child programs the computer* and, in doing so,

both acquires a sense of mastery over a piece of the most modern and powerful technology and establishes an intimate contact with some of the deepest
ideas from science, from mathematics and from the art of intellectual model
building.*

The arguments both for and against teaching programming are most con-
vincing; to date, however, there is little evidence either to support the contention
that programming enhances intellectual skills or to indicate that the converse is
true. In any case, teachers who involve their students in programming activities
soon discover that they love the challenge of writing programs and relish the
sense of control over the computer that programming provides. Obviously, few
teachers would involve their students in programming activities without first understanding the essentials themselves. There are various approaches to gaining
familiarity or competence in this area.

One way to learn about programming is to obtain a text on the subject (see
this chapter's references), sit down at the keyboard, and work carefully through
the various exercises. This approach takes considerable dedication and determination, but many teachers have learned the elements in this way. Some excellent
tutorials, available on disk, will teach the concepts in a very direct fashion. If you
prefer a more formal approach, on the other hand, you might wish to enroll in
one of the many classes offered by school districts, universities, and community
schools. Learning to program often involves a combination of several of the various methods. Becoming adept at this skill requires a considerable expenditure of
time and effort, and many educators find the payoff incommensurate with the
requirements.

Regardless of your approach, you will find that programming is much
more involved than simply sitting down at the keyboard and writing a program.
Possibly 90 percent of the work is actually done away from the computer in the
form of conceptualizing, developing algorithms, formatting, and so on. The following information should prove enlightening, whether or not you elect to pursue the topic further.

## BASIC

BASIC is the "native language" of most microcomputers; that is, it comes
built-in from the factory. There are, of course, exceptions: you must insert the
BASIC cartridge into the slot in the Atari 800 series before a program can be
written, and the Macintosh and the IBM have their BASIC on disks. Other languages, such as Logo and Pascal, can be loaded from disks so the BASIC is
bypassed.

---

*From *Mindstorms* by Seymour Papert. ©1980 by Basic Books, Inc., Publishers. Reprinted by permission of the publisher.

## Commands

Described below are some of the more important commands that are used to control and direct the computer. These commands are fairly straightforward; typing them on the keyboard causes the computer to react in a specific manner. Among the commands are those that enable the disk drives and the computer to work together as a system. Whether or not you write your own programs, it is useful to know at least some of the more common commands: with them you can do such things as save a program onto a disk, delete or change lines in a program that you or someone else has written, or see all the programs stored on a particular disk. Some of the common commands follow.

**CATALOG.** Typing CATALOG will signal the computer to display all the programs stored on a disk (the term FILES is used with some computers). From these you may select the specific program you wish to run.

**DELETE.** DELETE followed by the name of the program deletes that program from the disk (the term KILL is used on some systems). Be careful with this command: it completely removes the information, and there is no way to get it back. If the name of your file was "myprog" the command would look like this: DELETE MYPROG.

**LIST.** The LIST command is used when the programmer wants to see what the program looks like line by line. If the program is a large one that scrolls up the screen, it can be stopped with CONTROL-S (Apple), CONTROL-BREAK (IBM), or the BREAK key on other machines. LIST followed by a number causes that line only to be displayed; LIST 20, for example, results in a listing of line 20 from the program. This same command followed by two numbers causes the numbers indicated and all those between to be displayed: LIST 30,200, for example, displays all lines from 30 to 200 inclusive.

**LOAD.** Typing LOAD and the name of a program will load the program from the disk into the memory of the computer. It can then be listed so you can add to it or delete unwanted segments. An example is LOAD PROG1.

**RUN.** Typing the RUN command followed by the name of a program on the disk will load and run that program. An example is RUN PROG1. Typing RUN alone will cause the program currently in memory (if any) to run.

**SAVE.** Typing SAVE followed by a program name will save it onto the disk. An example is SAVE EPIC (you can use just about any name you choose).

## BASIC Statements

To begin writing a program you type a line number, which is typically expressed as an increment of 10 (e.g., 10, 20, 30) to permit the insertion of additional lines of instructions between successive line numbers if needed. You then enter one of the special words that make up the BASIC vocabulary, such as FOR-NEXT, GOTO, IF-THEN, LET, or PRINT. Some of these words are described in the following pages. Many others are available, but this selected sample will serve to illustrate how the language works. Next, an expression is generally used, either a numerical one or a word or words (called a string). The following is a complete BASIC statement:

| 10 | PRINT | 2 + 4 |
|---|---|---|
| the line number | the keyword | the expression |

This statement, which includes a line number (10), a keyword (PRINT), and an expression (2 + 4), is a fairly typical example of a program line. However, the structure tends to change somewhat, depending upon what the instructions are supposed to do. In the example above, the word PRINT tells the computer to display the results of the computation; in this case, the printout will be 6. If PRINT is followed by words or numbers within quotation marks (such as 10 PRINT "ADDITIONAL EXERCISES"), however, a literal printout of that material will take place. After the statement has been typed in and the RETURN or ENTER key pressed, the line will be sent to the computer's internal memory (RAM), where it is stored temporarily. Each line of the program is stored in like fashion, and the program only executes when the command RUN is entered.

So far we have considered but one of the special words with which the computer works (PRINT). Following are additional words and a description of what each of them accomplishes.

**FOR-NEXT.** When a FOR-NEXT loop runs it begins at FOR and ends at NEXT, where it loops back to FOR and continues until the specified condition, set following the FOR statement, is met. The typical way to specify the number of loops is illustrated below:

```
10 FOR N = 1 TO 10
```

This indicates that the loop should be executed ten times, but there is no loop as yet, so we will create one:

```
10 FOR N = 1 TO 10
20 PRINT N
30 NEXT N
```

When the command RUN is given, the number at line 10 is 1; this is printed at line 20. Then line 30 instructs the computer to loop back up to line 10. Because the condition at line 10 instructs the computer to repeat this process until the number 10 is reached, the printout at line 20 will represent first the number 1, then 2, 3, and so on up to 10.

**LET.** The computer's memory is made up of a large number of spaces, each of which is identified by an address. Values, such as numbers or strings, can be assigned to (or placed into) these spaces. A useful analogy is that of many empty boxes such as those in a post office. Things can be placed in these boxes, each of which has a unique address. When the stored items are needed, they can be found rapidly and with little difficulty. A standard system is commonly used for numbering the boxes, such as letters in various combinations, with numbers appended as needed to provide additional combinations. These labeled boxes are called variables; their contents are values.

Placing a specific item into one of the storage boxes is called assigning a value to a variable. Using the post office analogy, we might say LET the box labeled PC contain a postcard. An important distinction between the memory spaces within the computer and the boxes in the post office should be noted: unlike the boxes in the post office, computer boxes can accommodate only *one* item at a time; thus, if another postcard is pushed into box PC, the one that was there previously is forced out. In actual practice, if memory space PC contained 10, for example, and 15 was then assigned to variable PC, the 10 would be destroyed and the 15 would be installed. Thus

```
20 LET PC = 10
```

means that space PC holds a 10, but the following line changes that:

```
30 LET PC = 15
```

Now variable PC holds 15; the 10 has been replaced.

To hold a word, variables must be modified by adding a dollar sign ($) to a standard variable: A$, D$, or X$, for example. The correct way to write a LET statement using a string variable is

```
10 LET B$ = "BOB"
```

The symbol B$ is called "B string." Now, let's consider how the contents in all these boxes are moved about. Here is a short program using the statements we know:

```
10 LET R$ = "RICHARD"
20 PRINT R$
```

The output is RICHARD (the contents of variable R$)—not R$, as one might expect. With nothing more than the LET and the PRINT statements, it is possible to write some programs that actually do things. As an example, let's try some math.

```
10 LET X = 4
20 PRINT X
30 LET X = X + 1
40 PRINT X
```

```
50 LET Z = X
60 LET Y = X * Z
70 PRINT Y
```

Run through the program in your mind to see if you can come up with the quantities that will be printed at lines 20, 40, and 70 before you read the following explanation.

In line 10 the value 4 is assigned to variable X. Line 20 prints out 4. In line 30, 4 is incremented by one, becoming 5; this value is printed out in line 40. Line 50 introduces a new variable, Z. The value in X, which is 5, remains unaltered, but variable Z now contains 5 also. In line 60 another variable, Y, is introduced; it will hold the results of the calculation X * Z (note that * means multiplication in BASIC). Finally, in line 70 the contents of variable Y are displayed. The printout looks like this:

```
4
5
25
```

**GOTO.** The GOTO statement directs the computer to go to the line number that follows this statement and then to continue with the execution of the instructions in sequential line number order. The correct line number must follow the GOTO if the branch is to be completed properly. Here is a sample of the use of GOTO:

```
10 LET R$ = "REBECCA"
20 PRINT R$
30 GOTO 10
```

When this program is run, the string REBECCA will be printed out at line 20, then line 30 will direct the computer to return to line 10; it then moves to line 20, where REBECCA is again printed, and so on forever. This is an example of an infinite loop—stop it by pressing CONTROL-C, BREAK, CTRL/BREAK, or RUN/STOP (depending upon the kind of computer being used).

It is very easy to overuse GOTO, which makes the written program both cumbersome and difficult to interpret. A much better approach is to use subroutines, which are described later, in place of GOTO statements where possible.

**IF-THEN.** IF-THEN is used in conjunction with conditions that enable the computer to make decisions. For example, we can inform our machine that if some condition prevails, then it should perform a specified task. To do this, we must use standard symbols to indicate such conditions:

|  |  |
|---|---|
| < | less than |
| <= | less than or equal to |

|       |                       |
|-------|-----------------------|
| >     | greater than          |
| >=    | greater than or equal to |
| =     | equal to              |
| < >   | not equal to          |

By using the IF-THEN statement we now have a way to get out of an infinite loop without having to resort to the use of CONTROL or BREAK keys:

```
10 LET R$ = "REBECCA"
20 LET C = 0
30 IF C = 6 THEN 70
40 PRINT R$
50 LET C = C + 1
60 GOTO 30
70 END
```

When this program is run the name REBECCA will be displayed six times, then the program stops.

**INPUT.** The INPUT statement is useful because it permits the user to interact with a running program, inputting information as the computer asks for it. As you will recall, two kinds of input are used—numeric and string—which vary in the way they are written:

|         |                |
|---------|----------------|
| numeric | 10 INPUT A     |
| string  | 20 INPUT A$    |

When waiting for input, the computer stops executing the program until it receives a response from the user. Generally a question will be displayed on the screen. Here is an example of a typical INPUT statement:

```
100 INPUT "WHAT IS YOUR GUESS? ";G
```

There is a unique characteristic about this statement that is worth mentioning. Note that the input statement works very much like a PRINT statement; that is, the message WHAT IS YOUR GUESS? will be displayed on the screen. When you type your guess and press the return or enter key, it is stored in memory space G.

You can also use the INPUT statement to give control of the pacing of the program to the user. An INPUT statement followed by a message such as PRESS RETURN TO CONTINUE will hold the display on the screen until the student presses the return key. The line looks like this:

```
50 INPUT "PRESS RETURN TO CONTINUE";P$
```

Here is an example of a string input:

```
10 PRINT "HI, I'M THE COMPUTER."
20 PRINT "WHAT'S YOUR NAME?"
30 INPUT N$
40 PRINT "PLEASED TO MEET YOU "N$
50 END
```

When this program is run, HI, I'M THE COMPUTER. WHAT'S YOUR NAME? is displayed on the screen, then the computer stops and waits for your response. When you type your name, it is stored in the memory space labeled N$. Whenever N$ appears in the program, its contents (your name) will be printed out. When the program above is run, here's how it looks:

This shows on the screen:

```
HI, I'M THE COMPUTER.
WHAT'S YOUR NAME?
```

You type your name:

```
PATRICIA
```

The computer responds with:

```
PLEASED TO MEET YOU PATRICIA
```

(note that it prints the contents of memory space N$ which is "Patricia").

**GOSUB-RETURN.** A subroutine is a self-contained module in a program. Using this statement permits you to branch to the subroutine from almost anywhere in the program. Here is an example:

```
10 REM GOSUB EXAMPLE
20 HOME
30 GOSUB 1000
40 PRINT "  AUTUMN COLORS"
50 GOSUB 1000
60 PRINT "   ORANGE,GOLD"
70 GOSUB 1000
80 PRINT "   WARMER THAN"
90 GOSUB 1000
100 PRINT "BLUE WINTER'S COLD"
110 GOSUB 1000
120 END
```

```
1000 PRINT
1010 PRINT "     !!!!!!!!!!      "
1020 PRINT
1030 RETURN
```

When you run the program the result should be:

```
                    !!!!!!!!!!

                 AUTUMN COLORS

                    !!!!!!!!!!

                 ORANGE,GOLD

                    !!!!!!!!!!

                 WARMER THAN

                    !!!!!!!!!!

              BLUE WINTER'S COLD

                    !!!!!!!!!!
```

The GOSUB statements cause the subroutine, which begins on line 1000, to be executed. A blank line is inserted, then a line of exclamation points, and then another blank line. The RETURN statement on line 1030 causes the program to pick up where it left off—that is, immediately following the last executed GOSUB statement. Thus, following the execution of the first GOSUB at line 30, the program continues with line 40, and the words AUTUMN COLORS are displayed, then the next GOSUB is encountered. This sequence continues until the program ends. Subroutines are generally placed after the main program, which is often very short when several subroutines are included.

GOSUB statements are generally more involved than the sample shown here. For example, you might wish to work out grades for each of your students based on a number of test scores. A subroutine could be designed to add together each student's scores, divide the sum by the number of exams, and match this number with a predetermined scale to produce a letter grade for each student.

Note that there are two new statements in this program. Line 10 introduces the REM (remark) statement, which is used frequently as a prompt or reminder of what the various statements are supposed to do. REMs make the program easier to read and understand and are a common form of documentation. The HOME statement in line 20 is an Apple term that automatically clears everything off the screen in preparation for the run of the program; you would use CLS for the TRS 80 and IBM, and PRINT "CLR/HOME" for the Commodore (these differences are explained in more detail in the sample programming exercise in appendix I).

Here is an example of a short program that uses many of the statements discussed above:

```
10 REM KITTEN PROGRAM
20 REM K = TOTAL KITTENS
30 REM G = KITTENS GIVEN AWAY
40 REM R = KITTENS LEFT
50 HOME
60 INPUT "HOW MANY KITTENS DO YOU HAVE? ";K
70 GOSUB 1000
80 INPUT "HOW MANY DO YOU WANT TO GIVE AWAY? ";G
90 LET R = K - G
100 IF R <= 0 THEN 150
110 GOSUB 1000
120 PRINT "YOU NOW HAVE "R" KITTENS LEFT."
130 PRINT
140 GOTO 60
150 PRINT "YOU'RE OUT OF KITTENS."
160 END
1000 PRINT:PRINT
1010 RETURN
```

When you run the program it will ask the number of kittens you have and wait for you to answer (line 60). You will then be asked to type in the number you want to give away (line 80). This amount will be subtracted from the current number of kittens (line 90), and the number remaining will be printed (line 120). This loop is repeated until the condition at line 100 is met (all the kittens are gone); then line 150 "you're out of kittens," will be printed. Note the REMs on lines 10 through 40. These have nothing to do with the way the program runs, but they give useful information about it. The subroutine on line 1000 simply inserts two blank lines between the lines of text. Note that a colon (:) can be used to separate two or more statements so they can be placed on a single line.

If you are intrigued with BASIC programming at this point and would like some more extensive hands-on experience, turn to appendix I, where a BASIC exercise is found. Merely type it into the computer just as it is written to see how the various instructions work. Incidentally, this can be a useful way to get acquainted with programming. Books are available that provide complete line-by-line listings of a variety of programs. Also, many journals include listings that can be typed into the computer and run.

## BASIC IN THE CLASSROOM

BASIC programming is typically undertaken in math classes, but it can be used elsewhere as well. Special graphics statements like HLIN (horizontal line) and VLIN (vertical line) can help create colorful graphics and can present art and design students with a new challenge. Programming might also be introduced in conjunction with a careers unit in which positions in the computer industry are being discussed. Various aspects of programming can be most useful in the study of physics: many equations can be included in functional programs to be run on the microcomputer. Programs can also be written to control a programmable robot; the results are much more dramatic than are those displayed on the monitor screen. BASIC can be used to generate sounds in addition to visual displays. Music students will enjoy creating high-tech compositions on the micro—some machines provide a highly capable sound synthesizer as part of the standard equipment.

There are a number of approaches used in the teaching of programming. One is simply to concentrate on one statement at a time, then to tie them together. The opposite extreme involves seating the students at the computers and letting them find their own way. Somewhere between these two is the most common approach: the student works through a series of exercises that proceed from the simpler concepts to the more complex ones. The instructor must be certain that the exercises are bug-free (if they're typed in properly, they will work), but the rest is up to the student. A useful exercise of this type will be found in appendix I. Note that the lesson should be undertaken only after some discussion and after the student has learned the various system commands and has run several disk-based programs. Any number of exercises of this nature can be constructed.

Also useful are debugging exercises in which intentional mistakes are built into the program to prevent it from executing properly. The students correct the bugs and make the program work—this is an excellent project. The actual writing of programs is an enjoyable activity. A specific outcome is described, and the students employ their own selection of statements to produce the desired results. They also enjoy creating their own programs from scratch, with no specific prior instructions from the teacher as to what the programs must do. The results of such exercises are often surprisingly sophisticated.

In another exercise the teacher or capable students type short programs that are displayed on a large monitor (so the class can see the programs as they evolve). The class is divided into teams, which try to figure out what the results of a given program will be when it runs. After all the guesses are in, the teacher or student types RUN to display the results on the screen; a discussion period follows, during which correct answers are acknowledged and incorrect ones analyzed.

A similar exercise can be conducted without a computer. The short programs are printed on sheets of paper that contain a "blank screen" with each program (see fig. 7.4). The student writes the output, including correct spacing,

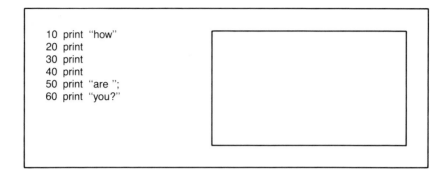

```
10 print "how"
20 print
30 print
40 print
50 print "are ";
60 print "you?"
```

FIGURE 7.4  An Example of a Programming Exercise and a "Blank Screen"

formatting, and so on, on the "screen." During the class discussion that follows each program is analyzed and the correct results displayed or written on the chalkboard.

Many of the BASIC statements and commands presented in this chapter can be taught through the use of analogies. A few examples are offered in the following discussion.

Using the analogy of computer memory spaces as mailboxes in a post office makes the LET statement easier to comprehend. The statement LET P = 10, for example, is interpreted as "let the mailbox labeled P contain a 10." The concept that, unlike mailboxes, a memory space can hold only one quantity at a time can be explained by saying that inserting a new letter (a value) into an occupied mailbox (a memory space) pushes the old contents out.

The PRINT statement is easily understood using the analogy of a typewriter. The importance of the quotation marks in relation to literal printout should be noted. A literal printout occurs only if quotation marks enclose the information. To emphasize their use you can play a game of "Simon Says" giving the directions "quotes" and "no quotes."

The GOTO statement is so straightforward that it requires little explanation. However, you can devise a treasure hunt in which this keyword is used to direct students to various places on a map. This statement can also be related to many of the common dice and spinner games in which players go to a particular space on the basis of the number from the spin or die toss.

The IF-THEN statement can be explained using everyday occurrences. For example, if it is cold outside, then I'll wear my coat. It should be stressed that an alternative *must* follow an IF-THEN statement. In other words, if it is cold outside, then I'll wear my coat; but if it is not cold, then I'll merely go to school (move to the next line) without donning my coat.

With a bit of imagination, the concept of BASIC keywords, statements, and commands can be made more concrete and therefore easier for the students to comprehend, remember, and utilize.

## LOGO

Logo, unlike PILOT and BASIC, is not an acronym. The name is taken from the Greek word *logos,* which means a word or a thought. The philosophy underlying this language was greatly influenced by the ideas of Piaget, who maintained that children learn by being actively involved. Logo, like PILOT, must be loaded into the computer's memory from a disk. Rather extensive documentation accompanies the program, but it is not necessary to spend much time with it; indeed, it's possible to control the turtle (a triangular cursor) the first time the language is used. However, Logo is not just turtle graphics; to realize its full potential takes quite a bit of effort and study. One of the nice things about Logo, though, is that a child can have fun and learn with it from the first press of a key while a high school student can be challenged by its powerful mathematical features that have applications in geometry, trigonometry, algebra, and calculus: it is a friendly, interactive, extensible tool.

The most common application in the schools is that of creating various geometric figures with the turtle (fig. 7.5). Directions are given using a set of words

FIGURE 7.5  A Design Created with Logo

called primitives—everyday, descriptive words such as *forward, right,* and *repeat*—
that the turtle understands. One way to teach Logo to children is to have them
walk through the commands; by following the moves themselves they are better
able to comprehend what the turtle will do.

To direct a friend using the language of Logo, you might say "go forward
10 steps; then turn right 90 degrees." If you give this same set of directions four
times, your friend will walk in a square and end up where she started—this is just
what the turtle does when it is given the same set of directions. Here is how the
program looks:

```
FORWARD 10
RIGHT 90
FORWARD 10
RIGHT 90
FORWARD 10
RIGHT 90
FORWARD 10
RIGHT 90
```

Later, you will learn a shorter way to accomplish such repetitive tasks; but for
now, we have just written our first Logo program. The words used (forward,
right) are primitives—they are part of the turtle's original vocabulary. Here are
some additional primitives:

| | |
|---|---|
| SHOWTURTLE | Causes the turtle to appear on the screen. |
| HIDETURTLE | Causes the turtle to disappear. |
| PENDOWN | Causes the turtle to draw a line as it moves. |
| PENUP | Allows the turtle to move about but leaving no line. |
| PENCOLOR | (SETPC, followed by a number from 0 to 5) Determines the colors of the lines that are drawn (SETPC 5, for example, results in a blue line). |
| PRINT | Prints whatever follows, as long as it is encased in brackets (PRINT [I LIKE YOU]). |
| LEFT | Causes the turtle to turn left the number of degrees specified (LEFT 90). |
| RIGHT | Causes the turtle to turn right (see LEFT, above). |
| FORWARD | Causes the turtle to move ahead a specified distance (FORWARD 6). |

| | |
|---|---|
| BACK | Causes the turtle to move backward (see FORWARD, above). |
| REPEAT | Repeats a procedure a specified number of times. |
| TO | Precedes a new word (not a primitive) that you will invent. |
| CLEARSCREEN | Clears the screen; the turtle remains in the center, ready to go to work. |
| END | Used after a procedure has been defined. |

Combinations of primitive instructions can be used to create an endless array of geometric designs and graphic displays. Children, and even adults, get caught up in the process and develop a sense of control as they learn to manipulate the turtle. The deeper power of Logo is not realized, however, until its extensibility is brought into play: beginning with the primitives, students can create a whole new vocabulary that the turtle understands. The new words, called procedures, are made up initially from elements of the original language; however, once introduced, they work just as if they had always been there.

In the following exercise a short program is used to create a geometric shape. Once the precise set of instructions has been established, the set, in toto, is given a name; it is then a procedure and becomes a part of the turtle's vocabulary. Whenever the procedure name is used, the product of the total instruction set that made up the procedure will be displayed. It is possible to create some striking effects by combining a number of procedures.

To begin, insert the disk in the drive and boot it. A few simple instructions will appear on the screen; following them causes a blinking cursor to appear, which indicates that the computer is waiting for some input. Typing SHOW-TURTLE produces the turtle in the center of the screen. A program can now be typed; here is a simple one:

```
FORWARD 80
RIGHT 90
FORWARD 10
RIGHT 90
FORWARD 80
RIGHT 90
FORWARD 10
```

The product of this little program is an elongated rectangle, as shown in figure 7.6. We are now ready to create a procedure. First we must select a name—LONGREC, for instance, for long rectangle. To define a procedure, follow these steps:

| | |
|---|---|
| TO LONGREC | (TO followed by the name is the first line of a procedure) |

```
FORWARD 80          (These are the same lines used in the
RIGHT 90            original program)
FORWARD 10
RIGHT 90
FORWARD 80
RIGHT 90
FORWARD 10
END                 (END is the last line in a procedure)
```

The computer will respond with the words "LONGREC defined."

You should normally finish a procedure with the turtle facing in the same direction as it began. In this case, however, we want to continue to enlarge upon the initial procedure and have thus left the turtle pointing in the direction of its next movement.

Now we can simply type the word LONGREC to have the rectangle displayed on the screen. In other words, a new command has been created that gives a predictable output whenever it is used. The magic of Logo begins to emerge when we realize that our new procedures can themselves be used to create additional procedures. To illustrate, LONGREC will be used as the main component in a new procedure we'll call WINDMILL:

```
TO WINDMILL
REPEAT 4 [LONGREC]
END
```

Once again, Logo will respond with "WINDMILL defined," to indicate that this procedure is now a part of its vocabulary. To see what WINDMILL looks like, we simply type that word; the turtle, obeying the instructions to repeat four longrecs, will draw the graphic shown in figure 7.7 on the screen.

This short exposure to Logo scarcely seems adequate for a language with so much potential, but if it has been of interest, you may want to learn more. One of Logo's most valuable features was alluded to but not demonstrated, due to lack

FIGURE 7.6  A Turtle Graphic

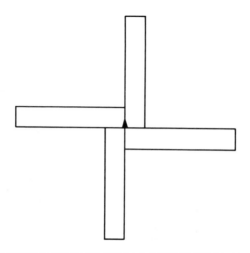

**FIGURE 7.7**  The "WINDMILL" Graphic

of space: it is highly capable of manipulating words and sentences through the use of a built-in tool called a list. Using lists effectively is reserved for those willing to spend the time and effort to learn the additional commands and the more complex syntax involved; those who have done so speak enthusiastically of Logo's capabilities.

## LOGO IN THE CLASSROOM

Logo is a sophisticated and powerful language that is said to have "no floor and no ceiling": its potential is nearly unlimited. It is probably the most interactive of the computing languages used in education, lending itself readily to experimentation. It encourages exploration and is friendly toward mistakes. Ideas can be worked through virtually at the point of inception; results are immediate and often dramatic.

Much of what the student learns is unintentional: the Logo experience should be based on the idea of discovery, avoiding the notion of structure in the sense of prescribed goals or objectives. Thus, interacting with the language itself is the primary activity when students use Logo. They conquer the computer and come to control it. They learn about the logic of programming, and they think about thinking.

There are, however, serious problems involved with discovery learning. Quite a bit of time can be spent in "discovering" anew concepts that are commonly known. The demands for accountability often preclude extended use of strategies that lack clear-cut objectives and outcomes. Perhaps the most satisfactory approach could be termed guided discovery, in which the teacher intervenes as needed; the student is not simply turned loose with the language.

Rather than being used in isolation, Logo is typically part of a wide range of learning experiences.

The fact that the turtle spends much of its time making turns indicates that students should know about angles if they are to be successful in their programming efforts. Of course, since Logo is discovery-based you might just turn them loose to experiment, but it is more effective for some students (though not all) to give them some help. A useful concept is the relationship of the turtle's turns to the 360 degrees of a full circle.

Most children have little difficulty understanding that the four 90-degree turns the turtle makes when drawing a square add up to 360 degrees. In essence, the turtle completes a circle even as it draws a square. This same idea applies to the construction of many other closed figures besides the square, but it is easiest to see with regular polygons. Equilateral triangles, pentagons, hexagons, and other polygons are simple to construct using a formula to figure the angle of the turns the turtle must make. An equilateral triangle has three sides and a turtle trip is 360 degrees, so the turtle must make three turns of 120 degrees to draw the triangle and come back to rest in its starting position. To figure the number of degrees for each turn (angle) of a pentagon, you simply divide 360 by 5 to arrive at five turtle turns of 72 degrees. A hexagon requires six turns of 60 degrees, and an octagon has eight 45-degree turns. It is easy to construct a useful tool for teaching the concept of degrees (see fig. 7.8). Begin by drawing two circles on pieces of cardboard. Using a protractor, mark off the degrees at various

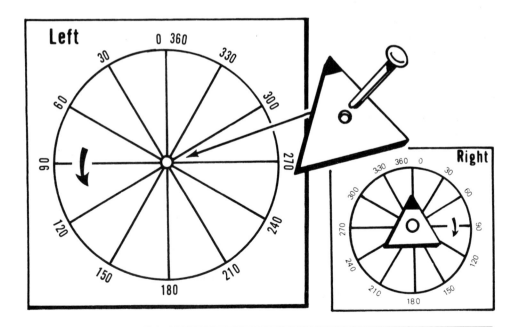

FIGURE 7.8 Making a Pair of Turtle Compasses

intervals around the edges of the circles (in a clockwise direction for one circle and counterclockwise for the other) and draw lines radiating from the centers to the degree marks, thus dividing the circles into segments. Cut out two triangular "turtles" and fasten them to the centers to act as spinners. Students can use these devices in conjunction with the computer to move the turtle in predefined ways.

Teachers employ a variety of techniques for introducing Logo to their students; we'll mention but a few. Giving turtle commands to children to act out, which we discussed earlier, can become gamelike if teams compete to see who can execute a secret figure, or reach a spot in the room or on the playground, on the basis of directions given by the team leader. A similar game offers a greater challenge by having the players execute the program blindfolded. By placing masking tape in a pattern on a tile floor it is possible to delineate a turtle program, with each tile representing a turtle step. You can construct progressively more complex mazes with additional strips of tape. Students must write the program from the "tracks" the turtle has left on the floor.

A treasure hunt can be conducted using the screen turtle to move from point to point on a terrain map drawn on transparent plastic and taped over the screen. A second map (the pirate's map) or a set of instructions is drawn or written on paper; as the directions are interpreted, the turtle is directed from one point to the next on the plastic screen map. This procedure gives students practice in estimating angles and distances.

Logo can also be used in conjunction with a unit on astronomy. After studying the constellations, students recreate them on the computer screen. Procedures can be developed and named after the constellations they represent or to generate geometric shapes (squares, triangles, and circles, for example) to be used as components in the construction of more complex figures. The basic shapes can be combined in numerous ways to form objects such as houses, animals, and people. This idea is useful for illustrating the concept of modular programming.

Another exciting use of Logo is to control a robot. One of the more popular classroom robots is Turtle Tot, shown in figure 7.9; when attached to a computer with a special flexible cable, it can "feel" with touch sensors, move in all directions, draw with a marker, and even speak, using a special speech chip that is available in several languages. Valiant Turtle, shown in figure 7.10, with its turtlelike head and body, is a second Logo-controlled robot. Unlike the Tot, this model is not physically attached to the computer—it is totally remote-controlled. The shape of Valiant is practical: there is never any doubt about the way it is facing, so children know exactly which command to use to move it backward, forward, right, or left. An infrared transmitter on the computer sends the signals that control the turtle's actions. The robot itself runs on a set of ten rechargeable, long-life nickel cadmium batteries that are easily replaced. Logo has special meaning to young programmers when it is used to give life to a Turtle Tot or a Valiant Turtle.

Many additional ideas for introducing and using Logo can be found in the references listed at the end of this chapter.

**FIGURE 7.9  Turtle Tot** (Courtesy of Harvard Associates, Inc.)

## PILOT

To this point emphasis has been on programming languages. PILOT, on the other hand, is an authoring language and thus differs in various ways from languages such as BASIC and Logo. A discussion of certain of these differences is found in the introduction to this chapter.

Since BASIC is, with few exceptions, the microcomputer's native tongue, the computer must learn a new language to write a program in PILOT. This is not very difficult—the language is stored on a disk called the author diskette and must simply be loaded into the memory. A second disk, on which the created lessons are stored, is called the lesson diskette. When the PILOT or SuperPILOT package is acquired, it will include extensive documentation (sometimes a book or two) detailing how to author a lesson; the information given here must, of necessity, be brief.

You will need two disk drives to write the lesson (drive one holds the author disk, drive two holds the lesson disk), but after the lesson has been created, it can be run using a single drive.

When PILOT is loaded into the computer's memory, a number of different options will be displayed on a series of menus. Once you have made your selection, press the letter key representing that option. Pressing key L, for example,

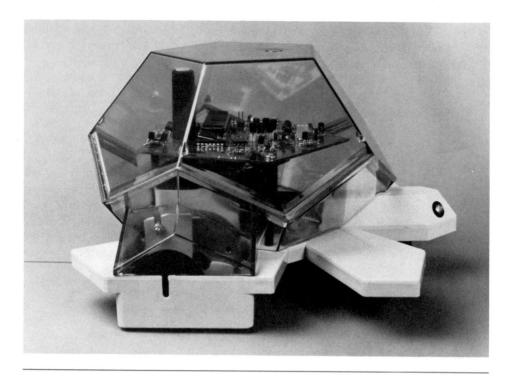

**FIGURE 7.10  Valiant Turtle** (Courtesy of Harvard Associates, Inc.)

puts the computer in the Lesson Text Editor, which lets you write a lesson—this is the most widely used option. When a letter key is pressed, the main menu is replaced by the menu for whichever editor is selected. At this point prompt lines will appear on the screen; pressing the appropriate keys in response will eventually get you into the Insert Mode, where the lesson is actually written.

The PILOT instruction set consists of a total of about forty-five abbreviated commands, most of which you would not use until you have become quite familiar with the language.

The primary purpose for using PILOT is to create interactive instructional programs tailored to meet the specific curricular needs of the instructor who writes them. PILOT makes the extensive use of text a relatively simple matter—developing a computer-based dialogue is much easier with this language than it is with most others. It offers the user other powerful capabilities as well: an excellent graphics editor and one for sound both greatly enhance a program. (See appendix I for a sample PILOT lesson.)

## SUMMARY

Arguments both for and against programming have been presented in this chapter. Basically, proponents maintain that this activity enhances the students' ability to think logically and analytically. Opponents maintain that few students will become professional programmers so students can better spend their in-school time mastering the basics.

The nature of computer literacy courses is changing. While these classes continue to be popular, programming activities are giving way to such things as word processing. On the other hand, a strong trend appears to be developing toward offering programming as an elective class to serve the needs of science-oriented students. At the same time, teachers with programming skills are integrating this activity into the traditional curriculum in various ways.

Two programming languages were described in this chapter: BASIC and Logo. BASIC was emphasized because most classroom computers have this language on board. A selection of essential statements and commands was provided to enable the creation of simple programs. A discussion of the authoring language PILOT was provided and the differences between authoring and general purpose programming languages were discussed. Those who wish to try writing more complex programs will find the following references useful.

## REFERENCES

Abelson, H. *Apple Logo.* Peterborough, NH: BYTE/McGraw-Hill, 1982.

Albrecht, B., Finkle L., and Brown, J. *BASIC for Home Computers.* New York: John Wiley and Sons, 1978.

Apple Computer Company. *Apple PILOT Editor's Manual.* Cupertino, CA: Apple Computer Company, 1980.

———. *Apple PILOT Language Reference Manual.* Cupertino, CA: Apple Computer Company, 1980.

———. *Applesoft Reference Manual.* Cupertino, CA: Apple Computer Company, 1978.

———. *The Applesoft Tutorial.* Cupertino, CA: Apple Computer Company, 1981.

Babbie, E. *Apple Logo for Teachers.* Belmont, CA: Wadsworth, 1984.

Barnett, M., and Barnett, G. *Personal Graphics.* Boston: Little, Brown and Company, 1983.

Bateson, R., and Raygor, R. *Basic Programming for the Apple Computer.* St. Paul: West Publishing Co., 1985.

Bearden, D., Martin, K., and Muller, J. *The Turtle's Source Book.* Reston, VA: Reston, 1983.

Bitter, G., and Watson, N. *Apple Logo Primer.* Reston, VA: Reston, 1983.

Clark, J., and Drum, W. *BASIC Programming: A Structured Approach.* Cincinnati: South-Western, 1983.

Culp, G., and Nickles, H. *An Apple for the Teacher.* Monterey, CA: Brooks/Cole, 1983.

Dachslager, H., Hayashi, M., and Zucker, R. *Learning BASIC Programming: A Systematic Approach.* Monterey, CA: Brooks/Cole, 1983.

Dunn, S., and Morgan, V. *The Apple Personal Computer for Beginners.* Englewood Cliffs: Prentice/Hall, 1982.

Elgarten, G. "Programming Perimeters." *Classroom Computer News* (March 1983): 68–69.

Friedman, B., and Slesnick, T. *Teaching BASIC Bit by Bit.* Berkeley, CA: Lawrence Hall of Science, 1981.

Grammar, V., and Goldenberg, P. *The Terrapin Logo Language for the Apple II, Tutorial.* Cambridge, MA: Terrapin, Inc., 1982.

Heller, R., Martin, C., and Wright, J. *Logoworlds.* Rockville, MD: Computer Science Press, 1985.

Kuechle, N. "BASIC Adventures." *Classroom Computer Learning* (January 1984): 66–67.

Lough, T. "Exploring New Horizons with Logo." *Electronic Learning* (April 1983): 71–75.

————. "Logo, Discovery Learning with the Classroom's Newest Pet." *Electronic Learning* (March 1983): 49–53.

Lough, T., and Tipps, S. "Logo Notebook, Lesson One: Introductory Activities." *Teaching and Computers* (September 1983): 38–39.

Luehrmann, A. "Microcomputers in the Junior High School." *Proceedings of the Annual Summer Conference on the Computer: Extension of the Human Mind II.* Eugene, OR: College of Education, University of Oregon, 1983.

Luehrman, A., and Peckham, H. *Computer Literacy: A Hands-On Approach.* New York: McGraw-Hill, 1983.

Mandell, S. *Introduction to BASIC Programming,* 2d ed. St. Paul: West Publishing Co., 1985.

Marateck, S. *BASIC,* 2nd edition. San Diego, CA: Coronado Publishers, 1982.

Nelson, H. "Learning with Logo." *On Computing* (Summer 1981): 14–16.

Nickles, H., and Culp, G. *Instructional Computing Fundamentals for the Commodore 64.* Monterey, CA: Brooks/Cole, 1985.

Orwig, G. *Creating Computer Programs for Learning.* Reston, VA: Reston, 1983.

Papert, S. "Computer as Mudpie." *Classroom Computer Learning* (January 1984): 36–38, 40.

————. "New Views on Logo." *Electronic Learning* (April 1986): 33–36, 63.

————. "Spearheading the Computer Revolution." *On Computing* (Summer 1981): 10–12.

Shane, J. *Apple II BASIC.* Boston: Houghton Mifflin, 1983.

Shelly, G., and Cashman, T. *Introduction to BASIC Programming.* Brea, CA: Anaheim, 1982.

Swett, S. "Logo Offspring: A Look at Modified Versions of Logo and Turtle Graphics Programs." *Electronic Learning* (May/June 1983): 72–75.

Tipps, S., and Lough, T. "Logo Notebook, Lesson Two: Grids, Mazes, and Maps." *Teaching and Computers* (October 1983): 51–52, 59.

Waite, M., and Pardee, M. *BASIC Programming Primer,* 2d ed. Indianapolis: Bobbs-Merrill, 1982.

Watt, D. *Learning with Logo.* New York: McGraw-Hill, 1983.

————. "Learning with Logo." *Classroom Computer News* (April 1983): 40–43.

# 8

# PLANNING AND IMPLEMENTATION

## INTRODUCTION

Many schools have no systematic plan for acquiring and using micro-computers. They might purchase a basic system with money from a variety of sources and then turn it over to an interested teacher to use as she sees fit. Little planning and practically no staff involvement are necessary with this approach. But when a school makes a serious decision to develop a functional microcomputer program, the situation changes dramatically—a host of questions must be dealt with.

A number of questions concern support. For a program to be successful the majority of teachers and administrators must be convinced of its usefulness: how can this be achieved? How will teachers, administrators, and students acquire the necessary training to enable them to work and learn most effectively with the computers? The question of funding is a critical one. Where will the money to purchase the hardware and software come from? Who will be responsible for acquiring the needed equipment and programs? After these have been purchased, where will they be housed? The location of the systems, who has access to them, and when access will be provided are factors that will determine the amount of use by the students and staff. Provisions for maintenance, safety, security, and service may well determine how available computers will be to the teachers, students, and administrators. The arrangement and location of the microcomputer center (if the computers are housed in a central location) will also determine the extent of use.

Solutions to these crucial concerns are needed if the program is to reach its full potential as a viable methodology for changing students' behavior. This chapter will provide information about developing and implementing a microcomputer program and will offer suggestions for coping with the various problems that arise.

## HOW TO ACQUIRE A MICROCOMPUTER SYSTEM

The exact procedures followed to acquire a microcomputer system are unique to each school; however, the decision-making process can be either centralized or on an individual school basis.

### Centralized Approach

Many school districts acquire their equipment and supplies in a centralized administrative fashion, moving from the superintendent down to the individual school principals. The process of selecting machines, funding them, and placing them in the school is thus directed by the central administration—generally the district educational media director and his staff. An emerging role in some school districts is that of a specialist whose only responsibility is the direct administration of a microcomputing, computer literacy, or district computer program.

The logic of a centralized approach is clear and understandable. The expenses involved and the large numbers of people and equipment needed to establish and maintain a microcomputer program require the coordination, expertise, and accountability available in a centralized administrative structure. The rationale for centralized administration of the microcomputer program after it has become operational is not so logical, however. The program is best administered on an individual school basis, with the coordination and cooperation of the central administration.

Several advantages can accrue from the purchase and installation of a microcomputer system on a district basis:

1. The possible financial advantage when a school system bids to purchase a large number of microcomputers and peripherals, compared with each individual school purchasing a smaller number of microcomputers (especially of several different makes or brands).
2. The availability of specialists to train teachers and administrators in the use of the microcomputer systems, to answer technical questions about their equipment, and to set up workshops on how to install, use, and maintain the equipment.
3. The availability of service centers, with reasonable repair rates, that provide maintenance and repair to districts and individual schools.

4. The advantage of large-volume purchase of software programs: some districts are able to realize substantial savings on the purchase of multiple sets of programs, just as they are able to get books, filmstrips, slides, or transparencies at reduced rates.

There are also coordination and cooperation advantages when microcomputer programs are handled centrally:

1. The improved coordination of curricular uses of the microcomputer program so students are not taught the same things about or with microcomputers in more than one grade—a coordinated computer literacy program.
2. The availability of a trained staff for in-service programs for individual school teachers and administrators, under the direction of the central administration.
3. Procedures for obtaining preview software on a district basis, including the creation of locally produced software and the production of teacher guides for software packages.
4. The establishment of a hardware maintenance facility (where feasible) for repair of monitors and other peripheral devices.
5. A districtwide evaluation process of microcomputers and peripherals for durability and reliability; it can also be used to evaluate the CAI program and to recommend appropriate modifications, revisions, and updates.

## Individual School Approach

Many microcomputer programs were started by individual teachers or parents (especially at the elementary level), sometimes acting alone, sometimes in conjunction with their colleagues, and always in cooperation with the school principal. These programs generally occur in small school systems, rural areas, or suburban areas where parents are anxious to have their children use microcomputers and the principals have considerable autonomy over their budget and curricula.

Among the advantages of the individual school approach over the centralized approach are the following:

1. The teachers have more control of the curriculum, and the district has less say about the software to be used.
2. Individual teachers are less dependent on the judgment and decisions of others and more involved in the selection process.
3. Teachers and schools have more influence concerning the equipment that is acquired (when a district determines that a certain brand of computer will serve all needs, many compromises must necessarily be made).
4. Teachers and schools have greater access to microcomputers and district assistance if they are free to determine which programs should have

priority—when the central administration establishes priorities, resources may be allocated in an inequitable manner (the high school business classes, for example, may get most of the microcomputers).

The individual school microcomputer acquisitions program must be a combined effort. Because funds are generally insufficient to implement all new programs desired, a school must establish priorities, set goals, and undertake a logical course of action. The effort must be a coordinated one: microcomputer programs that depend on the energies, enthusiasm, expertise, and presence of only one or two persons are unlikely to survive. A joint fund-raising effort involving the school PTA, local civic clubs, business owners, heads of departments, and the school administrators, students, and teachers will most likely succeed.

It may be necessary to begin modestly, with only one or two microcomputers, monitors, disk drives, and some software the first year. Long-range plans, however, should provide for the acquisition of the total system within two to five years. Because all microcomputers do not have the same capabilities or available software, be sure that the brand of microcomputer system purchased will handle as many needs of the emerging program as possible and that it is not so limited that after the newness wears off it will sit idle.

## FUNDING FOR MICROCOMPUTER SYSTEMS AND SOFTWARE

Computers—and news about them—abound. Tiny microprocessors found in modern automobiles, kitchen appliances, high-fidelity and video equipment, and children's toys are increasing our awareness of the current computer revolution. Personal computers are now found in thousands of American homes. More and more school board members and other officials in positions that critically affect education are showing a great deal of interest in computers, thus making computers and their various applications timely, school-related issues. As a result, funding for school microcomputer projects is generally less difficult to obtain than funding for other educational projects.

The prices of most microcomputers, peripherals, and many good software packages have declined dramatically, making it possible to acquire a computer system for hundreds rather than thousands of dollars. Consequently, many schools and districts are now able to integrate the purchase of computers into their budgets under tax-levy funding—a regular part of the operating budget of the school or district. Because, in most cases, outside funding is needed to set up a microcomputer system, we will identify several sources: public funds, private foundations, local support, and the individual school. It will be advantageous to tap as many sources as possible, because funding for education is still under par. The following sources and ideas can be helpful in obtaining funding for microcomputer projects.

## Public Funding

The enactment of the Educational Consolidation and Improvement Act of 1981 brought about significant changes in sources for public funding of educational projects. This legislation substantially reduces the federal fiscal role and also limits its regulatory role, giving states and local districts much greater autonomy in planning, maintaining, and monitoring educational programs. The Elementary Secondary Education Act, Title 1 (now defunct), was reworked as Chapter 1 of the new act. Although funding was reduced, local educational agencies are much less restricted in how they can utilize the funds they receive. Monies forthcoming under the new Chapter 1 of the Educational Consolidation and Improvement Act can be earmarked for a variety of microcomputer programs.

Chapter 2 of the act sets up the block grant concept, whereby federal money comes to the states in one large block rather than being allocated in several specific categories. These block grants now filter down to the districts and schools, where they are used at the discretion of local authorities. The specified categories of activities that may be funded through block grants—special projects, basic skills, support services, and educational improvement—provide adequate leeway to permit the use of funds for microcomputer projects. Federal funds are also available under the Special Education Act, Public Law 94-142, for use in mainstreaming and special programs for the handicapped student; here, again, implementation of the law is flexible enough to provide financial assistance for microcomputer programs.

To tap into these funds you will need the most up-to-date list available of major public funding sources. You can obtain such a list by writing to or visiting the appropriate person at your state education department; you should then request the following information from the organizations on that list:

1. Titles of federal and state programs that provide public monies to local schools.
2. Authorizing legislation (Public Law 94-142, for example).
3. Name of the contact person, with address and phone number.
4. Total amount of funding available during previous and present fiscal years (to give you an idea of emphasis in any particular fiscal year).
5. Total amount of funding allocated to computer projects during the previous fiscal year (again, to identify areas of emphasis).
6. A brief description of the particular funding program's mandate (how to secure the funds, what is the intent of the program, and such).

In some cases a proposal must be written to obtain public funds, so some skill in grantsmanship will help. Many school systems have a specialist to assist in writing and securing grants: be sure to see if this help is available, either at the district office or in your own school. If not—and if you do not have the necessary experience yourself—solicit the aid of a colleague who has prepared a grant proposal or two.

## Private Sources

A number of foundations (such as Ford and Carnegie) provide schools, school districts, universities, and colleges with financial support for educational activities. The larger foundations are well known; however, hundreds of smaller agencies also welcome worthy proposals, and although they have fewer dollars to share, they also receive fewer applications. The smaller foundations are more apt to support microcomputer projects because they tend to fund a wider variety of activities.

An easy way to identify private funding sources is to examine a current foundation directory—available in most public and university libraries (it is updated annually)—which lists the name of virtually every private foundation in America. The directory provides the information needed—address, contact person, restrictions, types of projects funded, extent of written proposals needed—to decide whether to contact a particular foundation regarding a microcomputer project.

Along with the private funding sources and foundations already mentioned, the microcomputer corporations (Apple, IBM, Tandy/Radio Shack, and Atari) have funding programs for instructional applications of computers. These companies furnish hardware, software, and funding for instructional applications of their products.

If your district's central administration has a grant specialist, be sure to contact her for assistance, coordination, and cooperation regarding obtaining funding through a foundation (in some districts, you must get initial permission from this person before you begin to apply for outside funding).

Another way of locating active funding organizations is to talk with local schools, districts, and educational agencies that have already succeeded in securing funds for their projects. The following suggestions may help identify these sources.

1. Read relevant magazines, journals, and newsletters. Many publications contain articles that provide the names of schools or districts that have implemented successful microcomputer projects.
2. Attend relevant lectures, workshops, and conferences with the idea of contacting people who have been successful in funding their projects. Do not be reluctant to ask these people how, who, when, and where in relation to their successes.
3. Join one or more appropriate microcomputer organizations. If you have a state organization, you can make valuable contacts attending conventions, meetings, or workshops. It is also a worthwhile investment to join a national organization—if you become active the district will often fund your trip to a national convention, workshop, or special meeting. The contacts made at these meetings are a great source of ideas of all kinds— not just funding.
4. Obtain a copy, from your local university or college, of the *Microcomputer Directory: Applications in Educational Settings*. In it are listed, by states,

brief descriptions of hundreds of educationally relevant computer projects, along with the names, addresses, and phone numbers of contact people.

5. Solicit advice from faculty members at your state or local college or university who may be eager to share their knowledge, experience, and advice. They may be interested in helping you write the grant proposal or even in submitting a proposal whereby the college or university will work jointly with your school or district in a microcomputer project.

## Local Support

The financial support that parents and civic groups can provide is generally insufficient to underwrite a major microcomputer project. These groups can, however, provide seed money for acquiring some basic equipment and getting the program started. When appealing for assistance to either a PTA or civic group, the following suggestions may help:

1. Make the proposal brief, to the point, and specific. Avoid technical jargon—you need to communicate with your potential benefactors, so don't try to impress them with esoteric computer terms.
2. Organize a workshop and invite a vendor to demonstrate, using an actual microcomputer, at least one of the machine's more dramatic uses.
3. Seek out parents or civic group members who use or own microcomputers and invite them to take an active role in the planning and presentation stages of your proposal.
4. Include your students who are already involved in microcomputing. They will be the best spokespersons of all. An interested student can influence a parent who may be the civic club president.
5. Include your principal and colleagues in the proposal and presentation. If you have the support of the administration, many teachers will also fall in line and offer their support.

After you have made the proposal to the PTA and one or more civic groups, present it to the school board. The school board members may be business people from the community who are currently using computers and who therefore realize their importance in education.

Business contributions to schools enhance public relations and can be good advertising. Many schools have been successful in funding medium-to-large microcomputer projects through business contacts. As you contact a local business regarding funding, point out some of the ways the school can reciprocate that will benefit the business.

1. Thank the contributors for their support at public gatherings such as a PTA meeting, a back-to-school night, intermission during a school play, or during halftime at a basketball game.

2. Invite a representative from the business to formally present and dedicate the microcomputer system (or whatever they purchased) at a public meeting or a special assembly held for that specific purpose.
3. Print an announcement or article in the school's newsletter. Special mention, including pictures, could be made in the yearbook, activities book, or any other school publications.
4. Have students make posters or other artwork based upon the contribution to the school; these can be displayed in the school or even at the place of business.
5. Send a press release about the contribution to the local newspapers, accompanied by a photograph of the key persons involved. You could also arrange with the local TV station to have a human interest spot on their local news broadcast or public forum program.
6. Provide the community with monthly, bimonthly, or quarterly reports, using the above-mentioned sources, detailing such things as how the equipment is being used, the success of the program, how many hours the program is being used, and students' anecdotes.

## Individual School Support

As we have mentioned, district funds can be used for the purchase of microcomputers and software—your school principal will be aware of these. Additionally, several departments or teachers may be persuaded to allocate some portion of their budgets for microcomputer hardware or software purchases. The discretionary funds controlled by the school principal may also be available for the microcomputer program (in some large schools this could represent a considerable sum).

To be successful in obtaining funding, develop a well-defined plan of action and be aggressive in promoting your plan. Once the program begins to gain momentum, the funds available within the district may be sufficient to support the continuation and expansion of the ongoing microcomputer curriculum and facility.

## IN-SERVICE PROGRAM—PREPARATION OF FACULTY AND ADMINISTRATORS

As the program expands, an in-service training program to provide all interested persons with the skills needed to use the microcomputer system will become necessary. Some faculty members will not look forward to having the microcomputers introduced into the school—they may still view microcomputers with suspicion. A well-planned, meaningful in-service program may therefore help allay some of these fears.

Following are some points that are worth considering in the preparation and administration of an in-service program.

1. What are the objectives? You will not find a ready-made course or program that will exactly suit your needs. Portions of a course or program prepared by some other school or district may be useful, but they will have to be modified. It is wise to set your own in-service objectives by asking the following questions.

   a. What is the topmost priority? You will be operating within limits set by the school's schedules of classes, budgets, and available resources. You must therefore establish priorities for the role the microcomputers will play in the school curriculum. It may be better to concentrate on specific areas rather than to try to cover an entire literacy program —CAI for fourth, fifth, and sixth grades, for instance, Logo in grades kindergarten through three, and a special program for the ninth grade only.

   b. How much computer literacy should be provided for the faculty? Knowledge of the workings of the microcomputer system? the computer's impact on society? programming skills? software selection and evaluation skills? As you plan your training program, you and your colleagues will need to decide exactly what to include in the in-service program.

   c. Where should the program be in five years? Plan a long-term program that reflects the ideal; then work backward, year by year. What you have for the first year is the starting point; the long-term plan will guide the development of the total program.

2. Who should receive the in-service training? You must be realistic here. It would be nice to include everyone in the first training session, but that is not always practical. Concentrate on those members of the faculty and administration who are most interested and could be most beneficial to the continuation of the program—teachers, school and district-level administrators, and decision makers. It might be wise to divide the in-service program into two elements: introductory sessions for both teachers and administrators, and intense hands-on work that focuses on the applications specific to each group (CAI for teachers and CMI for administrators, for example). Decisions about which teachers in which grades or departments are to receive the in-service training will depend largely on priorities and resource limitations. Selectively limiting computer use to specific departments and individuals may make better use of scarce resources, but care must be taken that the computers are not regarded as the domain or property of any one department. The first in-service program may be most successful if it is limited to those who display a sincere interest in the school CAI program.

3. Who should do the instructing? There are several sources for instructors. A teacher who has taken a class and has a basic understanding of the microcomputer and its use in a CAI program could be an effective instructor. The media specialist or coordinator in your school may be

qualified, but if this person is not interested, a teacher who could attend seminars, classes at the university, or conferences might become qualified to conduct the training.

The best source may be an outside consultant, perhaps someone from the state department of public instruction, a state college or university, or even a local organization. Select wisely and be sure of the person's qualifications, both in subject matter and in methods of conducting the in-service program. Nothing will be more deadly to your in-service program than someone who simply lectures rather than providing hands-on experience and other interesting and exciting methods for learning about concepts and applications.

One problem with outside consultants is that they are not members of the school staff and therefore lack a sense of commitment—they may conduct a session and then hurry away. Before leaving, however, these consultants should have trained one or two members of the staff well enough to carry on for them after each session and after the conclusion of the workshop.

4. Should participants learn to program the microcomputer? This critical question always arises in an in-service program. Its answer should be determined by the school's software policy: is the plan to purchase most of the needed software from commercial sources, or will teachers help develop and program materials in-house? It is critical that the in-service program teach software evaluation and selection skills; the amount of time devoted to programming skills, however, will depend on the overall objectives. Keep in mind, though, that most students will want to learn to program; some basic programming skills instruction may therefore be necessary so teachers will be able to assist their students at a basic level.

5. Should parents and other lay people be involved? If the PTA, civic groups, or business people have contributed financially to the microcomputer program, they must be included in the in-service training, if they are interested. Their interest and support can be long-term if they are involved from the beginning of the program. They may only attend one or two sessions, but the public relations value will be well worth the effort of inviting them.

6. What about the future? Even the best workshops will fail to answer everyone's needs or to take them as far as they want to go. At the onset of the program, plans should be made for the participants' future growth. They can follow up by reading current periodicals in the field and new textbooks and monographs; access one of the commercial data bases; arrange methods and procedures for additional in-service training by the state university or college (even district-paid, if possible); or attend a local or national convention.

The ultimate proof of the in-service program's success will be whether the teachers use the microcomputers in their classrooms. The value and effectiveness of microcomputers as tools to help change student behavior are in the hands of the teachers: if they are not willing to use microcomputers to educate students, the machines will sit in a corner and draw dust. Teachers must also use them themselves—for keeping grades, recording student data, preparing lesson plans, and so on. Often the use of a microcomputer as a tool to ease the classroom management load is the first step toward eventual classroom use.

## FACILITY—LOCATION AND LAYOUT

For the great majority of our schools, the placement of the micros has evolved in haphazard fashion similar to the microcomputers' acquisition. In many cases the proposal for obtaining the microcomputers is presented in a bare-bones fashion so they can be purchased with funds from a parent-teacher organization, a civic club, a business establishment, or a local school administrator. Then the search begins for an old physics lab, a little-used classroom, a space in the media center or library, or any place secure enough to house the new microcomputer systems. The number of peripheral devices adds to the concern: plotters, joysticks, printers, larger monitors, and modems must be housed with, or at least near, the microcomputer, so room must also be found for these items. As the program grows and more equipment and software are acquired, the need for better facilities becomes apparent. Possible placement of the micros will differ widely from school to school, but a common set of factors will influence decisions about placement. Among these are the type and amount of equipment available; current long- and short-term instructional goals; the physical layout of the school; and constraints imposed by networking, available personnel, various uses of the micros (after-school hours, in-service, or community use, for example), and security or maintenance considerations.

The microcomputer program's long- and short-term instructional goals are so important in determining location that we will discuss three possible configurations for the placement and utilization of the micros. As we have discussed earlier, the main academic uses of microcomputers fall into three categories: CAI, the computer as a tool, and computer literacy training. Each one places its own requirements upon the placement and physical arrangement of the microcomputer facility.

### Central Location

The common thread in most CAI programs in schools is the self-paced approach. As a result, students need cubicles where they can spend undisturbed time working with the microcomputers and appropriate software programs to master the subject being presented. These cubicles can be as small as four by four feet and have a shelf and counter space to hold the microcomputer system (microcomputer, monitor, disk drive) plus a work area to allow for leaving books open and doing pencil-and-paper exercises. The traditional student study carrel, with some slight modifications such as a larger upper shelf and removal of the rear-projection apparatus, works nicely. The single power switch module built into the student study carrel reduces wear and tear on the microcomputer power switch. The student should have a comfortable swivel chair, which facilitates movement from the work area to the microcomputer and back. The cubicles might be located in the school media center or library because it is a secure area and the mechanism for checking in and out has long since been established. Several possible arrangements of study carrels are illustrated in figure 8.1.

The microcomputer system can also be set up on tables within the media center, although the individual study areas are more conducive to quiet, independent study. When two or three students need to work together at one station, the cubicle is, again, the most desirable arrangement. Figure 8.2 shows a possible placement of the microcomputers within the confines of the media center.

If there is not enough space within the media center or library to accommodate the cubicles, a classroom next to the media center or library should be converted into a microcomputer laboratory. If the wall between the media center and this new laboratory can be removed, enlarging the original space, management of the microcomputer laboratory will be possible with only one additional media center staff member—a microcomputer specialist. This arrangement will retain the management/storage/retrieval capabilities and availability of instructional materials common to the media center and will couple these functions with the new microcomputer capability. This administrative arrangement adds a totally new dimension to the capabilities of the media center. Figure 8.3 shows how a classroom might be incorporated into the media center or library.

Since each cubicle within the laboratory or media center will be drawing two to three amps of electricity, it is advisable to place them on an independent thirty-amp line. This will avoid spikes (changes in the electrical current coming to the cubicle), that can freeze up a microcomputer when any other piece of equipment or machinery starts up, often even in a location remote from the lab.

Teaching programming and conducting computer literacy instruction can be accommodated in the microcomputer laboratory with the addition of a chalkboard, a wall screen (perhaps an overhead projector), and a teacher's instruction

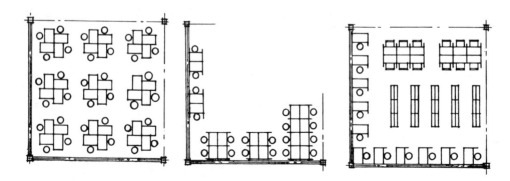

**FIGURE 8.1**  Arrangements for Study Carrels

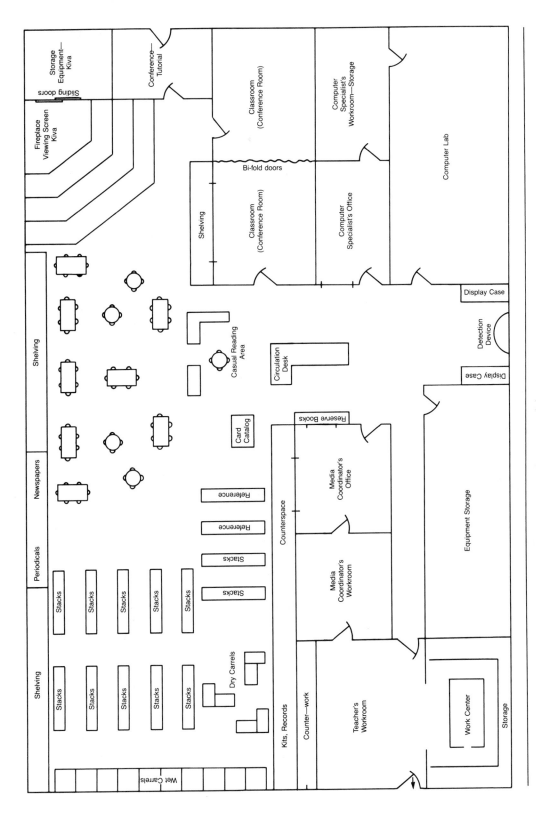

FIGURE 8.2  Placement of Microcomputers in Media Center or Library

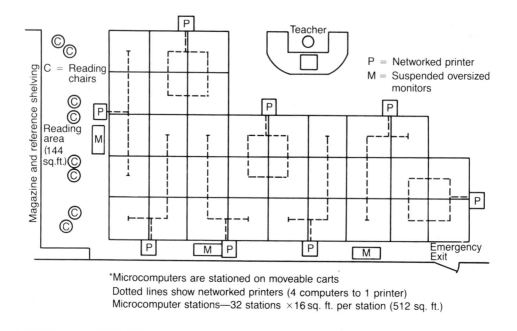

*Microcomputers are stationed on moveable carts
Dotted lines show networked printers (4 computers to 1 printer)
Microcomputer stations—32 stations ×16 sq. ft. per station (512 sq. ft.)

**FIGURE 8.3   Incorporation of a Classroom into a Media Center to Create a Microcomputer Laboratory**

station—including a microcomputer, two twenty-five-inch color monitors, and a double disk drive. By careful scheduling of the laboratory to avoid conflicts, this program can be maintained along with the independent study needs of the CAI program. It is advisable to have the teacher's station at the rear of the classroom so the students can swivel around for instruction and then turn back to the microcomputer in the cubicle for the hands-on portion of the class. It is extremely difficult to carry on instruction with the students looking over the top of the cubicles.

If you can afford both the laboratory and an instructional classroom, this is even better. In this situation students are instructed in the classroom with the teacher's microcomputer system only; they then go to the laboratory for hands-on practice.

## Location within the Classroom

For microcomputer use in a self-contained elementary classroom, the ideal situation would be one microcomputer, monitor, and disk drive for every one to three students. An effective program can, however, be carried on with a minimum of five microcomputer systems per classroom. In the self-contained classroom, scheduling can be controlled so students can do seat work between their scheduled times at the microcomputers.

The microcomputers should be located at the back or sides of the classroom so that those working on them will not disturb their classmates doing seat work, small group work, or individual reading. The computer literacy training can be carried on with the entire group; then students, on a scheduled basis, can go to the microcomputers for hands-on use. The CAI work can also be scheduled into specific time slots during the school day.

In the junior and senior high schools, where microcomputer use is totally integrated into the science, social studies, English, or mathematics curriculum, there will be a great demand for the computers. In such cases, five microcomputers located permanently in each classroom or department laboratory is an absolute minimum. The program should be designed to allow a maximum of three students per computer station at any one time.

The software that supports the microcomputer program should also be located within the classroom. It is not efficient use of resources, especially teacher time, to keep this specialized software in a central location such as the media center or library. Just as with textbooks, the program is best facilitated when the instructional materials that support the curriculum are right in the classroom. However, classroom storage and use will place a heavy burden on the teacher, who must see that care and caution in the utilization and storage of the diskettes and accompanying documentation are exercised.

Placement of the microcomputers in the individual classroom creates some special problems, one of which is the dust and dirt that tend to collect not only on the microcomputers but also on the disk drives and diskettes. The microcomputer system should not be located next to the chalkboard, nor should it, or the diskettes, be in direct sunlight. For this reason an overhead projector is recommended in preference to the chalkboard: exclusive use of an overhead projector greatly reduces the dust in the environment. Location in the individual classroom might also create security concerns, because a classroom is not as secure an area as a media center or library, for example. Some special security measures might be employed, such as a locked cabinet for the software and devices to lock the microcomputers, monitors, and disk drives to the carrel or tabletop. A microcomputer table can be purchased with detachable, locking hood that can be fastened in place when you are finished with the computer system but completely removed when the system is in operation. Figure 8.4 details a possible placement of the microcomputer system within a classroom.

In the preceding discussion we have detailed an ideal classroom situation. In many classes in the United States, however, the ratio is one microcomputer to one or two classrooms. In this situation the suggestions concerning group instruction and careful scheduling of student microcomputer time become even more important.

Some teachers use a rotating system wherein students are scheduled twenty-minute blocks of time on the microcomputer and then their name is moved to the end of the list. This system ensures that all students will have time on the microcomputer and that no one person will monopolize the time available. This plan can even assist in scheduling nonclass hours.

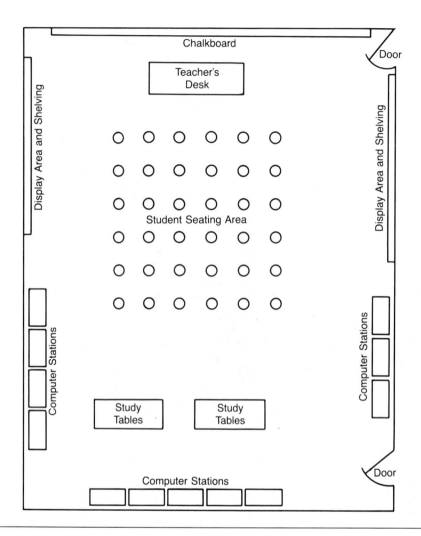

**FIGURE 8.4  Classroom Placement of the Microcomputers**

## Portable Systems

There may be a time when all the microcomputers need to be available at once in one classroom or area. Some elementary school teachers and secondary math or science teachers may want to use the computers in units designed to introduce students to computers or in a CAI remedial or accelerated program; such units may run from one week of intense, daily use to several weeks involving use of the computers for only one period a week. Since several classes might be involved in this endeavor simultaneously, it would be helpful if the microcomputer systems were on portable carts, self-contained, with extension cords and cables to connect all peripheral devices. These carts need to be stable and strongly constructed so there is no danger of tipping over or collapsing as they are moved from classroom to classroom. It is recommended that the microcomputer systems not be transported up or down flights of stairs—a stumble could result in damage to a complete system.

When microcomputer systems are placed on a portable cart, problems with security, particularly in regard to software, are increased. It is suggested that portable systems be locked up in one central location at the end of a school day and that the software be housed in a locking storage cart that accompanies the portable microcomputers; only those programs that are in use during any one period should be removed from the storage cart. The software programs in the storage cart can be arranged in a logical filing order (perhaps by Dewey decimal classification) so any single program can be located quickly and easily.

The use of portable systems for microcomputers and software will provide considerable flexibility for teachers throughout the building. The various constraints mentioned above are not insurmountable and should not rule out this procedure as a way to accomplish the goals of the program.

## FACILITY ADMINISTRATION

The management of the various functions needed for a successful program is an important concern. In this section we will discuss access and time allocations, rules and regulations, and basic hardware and software needs.

### Access and Time Allocations

Who will have access to the microcomputers? Students only, teachers only, both teachers and students, students in the computer literacy program only, students in the CAI program only, or anyone who has the time? The management pattern in American schools seems to be divided between allowing anyone to use the microcomputers—open access (except for scheduled periods)—and having an established procedure that limits access in some way (controlled access). Generally, schools new to computing and inner-city schools (with their special security concerns) have the most restrictions on access. As the faculty and students become more knowledgeable and comfortable with the computer facility and microcomputers, access is handled as it is in most media centers: availability is provided for the total school population, with an imposition of only those rules needed to maintain order and equipment and software security.

There is growing concern that the microcomputer facility is male territory exclusively. Many schools are experiencing a high percentage of female drop-out in computer literacy programs beyond the very basic introductory level. The problem is not so acute in the area of CAI, because both male and female students achieve success with drill-and-practice programs, tutorials, and such. A concerted effort should be made to include female students in the literacy program in programming classes and in management as student aides to help run the microcomputer laboratory. Many schools are succeeding in breaking down this male-territory image by developing a combined male-female orientation to the management and utilization of the microcomputers.

As the need for fulltime use of the microcomputers for classroom activities eases, administrators may desire to make use of the computers to perform CMI functions such as managing pupil and personal records, keeping inventory, scheduling, and processing and managing the budget. Schools will need to develop clear, precise guidelines regarding student and teacher rights to their own files and limits on access to these files by others. Students are adept at breaking codes, so a different and uniquely protected computer system should be considered for records that require any degree of confidentiality. Teachers who use software packages to maintain their daily classroom rolls and records, test scores, and so forth on diskettes must take precautions to protect these diskettes from student access.

Access to the microcomputers depends on the total number available, where they are located, the intent of the program, and the scheduling procedure followed in the school. In some schools computer access is allowed only during class, regardless of the kind of program involved; others allow computer use at times other than during the regular school day—perhaps one-half to one hour before and after school, and during all lunch periods. In other situations, schools provide free access only after school, since the microcomputers are used for classes during the day, including the lunch hour.

Some considerations that have proven helpful in developing access rules in school microcomputer programs follow.

1. Doing intense work on a microcomputer often requires much greater blocks of time than for most other educational tasks. Many students will desire to spend thirty minutes to two hours on CAI programs, especially drill and practice, tutorials, and simulation exercises. Programming activities may take up to three hours of sustained effort. If students are allowed to do instructional gaming, they can spend one to four hours at this activity, and word processing activities are notorious for the time they take.

2. If teachers are developing curriculum-related software, they will need to have one- to four-hour time blocks on the microcomputers. It is not uncommon for teachers to stay after school and even work on Saturday to keyboard their curricular material.

3. If the goals of the program dictate extended hours, who will staff the microcomputer facility? In the case of teacher use, those using the facility can be responsible when they are working alone; however, when students utilize the microcomputers, supervision will probably need to be provided. Many schools have been successful in supplementing the regular staff and teachers with community volunteers such as parents and retired citizens. In almost all schools with extended hours, reliance on students as computer room aides has been necessary. These students can be trained during the regular program and can not only provide super-

vision and assistance but also gain valuable work experience that may help them secure fulltime employment after they graduate from high school. This experience also helps many students as they enter colleges and universities, especially in institutions of higher learning where there is a strong emphasis on computer utilization.

## Rules and Regulations

Consideration must be given to some specific rules and regulations that will make the utilization of the microcomputer facility both fair to users and efficient in operation. These guidelines should provide procedures for administering the facility by addressing the following concerns:

1. **Priority of usage.** The question of who has first priority in using the microcomputers must be considered. This decision will depend on the goals of the program. All persons involved (students, teachers, administrators, parents, and lay citizens) must know exactly what the priorities are and why they were established. These should be discussed, formulated, and finally presented in written form so all patrons of the facility know what to expect. If the program was established for CAI only, for example, or strictly for student programming use, or for teacher and student use under certain conditions and at certain times, this needs to be detailed and a written policy issued so all users are treated as the policy dictates.

2. **Length of time allowed at a station.** The length of time allowed at the microcomputer is task-dependent; that is, it depends on the activity being conducted. Some tasks take more time at the computer than others, and it may take some experimentation to determine just how much time should be allowed for each type of activity. Once some idea of the needed time has been obtained, specific time limits should be assigned for specific tasks. Most schools do not have enough machines to allow students unlimited time on the micros. Many have completely eliminated game playing during regular school hours, relegating this activity to special after-school hours or very low demand time (if there are such times). In some schools the time allocation is controlled by the use of a pass from the teacher detailing what the student is to work on, how much time is allowed, what she must accomplish, and so on. In others the students must come to the microcomputer facility as a group. The pattern varies from school to school and is generally dictated by the overall goals and needs of the program. It is important, however, that a policy is established, that all patrons know the details of the policy, and that enforcement of the policy is uniform—no special favors should be granted.

3. **Number of students per station.** As part of the policy statement governing the use of the facility, there should be a statement concerning

how many persons are allowed at any one station, since this can affect the noise level in the facility and the general atmosphere of the room. The noise level is difficult to control because the very nature of some microcomputer activity calls for high levels of student interaction and discussion, sharing ideas, or asking for help. This is especially true when students are learning to program using either BASIC or Logo. The quality of the exercises can deteriorate when a group of five or six students crowds around a station and all want to get in on the activity. It is recommended that no more than three students be permitted at a station at any one time. This number allows for interaction, idea sharing, and problem solving without the noise and confusion that a larger number of students can generate.

4. Maintenance of order. Established rules of order and conduct for the microcomputer facility are critical to its operation. These rules should be formulated in consultation with students, teachers, and administrators. An excellent source would be a committee of representatives from these three groups plus a parent from the school's parent-teacher organization. Once the rules have been articulated and approved by the student council, the teachers, and the administrators, they should be written up, distributed to the student body and teachers, and prominently displayed in the microcomputer facility. This may seem like a lot of work; however, if all students, teachers, and administrators, plus the PTA, are involved in the formulation of the rules, enforcement is generally simplified because all feel responsible for the policy and thus tend to adhere to their own rules and regulations. Some items that could be included in this policy statement follow.

   **a.** No food or drink allowed in the facility.

   **b.** No loitering—microcomputers may be limited in number, so unnecessary time at the keyboard should be minimized.

   **c.** No loud talking, shouting, pushing, or shoving—all of which disturb others and might result in damaged computers and peripherals or injured students.

   **d.** Each student must have a legitimate reason for being in a facility, such as a pass from a teacher, counselor, or administrator (conduct could be controlled by asking the student to surrender his ID card, with misconduct resulting in the card being kept and disciplinary action instigated).

   **e.** A statement of the policy governing payment of fees for such items as word processing paper, data diskettes, and networking costs.

   **f.** A statement of the policy governing the copying of software. No pirating of software should be allowed, and anyone violating this policy should be permanently excluded from the use of the microcomputers and laboratory facilities and possibly subject to disciplinary or legal action.

### Basic Information Needed in the Facility

Within the microcomputer facility there needs to be a detailed set of instructions on how to use the microcomputer systems and the facilities. This can be presented either as data sheets in a loose-leaf notebook or as posters displayed on bulletin boards. Although this information will be presented in the in-service or literacy training program, the reminder in the notebook or on a poster will help reduce the amount of individualized instruction the staff will need to provide within the microcomputer facility. Some suggested items to include in the instructions follow.

#### Microcomputer

1. How to turn on and off; proper use of either study carrel or microcomputer switch.
2. How to handle diskettes or cassettes properly.
3. How to boot up the disk operating system.
4. How to initialize a data diskette.
5. How to access a particular program.
6. What to do when the microcomputer malfunctions.
7. Log-on procedures for time-sharing or networking.
8. How to secure the microcomputer when finished: lid or cover over the computer to protect it from dust and dirt, security process, unplugging power cords, and so on.
9. Any idiosyncrasies.

#### Monitors

1. How to turn on and off (it should be noted if microcomputer is attached to carrel plug or surge control device and left in the "on" position, so students won't use the monitor on/off switch).
2. How to adjust the color, contrast, vertical and horizontal functions.
3. How to plug into the microcomputer in case the plug is inadvertently loosened or unplugged.
4. Procedure for changing from a color to a black-and-white monitor if the student is doing work that is better facilitated without color (word processing or programming, for example).

#### Peripheral devices

1. Printer
   a. How to turn on and off.
   b. How to load paper into the printer.
   c. How to activate the printer—getting data from the microcomputer to the printer.

    **d.** How to secure the printer when finished—covering, handling paper, security concerns, and so forth.

    **e.** Any idiosyncrasies.

  **2.** Modems

    **a.** How to perform the log-on procedure.

    **b.** How to activate the microcomputer.

    **c.** Proper placement of phone handset in modem cradle.

    **d.** How to conduct proper log-off procedure.

    **e.** Accounting procedures (if needed).

  **3.** Joysticks, graphic tablets, mouse, light pen

    **a.** How to attach these items to the microcomputer.

    **b.** How to utilize these devices (e.g., use of mouse to pick up menu items).

    **c.** Special handling procedures (e.g., how to move the arm on the graphics tablet, move the joystick handle and fire button, maneuver the mouse, and use the buttons).

    **d.** Any idiosyncrasies.

In addition to instructions on how to use the microcomputer system, the facility should contain several additional items to assist users.

All the manuals that accompanied the microcomputer system—those for the microcomputer, the disk drive, the monitor, and any peripheral devices—should be catalogued, provided with a catalog card and pocket, and placed in a book rack within the facility, to be checked out as any library book. It is critical that the check-out procedure be followed because manuals have a way of disappearing—especially when they are most needed. In most microcomputer facilities, manuals are restricted to use *only* within the facility.

The facility's software should also be catalogued, and a card catalog, accession file, or some other system of listing the materials must be provided for the patrons. If a card file system is used, the software programs could also be listed in the media center or library card catalog. In filing the software programs, it is important to file the diskette or cassette and its accompanying documentation together as a set: with many programs the diskette cannot be used, or is difficult to use, without the documentation.

Information about new software or hardware purchases, or any changes in either, should be provided for all students, teachers, and administrators. Among the several avenues for disseminating the information are a bulletin board within the facility, newsletters to teachers and administrators, or an announcement over the school's public address system along with the daily news. The microcomputer center can provide a special service to students, teachers, and administrators by having available a selection of current periodicals, newsletters, and books. There is considerable debate as to whether these materials should be placed in the microcomputer facility or in the media center or library. If the microcomputer facility is a part of the media center, the debate, of course, is moot. If, however, there is a separate microcomputer lab, the materials are most often housed in the lab. The location may not really matter, however; what is important is that a good selection is provided for the patrons' use.

One final matter, which will help the management and general atmosphere of the facility, concerns the procedures for cleaning up and putting items in their proper place when a patron has finished. Most staff members and volunteer aides in the facility do not have the time (nor should they) to tidy up the desks and study carrels, push chairs back in place, replace diskettes in file drawers, match diskettes with correct documentation, replace specialized peripheral devices, or perform a variety of other housekeeping tasks. These necessary responsibilities must be stressed during the in-service or initial training program and should be enumerated on a poster and displayed in the facility.

## AMORTIZATION SCHEDULE

In developing the microcomputer program and securing and expending monies to purchase equipment and software and to maintain the program, a budget package must be prepared that covers system and software replacement and equipment repair costs. These maintenance costs must be included as a regular line item in the yearly school budget.

Maintenance costs, equipment repair, and the costs for cleaning, spare parts, extra cables, and expendable items should be budgeted at 8 to 10 percent per year of the original equipment cost. For example, a microcomputer system that cost $3,000 initially should be budgeted at $240–$300 annually for maintenance. If funds are left at the end of the school year, these can either be carried over to the next fiscal year or used to purchase supplies. Most service contracts provided by microcomputer stores or service centers are based on this 8 to 10 percent per year figure.

When a service agreement is written, it generally covers all maintenance and repair costs. The major problem with a service contract is that usually the microcomputer system must be delivered to the service center. Maintenance and repair service can keep the system from your school for two to ten days.

An amortization schedule should be a major part of any school maintenance budget. The microcomputer systems will eventually wear out or become obsolete because of new technologies, so a schedule of replacement, based on a four- to six-year cycle, must be prepared. Because most systems have not been in operation for four years, there are no studies or cost procedures to substantiate this schedule. However, most microcomputer specialists feel that a system will need to be replaced during the sixth year (maximum) of its use.

A maintenance budget is extremely important for the microcomputer program; otherwise several machines could be out of service at the same time during the school year. For most microcomputer programs, the loss of even one microcomputer system severely hampers the program's overall effectiveness.

## SECURITY

One final area of administration and management of microcomputer systems in a laboratory, media center, or classroom environment is the issue of security—of both the hardware and software and the information stored on the microcomputer.

It is mandatory that the computer facility be locked when it is not in operation, and when it is open it should never be left unattended. Software programs, peripheral devices, manuals, data diskettes, and the computers, disk drives, and monitors are all highly valued and desired items. Unattended areas provide temptations for people to help themselves to these items. As we have suggested earlier in this chapter, machines can be bolted to the desk, diskettes and manuals stored in lockable cabinets, and books, periodicals, and newsletters checked out using a proven system. In general, security problems are eliminated by providing supervision (by adults or reliable students) and procedures and practices to be followed by a security conscious staff, student body, and administration.

Data security is a different issue because it may involve different motives than acquisition of equipment or software for personal use or financial gain. Breaking through a data security system to steal or change information or to steal computer time is seen by some computer users as an intellectual challenge. Procedures must be developed to protect student records, log-on procedures, and access to sensitive materials. Security can be improved by being conscious of the problem and not leaving diskettes in unlocked drawers, disk drives, or other places where they can be accessed by unauthorized persons.

## STAFFING THE MICROCOMPUTER PROGRAM

Staffing patterns for a school's microcomputer program will depend on the program goals and objectives. If the program is a beginning one, the microcomputers may be housed in individual classrooms and controlled by the individual teacher. If the program is departmentalized and the microcomputers are housed in various departments, a department chairperson will be responsible for the program. And if the equipment is housed in the media center or a special microcomputer facility, responsibility will be assumed by a microcomputer specialist. In some circumstances, however, a combination of the above situations might exist. Regardless of the arrangement, the supervisory personnel must possess some basic competencies and provide some basic services for the program to succeed. We will discuss these services and competencies at three levels: the individual classroom, the department, and the microcomputer laboratory.

### Individual Classroom

A teacher who will be utilizing a microcomputer system in his classroom must possess some minimum competencies, including basic knowledge of:

1. procedures for the selection and evaluation of software programs;
2. sources of software programs—in subject areas;
3. how to incorporate CAI into the classroom environment and curriculum;
4. how to set up and provide basic maintenance for the microcomputer system, including the microcomputer, disk drive(s), monitor, interface boards, and any peripheral devices used;
5. standards for the selection and purchase of the microcomputer system;
6. how to initialize a diskette;
7. how to boot up the disk operating system;
8. how the microcomputer handles data;
9. programming skills (if basic programming is part of the curriculum)—perhaps Logo for kindergarten through fourth grade, introductory BASIC programming for fifth through ninth grade, and Pascal for ninth through twelfth grade;
10. how peripheral devices (e.g., graphics tablet, touch screen, mouse, joystick) work and how to make use of them in the curriculum;
11. sources of networks and bulletin boards and how to use a modem to access these data bases;
12. how to utilize CMI for roll keeping, test score maintenance, and use of the microcomputer system for generating reports to be used by students, parents, and administrators;
13. how to do word processing and use a printer (if the curriculum involves creative writing, theme paper production, and the generation of reports);
14. the latest sources of information in the field—titles of periodicals, newsletters, and text materials in the microcomputer area and an active reading program to keep abreast of the latest developments;
15. the various sources of funding for the procurement of the microcomputer system, software, and furniture; and
16. how to set up and manage classroom facilities for microcomputer use, including access and time allocations, rules and regulations, and security.

## Department

When the microcomputers are housed in a department, the person in charge will need to have the same competencies listed above for classroom teachers; she might also have to assume the following duties:

1. Be responsible for maintaining and administering the program at the department level.
2. Be the microcomputer literacy teacher for the program, responsible for teaching the various courses in the curriculum.

3. Be responsible for some of the in-service training of the school's teachers and administrators.
4. Produce a newsletter, weekly bulletin board, or other vehicle for keeping faculty members apprised of new software titles, changes in scheduling, and so forth.
5. Develop procedures for securing, previewing, evaluating, and purchasing software.

## Media Center or Library—Microcomputer Laboratory

A fully integrated microcomputer program that is part of the media center provides the students and teachers with a rich environment composed of not only the microcomputer hardware and software but also the total resources of the center, including research and study materials in all instructional formats—printed materials, filmstrips, pictures, slides, audio and video tapes, and microcomputer software. The fully integrated program will necessitate the addition of a microcomputer specialist, a technician (if the budget can accommodate this person), and some aides to the media center or library staff.

Within a fully integrated program, the pattern of staff organization and responsibilities will result in assignments that provide services to teachers, students, and administrators. The media coordinator and microcomputer specialist will work with teachers by:

1. Assisting in the selection and planning of educational experiences for students.
2. Keeping teachers informed about the latest instructional materials and media equipment (including microcomputer systems) available.
3. Participating as a team on curriculum committees, study groups, seminars, and panels at various grade levels, subject areas, and departmental levels.
4. Providing in-service programs in proper selection and use of all instructional materials, with special emphasis on microcomputer and other new technologies.
5. Providing interested teachers and administrators with information about the instructional technology field, especially microcomputer and new technologies, gleaned from reading current literature.
6. Identifying and applying suitable criteria for the evaluation of all types of instructional materials, including microcomputer software and media and microcomputer hardware.
7. Assisting in application for research projects conducted by teachers and administrators, analysis of data collected during the project, and final evaluation of results and findings.

Technicians and aides, under the direction of the media coordinator and the microcomputer specialist, will provide the following services:

1. Produce instructional materials and microcomputer programs—doing the production and keyboarding (the program components and design will be produced by the specialist).
2. Assist where needed in arranging classroom, media center, or microcomputer laboratory displays, exhibits, and bulletin boards.
3. Assist in designing and illustrating promotional items and publications for the school, a grade, a department, or a subject area.
4. Provide bibliographic searches and assistance in locating instructional materials, including microcomputer software and all aspects of information and materials processing needed to supplement the curriculum.
5. Do minor repairs and maintenance (under the guidance of the specialist) on all equipment used by teachers and students.
6. Prepare instructional materials (under the guidance of the specialist) used by teachers and students, including producing backup copies of software programs, initializing diskettes, and making copies of documentation (and possibly also recording audiotapes, doing photographic and darkroom work, and producing transparencies).
7. Assist in the operation of microcomputer systems and audio and video equipment for classroom or individualized purposes, as requested by teachers and students.
8. Secure and schedule the use of microcomputers, peripheral devices, instructional materials in all formats, and media equipment requested by teachers for both classroom and individualized purposes.
9. Prepare and distribute to teachers and administrators, for their ordering or information purposes, catalogs, brochures, newsletters, and announcements of microcomputer software, hardware, and peripherals, and inform them about other instructional materials, equipment, and services available in the media center or microcomputer laboratory.
10. Assist in the maintenance of the facility's physical environment in a manner that encourages and facilitates its use, including proper shelving and storing of instructional materials; cleanliness and order of study carrels, microcomputer areas, and word processing areas; and the arrangement of all other study areas.

When students, parents, and lay citizens are used as volunteer aides, the in-service program must be comprehensive and thorough. These volunteers will perform a valuable service in direct proportion to the degree and quality of their training. It is recommended that they be carefully and precisely trained in all aspects of the functions they are to perform and the tasks for which they will be responsible. This training may take several weeks; however, once there is a cadre of trained people, they in turn can assist in training the volunteers just entering the program.

Many media coordinators and microcomputer specialists present their volunteer aides with a certificate and identification card upon completion of the in-

> TECHNOLOGY SPECIALIST LICENSE
> MEDIA/MICROCOMPUTER CENTER
>
> has completed the required course of training,
> has demonstrated proficiency in operation of initial equipment, and shows
> a satisfactory understanding of classroom learning conditions.
>
> CALUTE HIGH SCHOOL DISTRICT

**FIGURE 8.5   Certificate and ID Card**

service training (see fig. 8.5), which identify the person as a special individual who is performing an extremely valuable service for the school. Most aides hold these items in high regard and are proud to be a part of the microcomputer team.

## SUMMARY

A recent report on the availability of computers in schools throughout America indicates that purchases have skyrocketed over the past three years. Not only are large urban schools purchasing computer systems, but others such as small rural or medium-sized inner-city schools are also. This increase in acquisition necessitates the development of an orderly, systematic approach to planning if the schools are to realize the maximum benefit from each dollar spent. Once the resources have been acquired, a further effort is necessary to develop efficient procedures for maintaining and utilizing both hardware and software.

In this chapter we outline systematic methods for obtaining funds and support for a microcomputer program, for acquiring hardware and software, and for establishing and operating a microcomputer facility. Specifically, funding sources are identified, including those from internal sources such as schools and districts, and from external sources including businesses and others. Federal money is also available, but grant proposals must be written to obtain these funds. Suggestions for writing a proposal are included in this chapter.

An in-service program is described that will not only provide teachers and administrators with computer-related skills but will also recruit advocates and supporters for the larger computer-based instructional program.

The essential nature of managing microcomputers so they are maximally available to those who wish to use them is emphasized. The availability of equipment and software for use by teachers, students, and administrators will directly determine whether the resources are used or are left to collect dust.

Three trends in microcomputer assignment are identified. Commonly, they are assigned to a specified classroom, which tends to diminish access to some extent. Often a department is given responsibility for the microcomputers (many times the math department). Finally, a special room is sometimes set aside as the computer center; this room might serve as a general resource center in which print and nonprint materials are housed along with the computers.

The problem of who should have access to the computers is also addressed. A routine should be established to ensure that girls have equal access with boys. Also, patrons, teachers, and others who have an interest in the program should be accommodated. In conjunction with the access issue, we emphasize the importance of establishing and publicizing appropriate rules and regulations. Security concerns are also identified.

In the final section of this chapter job descriptions for those who will be involved in running the program—the specialist, technician, and aide—are developed.

## REFERENCES

Beatty, L. F. *Instructional Media Centers.* Englewood Cliffs, NJ: Educational Technology Pub., 1981.

Bitter, G. G. *Computers in Today's World.* New York: John Wiley and Sons, 1984.

Brown, J. E., et al. *Administering Educational Media: Instructional Technology and Library Services.* New York: McGraw-Hill Book Company, 1972.

Coburn, P., et al. *Practical Guide to Computers in Education.* Menlo Park, CA: Addison-Wesley Publishing Co., 1982.

Dixon, S. "How to Organize an Efficient, Smooth-running Computer Room." *Electronic Learning* (December 1983): 64–65, 83.

Engstrom, T. "Data Security: Paranoia or Prescience." *Personal Computing* (August 1982): 67–70.

Harper, D. O., and Stewart, J. H. *RUN: Computer Education.* Monterey, CA: Brooks/Cole Pub., 1983.

Hentrel, B. K., and Hentrel, P. C. "Implementing Computers." *Educational Computing* (October 1983): 52–53.

Hughes, R. V. "Before You Leap into the Computer Age with Both Feet, Take These Five Deliberate Steps." *American School Board Journal* (March 1983): 28–29.

Jay, T. "In-Service: What You Need to Know before You Begin." *Electronic Learning* (September 1983): 90–96, 1a–8a.

Lopez, A. M., Jr. "Facilities for Microcomputers." *American Schools and Universities* (December 1981): 34–38.

Prostano, E. T., and Prostano, J. S. *The School Library Media Center.* 3rd ed. Littleton, CO: Libraries Unlimited, Inc., 1983.

Swartz, T. F. "Finding Funding for Your Computer Project." *Classroom Computer Learning* (March 1984): 36–41.

Vockell, E. L., and Rivers, R. H. *Instructional Computing for Today's Teachers.* New York: MacMillan Publishing Co., 1984.

# 9

# PROBLEMS AND PROMISES

## INTRODUCTION

The report *A Nation at Risk: The Imperative for Educational Reform*, which was prepared by the National Commission on Excellence in Education and presented to Secretary of Education T. H. Bell in April 1983, identified a wide range of problems in the American educational system. The report emphasized concerns of a cognitive nature, such as weak performance by students in the areas of math and science, but it failed to address the erosion of moral character that is everywhere in evidence. Citing the need to deal directly with this concern, a group of noted scholars and policymakers issued a manifesto to coincide with the observance of Thanksgiving 1984. Entitled "Developing Character: Transmitting Knowledge," but known unofficially as the "Thanksgiving Statement," the document emphasizes the critical need to teach about issues. The report points out that "schools in general are not doing enough to counter the serious decline in youth character," and "good character is not generated solely by more homework, rigorous traditional grading and better pupil discipline." While concentrating on such problems as out-of-wedlock births, suicide, and homicide, the report makes clear that the full range of moral and ethical problems must be addressed by the schools.

A unique set of ethical problems has evolved with the wide-scale introduction of computers and related technology into the society.

People are beginning to recognize that merely teaching about the mechanics of computer use is not enough—indeed, coming to grips with the many moral implications may ultimately prove to be just as important to the survival of our society as is technical expertise.

Because of the complexity and uniqueness of the problems spawned by the new technologies, people are experiencing considerable difficulty as they try to cope with them. The apparent benign nature of many of the issues has caused a number of lawmakers to underestimate the seriousness of the situation. Typically, computer crimes involve no violence, privacy issues have always been difficult to address, and the problem of computer equity is so new that most people are not even aware that it exists; it is thus understandable that more isn't being done to solve these problems.

Virtually every child will attend public or private schools, however, and it is here that the informed teacher can begin to make an impact. But in order to teach students about issues, educators themselves must understand what these are. Many issues affect students directly; others will have their impact as young people graduate and move into the work force. At the school level students are confronted with the ethical issue of software piracy, and those who are proficient with telecomputing routines must deal with the concern of privacy. There is also the problem of equity—who benefits from the technology and who is cut out. Later, students as workers might lose their jobs to computer-controlled robots, have their private records searched, or read that a confidential government data base has been penetrated by foreign agents. Students may themselves get caught up in various aspects of computer crime. Though most would never commit a robbery at gunpoint, the impersonal quality of computer crime makes an equivalent electronic holdup seem much less immoral. To gain a sense of the extent and variety of computer-related issues it is only necessary to browse through the daily paper. Figure 9.1 shows a representative selection of articles that were published in an urban newspaper over a short period of time. Although some experts would argue the point, many see the implications as being so serious and far-reaching that, unless they are addressed at all levels, the future of our open society could be in jeopardy.

As bleak as all this seems, it represents but one side of the picture. Every innovation brings with it promises along with the problems, and the computer is no exception. The positive contributions of the computer revolution, like those of the industrial revolution before it, greatly outweigh the negative ones and promise a better life for all.

The transition from an agrarian to an industrialized society was not very smooth, however. Because many of the problems were not dealt with directly and systematically, havoc often resulted as people tried to find solutions as best they could.

The industrial revolution came about as society found ways to supplement and replace muscle power with machines. Vast smokestack industries evolved, and with them came a dramatic change in the way people lived and worked. Christopher Evans, in *The Micro Millennium,* describes the power of the move-

FIGURE 9.1   Newspaper Articles on Computer-related Issues

ment as follows: "once the process of the Revolution was fully underway, its dynamic growth was remorseless, and no power, no man nor combination of men, could set it back against its course."

The transition to a high-technology information society has been made inevitable by the development of highly capable computers. Whereas the industrial society was characterized by the amplification by machines of muscle power, the high-technology information society will see computers amplifying the powers of the brain.

As with the industrial revolution, this new revolution will radically alter society. It will, in Christopher Evans' words, "have an overwhelming and comprehensive impact affecting every human being on earth in every aspect of his or her life." And, again as with the industrial revolution, there will be no way to stop or reverse its course. However, there is a significant difference between the earlier revolution and the present one: having survived one hectic transition we are in a unique position to control and direct the current one.

Past experience dictates that we make an effort to identify and deal with problems as they evolve, rather than hoping they will resolve themselves. The problems associated with the transition to a high-technology information society are not really new—they consist of moral and ethical issues of a perennial nature made unique by the new context. As a society we should begin to develop an awareness and sensitivity to these problems, and the schools can play a major part in this. By familiarizing themselves with what is taking place, teachers will be better able to encourage the open discussion of issues in their classes. Open dialogue is a traditional and effective technique for dealing with philosophical and moral issues, and it is appropriate for computer-related concerns. The following information is presented in the hope that it will serve as the catalyst to encourage issue-related classroom activities.

## AN OVERVIEW

Before moving on to the discussion of issues, let us review a few of the many benefits that have resulted from the introduction of the computer and related technologies.

Computers are routinely used by hospitals as monitoring and diagnostic devices. The recent advances in genetic engineering would have been impossible without computers, and the space program would be nothing more than science fiction had the computer not been available.

Computers are used by farmers to balance their improved production capabilities with such market variables as demand and operating costs. Computer-directed robots perform complex and precise factory work; they even load artillery shells for the army, thereby relieving personnel of this dangerous and tiring work. Through the use of computerized charge-card networks we are becoming a cashless society: anything from a cup of coffee to a new suit can be purchased without the need for the vendor to enter a single word or number manually. At the grocery store the clerk runs items across a scanner; the computer responds by recording the sale for inventory purposes. The customer is given a computer-generated printout listing the items purchased, the cost, the date and the store location—and there is often a polite thank-you once the bill is paid. Modern automobiles would not run without their on-board computers, and their improved gas mileage is a result of computers that balance the air and fuel mixture with such factors as engine speed and temperature. Computers even enable some cars to actually talk: they tell us when the oil is low or when we have forgotten to fasten the seat belt.

The striking artistic effects we enjoy on television and in the movies are products of the computer artist's electronic palette. In a different kind of studio, the electronic-age musician creates music and special sound effects using the computer. The descendants of the original Mayflower party now have so many ancestors (48,000) that they have turned to computers in an effort to keep track of them all. And a recent computer analysis of the Shroud of Turin indicates that this may indeed be the authentic burial cloth of Jesus Christ.

Examples such as these point to the marvels that are possible in the computer age. All is not entirely rosy, however; along with the good comes the bad— promises and problems. Thus, while the ubiquitous computer presents society with a promise of Utopia, it simultaneously introduces the threat of Big Brother.

Commissions have been appointed, laws have been framed, and dialogue is ongoing, but solutions to the concerns spawned by the wholesale integration of computers into society are difficult to come by. No one seems to know exactly what to do about the theft of information, for example. Although the commodity is stolen, it hasn't been physically removed—it remains in the data bank where it was initially. And what should be done about the *hackers*? Although this term formerly was used to describe someone who was hooked on computers, it now has a negative connotation and refers to those electronic interlopers who enter data bases illegally. When a burglar enters a home and wanders about, the statutes are quite clear concerning his punishment. What is the difference between this kind of trespass and a hacker breaking into a large data base filled with private records? Again, what steps should be taken to ensure that equal access to computers is enjoyed by all? Is the answer to be found in the allocation of equal blocks of time to every individual? Could such a cumbersome system actually work, and is it really necessary?

The complexion of the work force and the nature of the workplace will never again be the same thanks to the introduction of computer-controlled robots. What will be the short- and long-term impact of such technology from a humanistic perspective? What steps can be taken to make the transition less painful?

Finally, what of the fifth generation "thinking" computers? Not only do they promise to alter the manner in which humans perceive themselves, but they threaten to alter the way people actually think and to change the definition of intelligence itself. This may seem a bit farfetched, but before deciding whether any credence should be given to it, let us examine the evidence in greater detail.

## COMPUTERS AND THE INTELLECT

The early machines, you will recall, required that machine language be used for programming, and input was through a series of manually operated switches that generated binary code. This tedious approach has been replaced with keyboards, mice, and touch screens for input, and with higher-level languages for writing programs. Current efforts are directed toward developing even simpler and more human systems through applications based on artificial intelligence (AI) research. Artificial intelligence is a field devoted to creating programs that will enable computers to think like humans. Natural language input is one promising area where researchers are making progress; the same holds true for voice output. An interesting product of the AI labs is the expert system, which is built around an exhaustive knowledge and strategy pool gleaned from experts in a specific field and incorporated into a program. Computers can reach decisions in the manner of human experts with this system. Expert systems are still being refined, but several are currently being used in fields such as medicine.

Although highly sophisticated, expert systems still cannot replace the human expert because they are unable to deal with the vagaries found in even the most precise disciplines. More capable expert systems will become available as

computers gain in power, and some scientists predict that one day computer-based expert systems will truly be as competent as a human expert.

There still remains the concern as to how far such innovations can be carried before an impasse is reached between the ability of the technology to do things in human terms and the need to maximize the potential of that technology. To illustrate, let us consider what some claim to be the ultimate input medium, spoken English. Few problems exist as long as the words conform to a standardized set of discrete commands that are unambiguous to the computer. Ambiguity, however, is an inherent characteristic of the language unless context can be taken into consideration (as when humans communicate with one another). But computers are not yet very good at dealing with context, and there is a very real possibility that they will not be able to deal with it much better in the future, despite the best efforts of AI researchers.

The problem, to some, is one of preserving the complexity of the language when utilitarian concerns dictate that it be simplified. This is, in fact, not a new problem. Many attempts have been made to redo the English language along phonetic lines, with much of the effort directed toward the standardization of phonemes and the letter combinations that represent them: the word *nation,* for example, can be spelled *nashion* phonetically, or even *neishun.* But why even make an effort to preserve the nonstandard structure when it presents so many problems to the average user in spelling, grammar, and so on? Some would argue that a complex language is essential for the manipulation of complex ideas. Still other reasons are proposed, but the primary one typically relates to cognitive concerns.

Will the need to communicate with computers through the use of "computer friendly" English result in the creation of a simplified version that then becomes the language of interhuman communication? This seems a bit farfetched to be sure, but languages do change over time, and perhaps the computer will be the catalyst to speed up this process. Pessimists fear that this will be the case and that the consequence will be a loss of our language's versatility, which in turn will lead to a decrease in the quality of thought.

Isaac Asimov is one who takes the opposite point of view. He maintains that computers will indeed change the manner in which the English language is structured, but he perceives this as being a needed improvement over the inconsistent approach to spelling and grammar to which we have fallen heir. According to Asimov a large part of the difficulty people encounter as they attempt to read and to spell is directly attributable to the mess the language is in. He maintains that both the nation and the world would enjoy all manner of benefits if the subtle changes needed in spelling and grammar were built into the word processors of the millions of personal computers that will eventually "replace other techniques for writing books, articles, reports, correspondence, and so on." Asimov believes that the evolution would occur over an extended period of time and in a very natural way, as first a word here and then a word there is flagged by the computer and identified as needing to be modified to the updated spelling scheme. He does not feel that simplifying the structure of the language would in any way diminish its utility for use in complex reasoning activities; as a matter of fact, according to his line of thinking, the converse would actually be the case.

So, here we have two points of view. Which of them, if either, will be proven true? Obviously, only the passage of time will reveal the answer. But language is only one area of concern; what of the other traits that are perceived as belonging uniquely to the human domain? Is it actually conceivable that a machine can do intelligent things? That depends in large part upon how the term is defined. Not too long ago the ability to calculate was considered a prime indicator of intelligence, but the pocket calculator performs math functions more accurately and more rapidly than can the best human mathematician. Despite this fact, many teachers continue to insist that students memorize multiplication tables, derive square roots by hand, and practice long division. Others maintain that such skills are archaic and merely waste a lot of time, given the current state of miniaturized calculator technology. Clearly the pocket calculator is better in one narrow, restricted domain than its human counterpart—computation. But as these domains become broader, and as new ones are added to the computer's repertoire of capabilities, will the human intellect eventually become second-rate?

Many individuals who have considered the problem hold a more optimistic point of view. They believe that the implementation of artificial intelligence computer systems will have nothing but a positive effect on human thinking. They maintain that people won't be replaced; rather, their capabilities will be amplified.

The potential for the computer to assume roles that have always been assigned to the human intellect is everywhere in evidence. The computational example mentioned above is a well-known one, but there are many others. The need to know how to spell accurately has been eliminated, to some extent, by the spelling checker programs in some word processors. Programs of this kind work in conjunction with the word processor to locate misspellings by matching the words in the document being written with a built-in dictionary. Some spelling checkers locate a misspelled word and then give several options that range from replacing the entire word (sometimes with a synonym) to ignoring the prompts altogether.

If today's computers can find and correct misspelled words, give a list of options for replacement, list synonyms and antonyms, and do all this on-line as the manuscript is being composed, it is fair to ask what tomorrow's intelligent machines will be able to do. Is it conceivable that they might be able to locate and correct errors in syntax? Will they be able to compose a letter, or write a novel? When we consider the complexities of the English language it seems highly unlikely that a computer will ever write a sequel to *Huckleberry Finn*. On the other hand, it would be no great task for the machine to put together a credible business letter, a résumé, or a newspaper blurb.

Given the present and projected capabilities of the computer, will attributes traditionally considered quintessential to the human intellect be given over to machines? Most probably, the answer to the question won't be a simple yes or no. Some would say that our present definition of intelligence will have to be changed to emphasize those kinds of things that machines, even thinking ones, don't do very well. Machines can deal with all kinds of mathematics, and they can do this more efficiently than can a human; they can store vast files of factual information and recall them instantly; they are able to contend with mundane problems day after day without getting tired or bored; and they can do many other things of this nature. As a matter of fact, research using some extremely powerful machines (such as the VAX shown in figure 9.2) has come close to

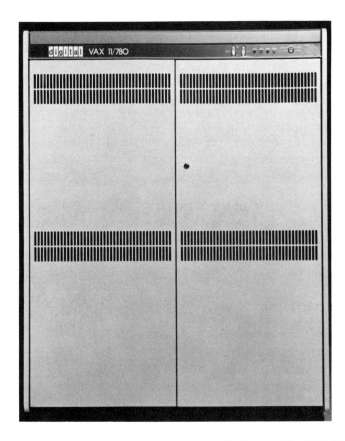

**FIGURE 9.2  A Powerful VAX Computer** (Courtesy of Digital Equipment Corporation)

producing what some might call a kind of intelligence—but these artificial intelligence systems are without many of the capabilities that humans take for granted: creativity, intuition, common sense, morality, flexibility, and the ability to capitalize on serendipity—all of these attributes belong within the human domain, and will most likely remain there into the foreseeable future. Optimists would argue that it is these latter qualities that humans should stress as a new model of intelligence is developed—not the traditional things such as the abilities to memorize and to compute, which should be given over to the computer permanently.

By now you are well aware of the speculative nature of this discussion. You have probably sensed the interplay of the pros and cons and have perhaps even taken sides. Such is the nature of the issues relating to computers and society—they are highly controversial. But great teaching and learning experiences are made of such controversies, so let us forge on to other issues and concerns.

## COMPUTER CRIME

Computer-related crimes range from acts that might be construed as pranks to international espionage in which the security of nations is put at risk. In San Diego a group of high school students gained access to the school's computer system via their home computers and, once inside, raised havoc with everything from grades to student records. Some records were destroyed, others altered. Grades were changed and some were simply obliterated. What should be done under such circumstances? The school viewed the act as the equivalent of a physical break-in and suspended those involved until the case could be examined in depth.

At the other end of the spectrum is the case of the Soviet scientists who apparently succeeded in breaking into two large computer systems in the West from their base in Central Europe. This incident and other related ones have led to the fear that the U.S. Defense Department computers, with their massive store of top secret data, are vulnerable to such penetrations.

A recent study by the American Bar Association Criminal Justice Section indicated that people are very much concerned about domestic computer-related crimes. Many have been victims, and the amounts of money involved are quite substantial. Some of the figures derived from the study are shown in table 9.1. (For those who wish to acquire the complete study, ordering instructions are given in the section on teaching about issues at the end of this chapter.)

### The Theft of Money and Goods

Most crimes committed with the aid of computers are not detected immediately. The various reasons for this state of affairs are all based on the uniqueness of the technology. When a gang of thieves tunnels into a bank and empties the vault over the weekend, the crime is discovered on Monday morning when the employees open the vault. When computer thieves rob a bank, however, the crime may not be detected for months or even years. The fact that data—which can

**TABLE 9.1  Figures from the ABA Survey** (From *Report on Computer Crime*, a publication of the ABA Criminal Justice Section)

| *Percentage of Respondents* | |
|---|---|
| 58 | Want a criminal code that deals specifically with computer crime |
| 48 | Reported that a computer crime had occurred within the past year |
| 41 | Consider losses nationally to be one billion dollars annually |
| 39 | Could not identify those who committed the crime |
| 28 | Had no method for monitoring computer crime |
| 25 | Reported some kind of loss from computer crime |
| 20 | Elected not to report the crime |

represent personal files, defense secrets, or even money—is stored in a relatively inaccessible fashion makes it possible for individuals to effect modifications in the information that are quite difficult to detect. An auditor is able to thumb through the corporation's books or count the cash and checks, but accessing the data in computer storage is a more formidable task.

Most people who operate computers know little about the inner workings of the machines and accept the output on faith, but experts are able to manipulate programs with relative ease and are therefore able to commit a variety of dishonest acts if they are inclined to do so. Such individuals are able to survive audit after audit because most auditors simply rely on a printout for their information, and the printout is merely a product of the manipulated program.

The amount of money stolen each year by "keyboard bandits" is highly speculative, but the figures range somewhere between $100 million and $3 billion, depending upon which reports are being quoted. One reason for this discrepancy is that many computer crimes go undetected for varying periods of time, and some are never discovered. Also, victims of such crimes are often reluctant to report them, for one reason or another. Indeed, it is not uncommon for the victim to hire the perpetrator in order to profit from his expertise—a person who is clever enough to execute a complex computer crime is most likely knowledgeable enough to assist in devising safeguards that will protect the system from similar crimes in the future.

According to FBI figures, a typical bank robber nets about $8,000 for his efforts. Computer bandits, on the other hand, average about $500,000 per robbery. The comparison of the two events is somewhat farfetched, since the bank robbery is a hit-and-run operation and the computer crime is extended over time, but both result in similar losses, though unequal in magnitude.

Numerous cases of fraud against the federal government are uncovered each month. Reports indicate that fully one-half of the fraud cases are found accidentally, whereas only about one-fourth are discovered through the use of built-in system controls. Such findings lead to the conclusion that innumerable computer crimes simply go undetected. Most of the reported thefts were committed by people who were less than affluent but had the necessary expertise to use the computer in an illegal fashion. In most cases nonqualifying parties obtained some type of federal benefit through the manipulation of records.

The list of computer crimes is virtually without end and includes all kinds of clever and even ingenious schemes. Thousands of dollars worth of products were rerouted and stolen from the Coca-Cola Company by a small group of employees who had access to the company's computers. A Social Security employee was able to use the computer to generate checks that ended up in the wallets of a group of her friends. A trusted employee of a stockbroking firm embezzled thousands of dollars by programming the computer to issue checks to nonexistent customers. A computer at the Internal Revenue Service was used to change the addresses on tax refund checks so they would be distributed to relatives of the computer operator. A claims manager for a federally sponsored medical program submitted false medical claims so checks were mailed to an office he maintained under a fictitious name. And on numerous occasions dishonest employees have pilfered and sold information files that frequently contain confidential material that is highly valued, particularly by those who sell their products through the mails, speculators, and certain government agencies.

The American Bar Association's survey of computer crime reveals some startling statistics (see table 9.1). Note that one-fourth of the 283 companies and government agencies surveyed reported losses from computer crime; close to one-half of the organizations believed that total losses were over $1 billion; and one-fifth of the victims had not reported the crime. Although some skeptics tend to downplay the magnitude of computer crime, surveys such as this indicate that the problem is not only real but also serious.

## The Theft of Hardware and Technology

The theft of money and goods constitutes the most common example of computer crime, but the theft of technology is also cause for much concern. Headlines were made when Hitachi, one of Japan's largest producers of electronic equipment, pleaded guilty to charges of conspiring to transport stolen IBM technology out of the United States. IBM was in full cooperation with the FBI in executing the carefully planned operation that led to the arrest of the Japanese agents at the moment they received the booty. Yet when the judgment was handed down, fines totaling a mere $24,000 were imposed. IBM was satisfied with the decision, however, because it sent out a clear warning to would-be technology thieves that such activities would not be tolerated.

The stakes are very high in this international game of electronic cops and robbers. Cadres of Soviet and other Eastern bloc agents swarm around the high-tech areas of Western and certain Asian nations in search of any small bit of information that might be of use to them. Sometimes they are lucky and obtain information about an entire system. Generally, though, they get bits and pieces that may ultimately fit together to form a total picture. But much of the high technology that flows from the West to the East is not stolen directly by agents. The culprits all too commonly are Western or Asian entrepreneurs who are lured into the web by the high stakes. This state of affairs may seem abhorrent to many; trafficking with the enemy, however, is by no means a new phenomenon. During many artillery duels along the western front in 1914–18 there were almost as many shells with the Krupp label fired at the German lines as fired toward France.

To a few individuals, good business apparently knows no nationality—it's the bottom line on the balance sheet that counts. Such an attitude has caused customs agents no end of concern. One huge computer system, an American-made VAX 11-782, was confiscated by customs agents in Hamburg from a ship that, it was claimed, had the Soviet Union on its itinerary. The reason for concern was the system's potential uses—among other things, the VAX is capable of guiding nuclear-armed ballistic missiles, conceivably to our own shores.

To counter such activities a concerted effort has been mounted by various Western governments, including the United States. Members of a special task force called Operation Exodus have successfully intercepted thousands of illegal shipments of high-tech equipment destined for the Soviet Union and its allies. Fortunately, there are high-tech companies that police themselves. Wang Laboratories is a good example of this emerging phenomenon. Company officials suspected that an order for several million dollars' worth of computer equipment had originated in the Soviet Union. Tracing the order to its source was complicated by the fact that the recipient was to have been India, which would have paid with a Yugoslav credit memo, which was drawn against an account in Liechtenstein, and so on. Such circuitous wheeling and dealing makes the task of tracking down international bandits a difficult one. Although Wang had received clearance from the Commerce Department and was under no obligation to refuse to sell the equipment, it elected to take the loss rather than be a party to the deal.

Many government officials feel that the Commerce Department does not maintain sufficiently strict controls over the issuing of export licenses, but Commerce defends its policies by saying that if the United States refuses to sell the technology to the Soviets, our allies in Europe and Japan will do it—and this seems to be the case. The answer to the problem lies in a coordinated international effort such as the COCOM agreement (Coordinating Committee for Multilateral Export Controls), an arrangement involving the United States, Japan, and thirteen NATO nations to control the flow of technology to the Soviets. This is a step in the right direction and should make the acquisition of Western technology at least a bit more difficult for the communist bloc.

## The Piracy of Software

Multimillion-dollar taps into international banks and the clandestine acquisition of computer technology by foreign governments are highly publicized events. But a much less dramatic and often overlooked problem is the illegal copying of disk-based programs. Although this activity is not as spectacular as the crimes already described, its critical nature becomes apparent when the extent to which it is being practiced is considered. Some estimates indicate that for every program acquired legally, ten are copied illegally (fig. 9.3). In addition to its illegality, copying provides unintended ethical models for students who observe it being practiced openly. Duplicating an entire book is both too costly and too time-consuming to make it viable, but pirating the equivalent of a complete book from a disk is both quick and inexpensive. The simplicity with which a program can be transferred from one disk to another causes many people to overlook the fact that the programmer spends as much time and effort creating his material as does the author of a traditional hard-copy textbook.

Recent reports conclude that more than 90 percent of the nation's schools now contain at least one microcomputer; thus the potential for copyright abuse is virtually universal. Though some teachers make a point of addressing the issue of software piracy, others actually assign the task of making copies to students—a practice that tends to legitimize the activity. Through condoning and even encouraging software piracy, educators may be teaching values that will transfer to other situations. If it is all right to steal people's creative works, is it therefore acceptable to steal other things from them?

**1 purchased          10 pirated**

FIGURE 9.3  The Ratio of Legally Acquired to Pirated Software (Estimated)

The long-term implications of mass copying are not pleasant to contemplate. Creative people must be compensated for what they do. If they are not, their tendency will be to stop turning out quality products. When this happens consumers, including the schools, will be the ones to suffer. In an effort to discourage the practice of illegal copying, many companies have devised plans for providing backup copies of programs; many of these, however, are quite restrictive and inconvenient. Much of the current copying is defended on the grounds that the producers have not done enough to provide workable backup plans. Nevertheless, the law is clear: copying is, for the most part, illegal.

School districts and software publishers are currently engaged in efforts to deal with the problem of piracy, and some positive results are being seen. Publishers have devised several plans to make their programs more widely available, one of which involves selling a site licensing plan to a school for each program purchased; the school may then either duplicate the program for each of its computers or load each machine in turn from the disk. An increasing number of publishers are making software available for use on networks; a central disk drive can then be used to load a program into all the machines on the network. Still other publishers offer a discount on multiple copies of the same program. And, though not a common approach, a few companies sell programs that can be copied freely.

Schools and districts are trying to do their part also. Some districts have negotiated contracts that permit them to duplicate programs centrally for distribution to the schools, in an effort to discourage illegal copying on the part of teachers by providing them with the software they need. Other districts stress the serious consequences associated with pirating software. Some have adopted the International Council for Computers in Education Guidelines, which prohibit copying software beyond the initial backup copy. The fact that they can be held liable for the illegal activities of teachers has caused some districts to enforce the rules strictly. Teachers have been reprimanded, and it is conceivable that the time will come when one or more might actually be dismissed because of noncompliance. In addition, some schools emphasize the moral issues involved. Students who are permitted to copy software, or who see the teacher involved in this activity, are getting the wrong message: it is acceptable to steal from another. Greater progress toward the solution of the piracy problem can be expected as consumers and producers work even more closely together to come up with an equitable and workable plan.

## Unauthorized Computer Entry

A problem that has gained national attention and much publicity is the entry into computerized data banks by unauthorized personnel. If the activity is shorn of its electronic accoutrements, the issue is one of old-fashioned trespass, infringement on personal privacy, and theft. The technique involves using the telephone lines to reach a data bank, where entry is accomplished through the use of a password or code. A number of methods have been devised for obtaining the passwords, one of which is the random generation of number combinations until one is found that works.

The worst possible case of illegal entry is illustrated by the movie *War Games*. Although the writers and producers took a certain amount of artistic license for the sake of entertainment, the basic idea is plausible to a degree. The computer system as depicted in the movie is quite unlike the actual North American Air Defense Command (NORAD) system, and the depiction of the computer making an independent decision to launch a first strike is a bit farfetched; but the potential for breaking into private communications systems is very real, and it happens all the time.

The film created a furor among computerphiles and the uninitiated alike. Most people let it go as entertainment, but two teenagers from California put together a real-life sequel. They were able to gain access to a research computer system, which enabled them to break into other systems, including one containing Defense Department data. Ultimately, the pair unwittingly caused over $200,000 in damage to some of the programs. When charges were brought they amounted to fourteen felony counts, a single count of theft, and one of receiving stolen property. The penalty for crimes of this nature is up to six years in prison and an unspecified fine. Thus, as the district attorney pointed out, this was "no childish prank."

A similar case was reported in Milwaukee, where a group of seven boys who dubbed themselves the 414s used nationwide computerized bulletin boards to post such information as passwords and other data that would permit others to gain illegal access to computer systems. Among their exploits was the accessing of the nuclear weapons laboratory at Los Alamos, New Mexico. The FBI cracked the case with the help of a security system that maintained a record of calls made

to a computer telephone network. At least sixty data banks were illegally tapped by the 414s using randomly generated code numbers. Members of the group were modest about their exploits and suggested that the computer operators inadvertently lent support to the scheme by neglecting to change the passwords frequently enough.

Joining the ranks of the hackers is relatively inexpensive and easy; it helps to be bright, but you need not be rich. The requisites for this kind of activity are rather modest—you need nothing more than a microcomputer, a modem, lots of time, and some knowledge of how to access a data base. The fact that these essentials are so readily available to so many has led to a phenomenal increase in the hacker population. The fascination hacking holds for its devotees is summed up by a statement from a member of the 414s: "It was like climbing a mountain: you have the goal of reaching the top or accessing a computer, and once you reach the peak, you make a map of the way and give it to everybody else." Most hackers harbor no malicious intentions when they enter a system illegally; they intend only to outwit the system. But there are those who, once inside, can't resist doing some kind of mischief. Then there are others who mess things up unintentionally—thousands of dollars' worth of programs and data can be damaged by doing very little.

Hackers have received so much publicity from the media—most of which has an aura of thinly veiled admiration—that a large part of the population looks upon these pranksters as electronic-age Robin Hoods. Something about the hacker and his self-proclaimed mission appeals to our love of the underdog: it's a case of David over Goliath. Large computers and the corporations that employ them have become the symbol of uncaring, brute power; the thought that a teenager could take their measure and then some is reassuring. But beneath this veneer of admiration lies the uneasy feeling that you or I could be next. Some hackers perceive their mission to be that of opening up an inaccessible system to those who lack access. While these proclamations may sound noble, the fact is that a citizen's right to privacy cannot be abridged—hacking is a crime.

## THE ISSUES OF PRIVACY

Concerns for individual privacy have brought about the formation of various organizations and the enactment of legislation to safeguard the rights of citizens. Despite the ongoing effort to ensure that the privacy of the individual is not compromised, the rise of our high-tech society has introduced problems that were not anticipated when many of the initial safeguards were put into place.

When records were kept in folders in filing cabinets the very nature of this cumbersome system made it impractical to access extensive data files efficiently and quickly; but the computer has changed all that. Little time and effort are required to conduct a search on virtually any subject or person. Massive personal files are maintained by a wide range of organizations. For example, TRW Inc.'s credit bureau can manage 325 thousand credit reports on 90 million households in a single day. The FBI has its own set of computerized records, as does the

CIA. There is a general feeling among taxpayers that the IRS computers know everything about everyone. Lockheed Corporation and McGraw-Hill control massive amounts of data but exclude most individuals from access; thus, another form of centralized power has evolved.

An effort is underway to match individual files in several data bases in an attempt to uncover cases of criminal activity. This seems innocuous enough until the potential for misuse of the data is recognized. Although the motive is a noble one, the fact that the private records of unsuspecting individuals are being examined without their knowledge or consent—and the information is perhaps being used for questionable purposes—makes this activity appear to be no more legitimate than that of the hackers.

Obviously, legal and well-intentioned uses of the data bases far outweigh illegal uses; nevertheless, the question of an individual's right to privacy frequently surfaces as a consequence of such searches. A case in point is the recent episode in which a computerized audit of the bank accounts of welfare recipients in the state of Massachusetts revealed that over two thousand welfare recipients had savings accounts that were sufficiently large to disqualify them from receiving benefits (one individual had over $64 thousand). If such a plan were to be adopted on a national scale, the savings could amount to nearly $500 million for the first year alone. Few people would support the practice of fraudulently obtaining welfare payments, and yet many would argue that the unannounced (though legal) entry into the privileged domain of bank accounts smacks of totalitarianism.

The case of the 414s points to the ease with which data bases can be accessed by unauthorized persons using, among other things, home-based microcomputers. This situation can also be reversed so the opposite condition prevails: if people at home are able to break into outside facilities, outside parties have the potential to break into records maintained in files at home. The proliferation of home computers, the development by private individuals and clubs of networks that employ electronic bulletin boards, and the burgeoning private use of telecommunications are making home-developed data much more accessible and therefore more vulnerable to unauthorized access and misuse than ever before. Fortunately, a home computer must be plugged into a telecommunications system for an unauthorized party to access it; machines that aren't hooked to the outside world are quite safe from break-ins.

Problems relating to privacy are compounded by the fact that it is next to impossible to develop a totally tamper-proof computer system. A variety of safeguards are built into most systems; but these tend to diminish, not eliminate, the problems. You will recall that the case of the 414s was solved by a security system that maintained a record of calls made to a telephone network: the inordinately large number of calls aroused suspicion, which ultimately proved to be justified. This case is most likely unique, however—the solution of most computer crimes comes about as a result of a lucky accident, not because of functioning safeguards.

Safeguards are becoming increasingly more sophisticated and effective, however. Also, the problems are being addressed at the social and philosophical levels. An interesting innovation is the insurance plan being offered by a handful of companies to counter the hackers and thieves. Traditionally, insurance policies have protected such things as automobiles, houses, and lives. But the age of technology has brought about a situation in which electronically stored information is of greater value than the storage mediums themselves. Thus, the data on a hard disk could easily be priceless, whereas the disk and drive could be replaced for a relatively small amount. The new insurance policies protect against both the person with criminal intent (our electronic bank robber) and the hackers or pranksters whose damage might be inadvertent.

Over the past several years many states have introduced sections pertaining to computer crime into their penal codes. Some state codes specifically address the problems of unauthorized computer access for purposes such as stealing money and services, committing fraud, or hacking. Placing a value on information stolen through illegal entry into computerized systems is a particularly difficult task. The case of IBM versus Hitachi illustrates the problem: IBM requested that the calculated base value of the technology be doubled to compensate for the projected spin-off profits that would supposedly be realized by Hitachi.

Due to the vagueness of the current laws, most computer crimes are never brought into the courts. As the laws become more clearly defined, and lawyers become more knowledgeable about high-tech crime, however, greater control will be exercised over this growing problem. At the national level two new bills have been written in an attempt to bolster and upgrade the laws already on the books—the Federal Computer Systems Protection Act, which makes it a crime to tamper with federal government computers, and the Small Business Computer Crime Prevention Act, which will establish a task force to safeguard business computers across the nation. In addition, the major computer-based information retrieval services have formed an association that is lobbying for tougher laws as well as taking steps to halt the unauthorized use of their systems and sharing information on known cases of unauthorized access.

A series of recommendations has been issued by a congressional panel formed to examine the problems of computer security. One suggestion was that a national commission be formed to deal specifically with safeguarding computer-based information. The panel further recommended that a much stronger federal commitment be made to the resolution of the security problem. They felt that the industry should assume a strong role that would include the establishment of universal hardware and software standards. Finally, it was recommended that stronger procedures be implemented for the selection and clearance of those who have access to sensitive information. All of this is an indication that society is starting to sense the seriousness of the problem and is gearing up to respond to the challenge.

## COMPUTERS AND JOBS

A statement in a small newspaper article probably went unnoticed by most readers, yet the implications are far-reaching: over the next twenty years computer-based automation will eliminate ten million jobs in the United States. That this dire prediction has some substance cannot be denied—the process has already begun.

In the first unfair-labor charge based upon the displacement of workers by robotization, local 644 of the American Federation of Government Employees filed a suit against a Department of Labor laboratory in Pittsburgh because a robot took the place of four workers, who were given various temporary assignments. Union officials agree that the robots are useful and desirable in many cases, but they maintain that labor should have a voice in decisions that affect job

security. At present unions have very little input into when and how technological innovations such as robots should be introduced.

Virtually all routine manual factory jobs can be automated through the use
of industrial robots (fig. 9.4). The automobile assembly line will never again look
the same, as robots take over such tasks as welding, painting, and assembling the
cars. Workers in other industries are affected as well: accounting and office procedures are being automated to a greater extent than ever before, and even such
creative endeavors as advertising and photography will increasingly feel the
presence of the computer. As a matter of fact, few—if any—jobs will be immune
from its impact. Predictions are that the number of robots in the United States
should reach between 50 and 100 thousand by the year 1990 and that each robot
will replace two workers.

Many changes will be of a positive nature, with various high-technology oc-
cupations increasing at a rapid pace. Jobs for computer operators, repair personnel, and systems analysts, for example, will skyrocket. When the broad picture is examined, however, the high-tech job segment will likely be a narrow one.
According to estimates only 6 percent of the newly created jobs over the next ten
years will be in the high-tech area. Although respectable numbers of people will
be employed by the high-tech firms, only about 20 percent will actually be di-

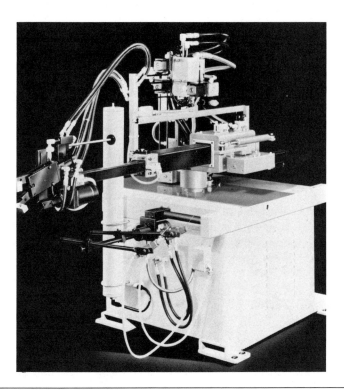

**FIGURE 9.4   An Industrial Robot** (Courtesy of Sterling-Detroit Company)

rectly involved in technologically oriented activities. The great majority will do such tasks as assemble components, work in the stock room, and do clerical work. Many experts predict that most jobs will actually require less training and a lower skill level than is currently the case.

Examples of this phenomenon can be seen in a variety of settings at the present time. Secretaries need fewer skills to be effective than was previously the case. Physicians rely on computers for much of their diagnostic work. Lawyers conduct computer searches using descriptors to find computer-base information on a particular case or subject—they scarcely need the traditional research skills that were so essential in the past. Computerized diagnostic machines are used by mechanics to pinpoint mechanical problems and by electronics repairmen to locate faulty modules.

Highly sophisticated electronic components such as IC chips are now manufactured by computer-controlled production equipment that can be operated by workers with minimal skills. Thus, many electronics companies have moved their operations to Korea, Singapore, Taiwan, and other Asian countries where labor is cheap. The end result is a loss of jobs for U.S. workers. In addition, advanced technology will most likely even decrease the need for so many computer programmers.

Despite predictions that computers will steal jobs from workers, many people take the more optimistic point of view. The current push by the nation's schools to implement computer literacy programs is indicative of the growing perception that people who do not know about computers will be disadvantaged. The emphasis on retraining in related technologies, particularly where laid-off workers are involved, is another indication that people have faith in the high-tech future. Many states are going out of their way to lure such industries; indeed, the competition has become fierce, to say the least.

## COMPUTER EQUITY

Women and the economically disadvantaged are among those who are being shortchanged as the computer revolution swings into full gear. This is not to say that the two categories are mutually exclusive, for there are certainly many women in the less affluent sections of our society; females have historically had less access to computers and computing, however, than their male counterparts (fig. 9.5), as have those who are financially unable to take advantage of the new technology.

Differences in the way boys and girls use computers begin to show up at an early age. Researchers at the Children's Television Workshop (the "Sesame Street" people), for instance, have found that as early as the age of three, boys tend to be more reclusive at the computer, preferring to use it in a one-on-one manner. In contrast, girls prefer to have a friend along and to work together on the machine—the interpersonal activity becomes an important part of the process. The boys prefer shoot-'em-up games in which there is an element of the chase and conquest, whereas the girls lean toward less violent types of software.

FIGURE 9.5   Boys Are Predominant in Computer Courses

Researchers suggest that though the differences are real, it is too early to attribute them to biological factors. Instead, the attitudes of role models such as parents, relatives, and teachers may be responsible.

Computers and math are often closely associated, and since math is perceived as being a male domain, girls tend to shy away from computer-related activities. The phenomenon is not a recent one. The mathematics prodigy Ada, the Countess of Lovelace, was discouraged from pursuing a career in this field by her tutor, who said that a mathematician must be capable of a "fierce concentration" and must have an "unremitting strength of intellect" in order to succeed. Both characteristics were held to be beyond the capability of a female. Ada persisted and, in the early 1800s, devised programs for the mechanical computers conceived by Charles Babbage—the first programmer was thus a woman. Ada notwithstanding, it seems that females have traditionally been perceived, even among themselves, as lacking real talent for mathematics. This tendency is reflected in studies showing that sex-related attitudes toward mathematical ability begin to emerge in the primary grades, with both boys and girls indicating that they think of mathematics as a male domain.

Depending upon the nature of the defined goals, a background in math may or may not be a prerequisite for achieving computer proficiency. But the perception generally persists that such skills are needed, and steps must be taken to correct this misconception. The stress on math proficiency is most likely a by-product of a number of factors, one of which is the preponderance of male math and science teachers among those who introduce children to computers. With the growth of computer use in the elementary schools, however, more female teachers will have a hand in this critical introductory phase and will come to serve as models for the girls.

Another reason for the phenomenon of male computer dominance is the different attitudes of parents toward male and female children. In a survey of twenty-three computer camp directors, researchers at Stanford University found that as the cost of a computer camp increases, the number of girls involved decreases. They also discovered that boys in families owning home computers tend to use the equipment two to three hours each day. Fathers are also involved in regular home computer use, and apparently serve as models for their sons, but mothers and daughters are virtual nonparticipants. The more aggressive behavior of boys has been identified as yet another factor. They tend to monopolize the limited classroom machines unless the teacher has the foresight to allocate hands-on time in an equitable manner.

Much of the available software tends to reflect a male bias. The use of stereotyped aggressive male behavior as the format of many programs has resulted in an abundance of violence-oriented game material, which seems to appeal to boys. A further Stanford survey revealed that girls and their mothers who evaluated a selection of seventy-five software programs felt that a mere 5 percent would have greater appeal to girls than to boys (many of the girls were actually bored by the programs, finding them uninteresting).

Schools should begin early on to attend to the problem of stereotyping. Evidence indicates that girls are as capable as boys when it comes to understanding and using the computer, but they must be convinced that this is so. One way to address this problem is to begin at the elementary level to familiarize students with women's contributions to the fields of math and computer science. Many outstanding programmers are women; some have their own companies. Women have made some noteworthy contributions to computer science: in addition to Ada, the world's first programmer, Admiral Grace Hopper developed the programming language COBOL, which is widely used for business applications. Visits by female computer science majors and women from industry would add a new dimension to a unit on technology.

At the secondary level it would be useful to identify computer-related careers that girls perceive as being attractive. Many traditional jobs are gradually becoming computerized, and it takes little effort to find a link between a girl's career choice and the computer. Once girls are aware of the importance of understanding technology regardless of career choice, it is much simpler to encourage them to get involved in courses they might otherwise shun.

When it comes time for hands-on activities, either in a classroom setting or in the computer lab, girls with little or no background often feel intimidated. One way to make the experience a positive one is to have girls with expertise help those who are inexperienced. Both tutors and their tutees learn from this kind of arrangement and typically find the social interaction an enjoyable bonus. As a rule, only girls should be included in these learning groups, because boys generally end up taking things over. After the girls gain confidence, they typically hold their own, and it is not uncommon, particularly in the higher grades and in college, to see both sexes working together at a computer.

The problem of equity or equal access also involves the underprivileged. These people, both adults and children, do not have access to the same resources as do middle-class individuals. If, in fact, the future belongs to those who are computer literate, then a large segment of the population does not have much of a stake in the future. This contention, as you may realize, is not universally accepted—there are those who do not subscribe to the idea that everyone should be computer literate. On the other hand, there is strong evidence that CAI is effective in the teaching of traditional subjects; thus, access to computers becomes an issue even though the goal might not be universal computer literacy.

Computer use differs between less and more affluent schools: the trend is to emphasize drill and practice in traditional skills in the former, whereas more creative applications represent the norm in the latter. The disadvantaged, in other words, are not learning to control the technology but are being controlled by it. The public schools are currently the best hope for bringing the disadvantaged into the mainstream. Some schools, however, simply cannot afford to invest in the technology. Even schools in affluent neighborhoods are having problems obtaining sufficient discretionary funds to put microcomputers in their classrooms. But these schools have something going for them that the less affluent schools do not—constituencies able to provide special financial packages to purchase the desired equipment. Home computers tend to imbalance the equation still further. A growing number of middle-income families have personal computers their children can use; but these machines are virtually nonexistent in less prosperous homes, so the disadvantage is compounded. Futurists predict that this condition will change, however, as computers become smaller and less expensive, and this phenomenon is already becoming apparent.

The middle class is also favored by having its culture, language, and values reflected in the software. Producers defend this tendency by pointing out that the largest market is in the middle-class sector. To help put the problem into perspective, consider that twice as many middle school students in the West have computer access as do those in the Southeast. Approximately one in three students in affluent schools have computer knowledge, as opposed to just over one in ten rural students. Disadvantaged students fare almost as poorly: a recent University of Minnesota study indicated that the twelve thousand most affluent schools surveyed were four times as likely to have microcomputers as were the twelve thousand least affluent.

The message is clear: though disadvantaged children are already behind in a society that has embraced traditional means for knowledge transmission, they will be even further behind as electronic technologies supplement and replace the older ones. In other words, those who are disadvantaged today will be further disadvantaged tomorrow. Yet there is a glimmer of hope for all those being left out of, or shortchanged by, the computer revolution. Pressure is being brought to bear on the schools to provide all students with the opportunity for equal participation. The movement has much broad-based support, but the schools obviously can't do the job alone—ultimately it is society that must meet the challenge. But here, too, the response is positive and growing.

## THE FUTURE

So far in this chapter we have dealt with the present and a bit of the past; the future has only been alluded to. We will now consider in greater detail what most likely lies ahead, using the best information futurists can provide as the basis for our predictions.

A peek at the future is available today in the form of the artificial intelligence (AI) research made possible by extremely fast and powerful computers like the one shown in figure 9.6. As even more powerful machines are developed, scientists believe they will have the potential to create programs that move ever closer to working like the human intellect. In the meantime, the development of programs has given the microcomputer some AI capabilities, which means that teachers and their students can begin to enjoy the benefits of this exciting new application.

Not only will the technology of the future be different, but society will change as well. Alvin Toffler, a foremost futurist and the author of *Future Shock* and *The Third Wave,* has some definite ideas about the future that include the microcomputer as one of the essential players in the scenarios. The "electronic cottage" will change the work habits, the workplace, and to some extent the products of the third-wave society (fig. 9.7). Rather than wasting time commuting to and from the office or factory, people will work at home with the aid of computers linked together by extensive telecommunications networks. According to Toffler, the problems of declining production in certain industries is merely an indication that the second wave—the industrial era—is giving way to the third wave—the high-tech information era.

The electronic cottage becomes an attractive substitute for the traditional workplace when such advantages as increased productivity and decreased transportation costs are considered. Cottage industries already exist in great numbers across the country. Most involve the production of personal articles such as knitware or custom-built items such as furniture. Beauty shops are maintained where the codes are flexible enough to permit them to operate, and typists ply their trade in homes from coast to coast. To these traditional cottage industries must be added the newly emerging ones that have become possible through the application of the new electronic technologies. Freelance writers, graphic artists, programmers, architects, accountants, and others are already riding the third wave as their homes become their workplaces. Mothers who desire to combine a career with raising a family find the concept appealing, as do some people with disabilities. The foundation is already in place for the electronic cottage—all that is needed is to tie all the parts together electronically.

**FIGURE 9.6 A Powerful Mainframe Computer** (Courtesy of Digital Equipment Corporation)

Information will be one of the largest commodities in the third-wave society, and the processing of that information will be among the most important of the cottage industries. Unlike most of the traditional home-based enterprises, Toffler's electronic cottage will actually take the place of the centrally located office or other work station rather than simply supplement it. Also, many electronic cottages will communicate among themselves and with a central business establishment rather than being independent or loosely linked, as most of them are today. Toffler coins the word *prosumer* to describe the new breed of producer-consumer that will evolve in the third-wave society. Prosumers will feed specifications into the computer to enable it to custom-design clothing, autos, appliances, and so forth. "It will be hard to tell the producer from the consumer," according to Toffler.

What of education in the world of the third wave? Will it be radically different from what it is today? Or will it simply be an embellished version of more of

**FIGURE 9.7   People Will Work at Home in the Third-Wave Society** (Courtesy of Apple Computer, Inc.)

the same? As one of society's most tradition-bound institutions, the educational complex has changed very little over the centuries. A twentieth-century teacher still imparts knowledge in much the same manner as did her ancient Greek and Roman counterparts. Will computers and their attendant technologies change all that? Toffler, for one, thinks so. He sees the classroom shifting to the home for a considerable number of students as the computer ties into videodisks and other interactive information storage systems. The computer will serve as a powerful tutor that can adapt to the needs and learning styles of individual students; thus, not only the workplace but also the schoolroom will shift to the home in the electronic world of the future (fig. 9.8).

Speculating on the effect this will have on familial relationships is a popular pastime. Some prognosticators suggest that the spread of computerized home work stations will strengthen the family by permitting more people to spend more time together. But others suggest that the reverse will most likely be true, as "computer widows" rebel against the technology that usurps so much of a spouse's attention and time. Jean Hollands, author of *The Silicon Syndrome: A Survival Handbook for Couples,* maintains that the home computer has made it possible for the over-involved professional to make his workday twenty-four hours long. She points out that this situation involves males, for the most part, and is a reflection of men's tendency to think of the computer as a companion of exciting and challenging dimensions. The end result in all too many cases is divorce and the disintegration of the family. Women, on the other hand, are more inclined to perceive the computer as a tool—when they have achieved the desired result, they turn it off and go on to something else.

**FIGURE 9.8  The Computer Will Bring the Classroom into the Home** (Courtesy of Apple Computer, Inc.)

Researchers at the University of California at Irvine have taken a careful look at the problem and have come up with some interesting statistics. In a survey of 282 computer club members who used computers extensively at home, two out of three indicated that they spend less time watching television than was the case before they became involved with the technology. Among families with children, three out of four stated that their viewing time had dropped. Approximately one-fourth of those studied indicated that they spent less time sleeping than before, and about half said that the time spent on other hobbies had diminished since they purchased a microcomputer. One-third reported that family members spent more time alone as they worked with the machine, and one-fifth said that the family spent less leisure time together than formerly.

These findings indicate that the habits of families change somewhat when the computer arrives. The computer, being the powerful, fascinating, logical device that it is, can be addictive to many. Knowing the machine and being able to control it give an incredible amount of ego support to some individuals, who often come to neglect human relationships in favor of interaction with the computer.

On the other hand, some argue, the need for interpersonal relationships is so great that no technology can hope to supplant human-to-human discourse. Indeed, a large percentage of students identify interaction with their peers as the primary reason for going to school. Researchers at the Bank Street College of Education in New York have found that students working together in small groups at a microcomputer are more talkative by far than are those working with traditional instructional materials. Thus, the computer is seen as a desocializing influence on the one hand and a force for stimulating social interaction on the other. Probably both points of view are correct. Studies indicate that the manner in which people view the machines has much to do with their psychological makeup. That there is room for concern is obvious—the answer to the problem most likely lies not in the technological arena but in the realm of the social sciences. But let us leave for now the electronic cottage, with its problems and promises, and consider additional projections by other futurists.

Computer networks will constitute the most common form of communication medium by the year 2000, according to some projections. People in the most isolated places will have access to these networks through a terminal that will be nothing more than an updated version of the television set. Individuals on the go will be able to use the networks to access data banks anywhere in the world through the use of small, compact pocket terminals.

The concept of the pocket terminal is not merely a pipe dream—it is both practical and possible to construct one using today's technology. Although somewhat removed from the versatile pocket terminal visualized by the futurists, two current innovations illustrate the potential for miniaturized applications. The first is a digital watch from Seiko that incorporates storage and retrieval capabilities along with certain computer functions. Input is via a tiny keyboard, and a dot matrix display provides output. The second device is widely known as the "smart card." It consists of a credit card containing a computer chip. Logic in the chip provides the card with a wide range of capabilities that are obviously lacking in the standard variety. Many of the laborious bookkeeping functions associated with the traditional credit card are managed automatically by the smart card system.

The move toward a popular information network has already begun to take place. Several companies have embarked on a plan to turn the TV sets in hotel rooms into computer terminals for use by business people and other guests. Using a keyboard hooked to the TV, a businessperson can communicate with the home office, address data bases, make airline reservations, and so on merely by typing one of his current credit card numbers to activate the system; billing takes place automatically, with the various principals each getting a percentage of the total fee. Major hotel chains have begun an advertising campaign to sell the idea —along with clean rooms and other amenities, they now speak of telecommunication capabilities.

Miniaturization has made it possible to create monitoring devices of such small dimensions that they are virtually invisible, such as one in current use that is embedded in the body and interfaced with the heart to keep it beating rhythmically. In the future a wide range of additional uses will be found for this technology. People in free societies, however, might find some of the suggested uses rather unsettling. For example, one application might be to track certain individuals by computer. Tiny transmitters would be surgically implanted where they could not be removed, and a central computer would pick up their signals, from which an accurate estimate of the individual's location could be made at any time.

The carriers might be emotionally disturbed individuals, or perhaps criminals on parole. Some would consider this a case of having an electronic parole officer on duty twenty-four hours a day. Perhaps the idea is not a bad one—perhaps the price (constant electronic surveillance) is not too great to pay to stay out of prison.

The greatest revolution, though, will result as computer technology and genetic engineering join forces. Through the use of this new technology, primitive biosensors have already been created. These amazing contrivances are able to sense the presence of various compounds using a biological substance. They then convert the information into electrical impulses, which are sent to the computer for analysis. The implications are breathtaking: biosensors could even serve as eyes for the blind and ears for the deaf.

Such applications as the life-supporting implant mentioned above for the control of heart functions will be greatly expanded in the future as the science is perfected. For example, biochips will be able to control the introduction of such chemicals as insulin and thyroxin into the bloodstream of individuals suffering from diabetes and thyroid problems and to monitor cholesterol in those with high levels who are on strict diets.

Research with biosensors might ultimately lead to the development of biocomputers, which would be built of organic compounds rather than silicon and metal. Such computers would be very small because of the vastly greater potential for miniaturization—biological cells are far smaller than are their silicon equivalents—and they could, theoretically, repair themselves and even reproduce. The molecules that make up the computer will be synthetically fabricated, organized into an interrelated mesh along with other elements, and then programmed. But the end result will most likely be quite different from that which we associate with present-day computers. For one thing, these biological devices may actually think for themselves. They may also be much less predictable than are today's machines, thus making systems analysis a difficult if not impossible task.

Because this book is written for educators, it is appropriate that we return to this subject for our final discussion about futures. You will recall that one of the scenarios projected for education depicts students obtaining most of their formal schooling at home in the electronic cottage. It is doubtful that this will ever become a popular trend, though, given our social nature. Schools will most likely be around for a long time to come, but they are certain to change.

Powerful, inexpensive, and tiny, tomorrow's microcomputers and their highly capable programs will be central to the uniqueness of schools of the future. Instructional programs will become increasingly intelligent as a result of the application of advances in AI research. Though this field remains highly theoretical in orientation, a number of successful applications (including the expert system) have been made.

In education, efforts are underway to meld AI capabilities with CAI programs to create what is termed intelligent computer-assisted instruction, or ICAI. In the future ICAI programs will be available that overcome the major problems of current CAI programs. For example, the new generation of tutorials will permit the student to bypass the keyboard and communicate with the computer using natural language. Also, the computer will be able to deal effectively with virtually any response, gently taking appropriate steps to get the students back on track if they stray too far afield. ICAI programs will be able to maintain an ever-expanding pool of knowledge which, like human knowledge, can be accessed as needed and when appropriate. In other words, future instructional programs will be more responsive and sensitive and will teach much as a human teacher does if the promises of ICAI research are realized.

The instructional hardware will be different also. Instead of a system that costs roughly one thousand dollars and sits on a desk, each student will have a compact, inexpensive unit with a flat screen that folds down for portability. The computers will be smaller than a standard textbook and will contain general firmware programs such as dictionaries, word processors, and spelling checkers. Beyond these basic applications, the programs will be tailored to the needs of individual students by simply plugging in different selections of chips. Telecommunications capabilities will be built in also, allowing students to access data bases in a vast, satellite-oriented network.

As a result of the expanded capabilities of technology, teachers will have different functions than they do today: they will spend more time attending to the needs of individual students and less time worrying about class norms; they will be relieved of tedious nonteaching tasks such as maintaining attendance and performance records; and they will become the skilled managers of complex instructional systems that bear little resemblance to today's classrooms.

Like the weather, the future is very difficult to predict. Given the phenomenal development of computer technology over the past several years, it is probably safe to say that any prediction we might make will have to take into account the potential for equally unanticipated developments in coming years. Thirty years ago who could possibly have guessed that a classroom in 1987 would contain the equivalent of all the computer power available in the United States at that time. And who could have believed a mere ten years ago that millions of homes would contain computers that were purchased for little more than the cost of most standard household appliances. Five years ago having students interact with a microcomputer as readily as they use a textbook was little more than a dream held by a few visionaries. In light of these developments, the futures we have projected do not seem so farfetched after all.

## TEACHING ABOUT ISSUES

One of the most exciting subjects for discussion to come up in recent years is that of computer ethics. The movie *War Games* caught the fancy of young and old alike and caused people to ask questions that most hadn't thought of before. Newspapers regularly run articles on computer crime and the international theft of technology. Many families have been touched by the on-rushing third wave —in some instances it has meant a loss of jobs, in other cases new and exciting careers have opened up. There can be no doubt that our general awareness level is higher now than ever before concerning computers and their impact on society. It seems appropriate to face the issues head on in the best of all places—the classroom.

Most educators agree that computer ethics is not a subject that lends itself to ready conclusions—right and wrong are often hard to distinguish. What is more important than firm conclusions, however, is the process involved as classes get caught up in dilemmas. The idea is to present short scenarios whose outcomes vary according to specific actions taken; as a result of these actions, legal and moral ramifications arise that lead to additional discussion and research, and the pattern continues to widen. Those who are most successful at teaching about issues do few of the traditional things. Instead, they stir things up a bit and then let the students take over. In essence, they identify issues, discuss typical instances of questionable computer-related activities, and describe some dilemmas; then they become moderators.

This is an excellent time to acquaint students with various laws that impact on computer-related activities. For example, the amended copyright law deals directly with such activities as the copying of commercial programs. As the discussion evolves, it may be constrained and focused somewhat by the framework created by the set of appropriate laws. However, the fact that certain laws exist should not discourage students from proposing a different, possibly more desirable, alternative. Also, the discussion need not always center around what is; it might evolve around the best and worst possible technological futures.

Many discussion topics are offered in this chapter, but other sources, such as newspaper articles and actual experiences, should be considered. An invaluable source of information on computer-related crime is the publication from the Criminal Justice Section of the American Bar Association entitled *Report on Computer Crime,* which can be obtained for $9.00 (prepaid) from Order Fulfillment 509, American Bar Association, 750 North Lake Shore Drive, Chicago, IL 60611, Order Number PC: 509-0017-01. The students themselves are often another good source of topics. Many are able to offer a variety of suggestions that can be enlarged upon in the classroom, such as the following actual examples. One girl talked about the fact that her mother, a stenographer, was attending a seminar to learn word processing in order to keep her job. A second girl wondered how it is that so much personalized mail reaches her home from companies her family has never heard of. A boy brought up the fact that his parents are angry with the computer at the natural gas company because it cannot seem to provide accurate bills. Another boy has heard his father, who works for a computer firm, express concern that some of the high-tech developments may have been stolen by a former employee. Still another student mentioned a newspaper article in which a hacker admitted to breaking into private data bases on over one hundred occasions. Student-generated concerns such as these provide a point of departure for class discussions.

Discussions can take the form of dilemmas—short scenarios involving imaginary individuals confronted with a computer-related problem. Various courses of action are provided, with different consequences accruing from each. The dilemmas are typically conceived by the teacher, but students are perfectly capable of generating their own. For more information on this approach, together with sample dilemmas, refer to the article "Teaching Ethics in the Computer Classroom," by Hannah and Matus. As the discussions progress, students frequently take sides, and things begin to heat up. On the other hand, activities can also slow down considerably as interest in a given topic wanes. In any case, the teacher must be actively involved in guiding and encouraging the discussion, at the same time avoiding the imposition of personal values or conclusions on the students. This takes practice, but the results can definitely be worth the effort.

## SUMMARY

Emphasis has been placed on the technological aspects of computer use to the near exclusion of related social and ethical issues. However, a growing awareness of the importance of these latter issues has caused many scholars and leaders to suggest that the schools assume a major part of the responsibility for addressing them. In order to involve students in meaningful discussions, teachers must be aware of the various issues involved. In this chapter we outlined several topics that can serve as the basis for class activities. A concern that is particularly pertinent to educators is how the computer will influence both how and what students learn. Computer crime, which continues to make headlines as money and goods are stolen through ingenious schemes involving individuals knowledgeable about computers, is another important subject to consider.

Technology is a big commodity for computer thieves, with both foreign and domestic organizations paying premium prices for stolen secrets. Less skillful thieves simply fill their pockets with chips, then turn around and sell them to the highest bidder. Hackers unlock protected data bases with their electronic keys and sometimes create havoc by altering information; at other times they silently slip away, leaving no trace of their unauthorized entry. Issues of privacy arise when masses of personal information—often of a sensitive nature—are accessed by strangers who sometimes use the information for unethical purposes.

As society changes from an industrial to a high-technology orientation, the displacement of certain segments of the work force is bound to take place. The situation is akin to the transition from an agrarian to an industrialized society that took place over a century ago. The question is, will society be better equipped to cope with the current phenomenon than it was the earlier one?

The problem of computer equity continues to persist, despite efforts to make opportunities more widely available to those who are being excluded. Females have traditionally not had the degree of access to computer-related training and jobs that males have enjoyed. Several reasons for this state of affairs have been identified, but the major factor appears to be sexual stereotyping. Socioeconomic status also has a bearing on the extent of a person's computer education. There is a direct correlation between annual income and computer literacy: the higher the income, the more likely a person will be knowledgeable about computers.

Predictions for the future include everything from electronic cottages to biochips that supplement human organs. The implementation of futuristic technologies will surely lead to radical changes in society as it currently exists. This, in turn, will generate social, moral, and ethical problems of a unique nature.

Teaching about issues typically takes the form of a class discussion. A dilemma can be devised by the teacher or students to pose a hypothetical problem with several alternative ways to proceed, each with its own consequences. The teacher serves as a moderator during class activities, offering suggestions, providing information and support, and maintaining control over the discussion as it progresses. Involving students in issue-related activities is a most important function of the schools—although great emphasis has been placed on the acquisition of cognitive knowledge, the area relating to moral issues has been ignored to a large extent. By including activities of this kind in the curriculum a better balance will be obtained, and students will be better able to cope with the technological future, whatever form it may take.

## REFERENCES

Asimov, I. "A Question of Spelling." *Popular Computing* (July 1982): 106–7.

Beyers, C. "Bridging the Gender Gap." *Family Computing* (August 1984): 38–41.

Brady, H. "Artificial Intelligence: What's in It for Educators?" *Classroom Computer Learning* (January 1986): 26–29.

East, P. "Ethical and Social Concerns." In *RUN: Computer Education*, by D. Harper and J. Stewart. Monterey, CA: Brooks/Cole, 1983.

Evans, C. *The Micro Millennium.* New York: Washington Square Press, 1979.

Fersko-Weiss, H. "The Intelligent Computer." *Personal Computing* (October 1985): 62–63, 65, 67–69.

Graham, N. *The Mind Tool.* St. Paul: West Publishing Co., 1986.

Hannah, L., and Matus, C. "Teaching Ethics in the Computer Classroom." *Classroom Computer Learning* (April/May 1984): 32–36.

Hollands, J. *The Silicon Syndrome: A Survival Handbook for Couples.* Palo Alto: Coastline Press, 1983.

Kreidler, W. "Teaching Computer Ethics." *Electronic Learning* (January 1984): 54–57.

Kurland, M. "Computers in Science Fiction." *Popular Computing* (March 1984): 102–9.

Miller, M. "Natural Language Interfaces." *Popular Computing* (June 1985): 52, 55.

Reinhold, F. "Sorting Out the Equity Issues." *Electronic Learning* (February 1985): 33–37.

Tinker, R., ed. *RUN: Computer Education*, by D. Harper and J. Stewart. Monterey, CA: Brooks/Cole, 1983.

Toffler, A. *Future Shock.* New York: Random House, 1970.

———. *The Third Wave.* New York: William Morrow, 1980.

Wyrick, W., Mathews, L., and Mathews, W. "Computer Equity Comes of Age." *Phi Delta Kappan* (January 1982): 314–15.

# A

# GLOSSARY

**Acoustic coupler.** A type of modem that uses the handset of a standard telephone and through which signals are sent to and received from remote computers (see also *Direct-connect modem*).

**Address.** A location within the computer's random access memory (RAM) into which data and instructions can be written and from which they can be read.

**Analog.** Continuous smooth-flowing electrical or physical currents (as opposed to distinct on/off pulses; see *Digital*).

**Applications software.** Programs written for specific applications, such as word processing.

**Arithmetic logic unit (ALU).** The part of the central processing unit that carries out both the arithmetic and the logic operations.

**ASCII Code.** The American Standard Code for Information Interchange; composed of combinations of binary 0s and 1s, this code is used to represent the standard alphanumeric characters (the letters, numbers, and symbols on the keyboard).

**Assembly language.** A low-level language that uses short, mnemonic words instead of the common words used for higher-level languages.

**Authoring language.** A language—PILOT, for example—whose structure lends itself to the in-house development of educational software such as tutorials and drill-and-practice lessons.

**Backup.** A duplicate of a program.

**Bandwidth.** The width, or total range, of the frequencies available for transmission of data on a specific channel (the total up-and-down movement of the wavelength as it is being transmitted).

**BASIC.** Beginner's All-purpose Symbolic Instruction Code—the most commonly used language for microcomputers, generally programmed into the ROM of the microcomputer.

**Baud.** A unit of speed equal to the number of discrete signals per second; that is, the speed at which bits are transmitted (e.g., 300 baud equals 300 bits per second).

**Binary.** The number system that computers use and that consists of the digits 0 and 1.

**Bit.** Stands for binary digit: the smallest unit of information—a 0 or a 1; combined in groups of eight to represent characters (see *Byte*).

**Boot.** Loading the operating system from the disk so large programs can be run; getting the disk operating system (DOS) up and running.

**Bug.** A problem in the program that keeps it from working properly (see *Debug*).

**Byte.** Eight bits combined to represent a coded character (e.g., *A, 8, @*); in some computers the word size is sixteen bits (two bytes) or even thirty-two bits (four bytes).

**Cell.** The space formed by the intersection of each column and row of a spreadsheet.

**Chip.** The small section of silicon that contains the etched-in integrated circuit (see also *Integrated circuit chip*).

**Composite.** A video signal sent to a cathode ray tube that consists of a picture signal, synchronization signal, and screen illumination signal all tied together into pulses that a microcomputer monitor can understand and translate into a picture.

**Computer-assisted instruction (CAI).** The use of computers in education for such exercises as drill and practice, tutorials, instructional games, and simulations.

**Computer-managed instruction (CMI).** The use of the computer for management functions such as diagnostic testing, record keeping, study, prescription generation, and scheduling.

**Courseware.** The program on a disk or tape and the printed material that supports it.

**Cursor.** The block of flashing light (or some other configuration) that indicates where the next character will occur on the screen.

**Daisy wheel printer.** A printing device that uses a matrix with multiple spokes (or petals) upon whose tips the characters are located; these are transferred when the spoke is hit by a small impact device.

**Data base.** A collection of information in a central location that is accessible to remote computers, generally through telephone lines and a modem.

**Debug.** To locate and correct the errors in a program.

**Demodulation.** The process of receiving tones from a transmitted sequence and converting them into electrical pulses that can be understood by the microcomputer (see *Modulation*).

**Digital.** The electronic system utilized by microcomputers that consists of distinct on/off pulses (rather than continuous electrical currents; see *Analog*).

**Direct-connect modem.** The device used to access remote data bases over the phone lines, but bypassing the telephone handset; it is attached directly to the computer and plugs into the phone jack (see also *Acoustic coupler*).

**Disk (or diskette).** A flat, magnetically sensitive storage device employed in the mass storage of data outside the computer; the most common format is currently the five-inch variety (see also *Hard disk*).

**Disk operating system (DOS).** The program that enables the computer and disk drives to work together in the storage and retrieval of data.

**Display.** The visual representation of data or graphics that is viewed on the monitor or TV screen.

**Documentation.** The printed (as well as the software-based) materials that serve as instructions for the proper use of the software and hardware.

**Dot matrix printer.** An impact printer consisting of a matrix of wires that can be activated selectively to form a character.

**Drill and practice.** A type of computer-based instruction that allows students to practice or study information with which they are familiar but not proficient.

**External memory.** Memory that resides outside the computer, such as on disks or tapes.

**Field.** The location of a specific item of information (e.g., a name, a birthdate) in a data base.

**File.** Related collections of data stored together under a common name in some kind of mass storage medium such as a disk.

**Firmware.** Programs in ROM that are wired in when the computer is manufactured (the BASIC interpreter, for example).

**Floppy disk.** See *Disk.*

**Form.** The common format for each record in a data base.

**Frame.** A self-contained visual display seen as a unit on the monitor; a screen.

**Function key.** A key that performs a specified task rather than printing out a character (some computers have numerous function keys and others have very few).

**Graphics.** A computer-generated pictorial display that may also be printed as hard copy; there are two common kinds—high-resolution (fine dots and lines) and low-resolution (blocks).

**Hacker.** Formerly used to describe one who was hooked on computers; now has the negative connotation of one who enters restricted computer data bases and does mischief.

**Hard copy.** Computer output on paper; created through the use of a printer or plotter.

**Hard disk.** A finely machined aluminum disk coated with a magnetic material; capable of holding millions of bytes of data; much faster and more efficient than floppy disks (see *Disk*).

**Hardware.** The mechanical components of the computer system, including the computer, disk drives, monitors, and printers.

**High-level language.** A programming language that uses common words in its vocabulary; must be translated into binary code by a program such as an interpreter or compiler.

**Initialize.** To place DOS commands on, and format the surface of, a new disk so it can store information.

**Inkjet printer.** A nonimpact printer that forms characters by forcing tiny droplets of ink through a matrix of holes.

**Input.** The activity of entering information into the computer; the most common input device is the keyboard.

**Instructional games.** A motivational strategy employed to achieve specific learning objectives that utilizes the unique capabilities of the microcomputer; requires a student to follow prescribed rules and includes some form of competition with either herself, another student, or the computer.

**Integrated circuit chip (IC chip).** The complete electronic system, consisting of transistors, diodes, and other elements formed together on a single silicon chip.

**Interface.** The go-between—such as between a printer and the computer or between two computers—that permits two different parts of the system to work together.

**Kilobyte (K).** When used to indicate computer capacity, K means 1,024 bytes or characters (even though it normally stands for 1,000).

**List.** A display of the actual program as it was written by the programmer.

**Logo.** A discovery-oriented programming language that uses a graphics mode (turtle graphics) for the introduction of geometric concepts; also incorporates a powerful text mode.

**Low-level language.** A symbolic programming language using coded commands rather than common words.

**Machine language.** A code that is directly understood by the computer; instructions and data composed of the binary 0s and 1s the computer deals with directly.

**Mainframe.** A large, powerful computer.

**Memory.** The area in which instructions and data are stored; also holds the results of processing (see *Random access memory* and *Read only memory*).

**Microcomputer system.** A system that consists of at least a microcomputer, a monitor, and an external storage device and that may also include additional peripheral devices.

**Microprocessor.** The part of a microcomputer that actually does the computing; a processor on a single chip.

**Modem.** Stands for modulator-demodulator: the device that not only converts binary code into audio signals that can be transmitted over telephone lines but also does the converse for input to the computer (see *Acoustic coupler; Direct-connect modem*).

**Modulation.** The process whereby signals are made compatible with telephone communication facilities; basically, changing digital to analog signals (see *Demodulation*).

**Monitor.** A video display device based on a cathode ray tube.

**Motherboard.** A printed circuit board containing the slots into which are plugged the various circuit boards that accommodate the addition of peripheral devices to the microcomputer system; can also be called a card cage.

**Mouse.** An input device used in place of the keyboard for certain functions such as selecting from a menu.

**Network.** Several computers and their peripherals that work together, over distances, through a common set of connections.

**Nonvolatile.** Used to describe memory that is not erased when power is removed (see *Read only memory*).

**Operating system.** A program that permits the computer to operate effectively with its peripherals; the disk operating system (DOS) is the most familiar variety.

**Output.** The information sent from the computer to any kind of peripheral (such as a monitor or printer).

**Parallel.** A way of managing the transmission and storage of a byte so all bits are handled together as a unit (see also *Serial*).

**Pascal.** A high-level, block-structured programming language consisting of two parts: a heading, which names the program and specifies the variables it will use, and the body of the program, subdivided into six sections.

**Peripheral.** An electronic device that is part of the total system but separate from the actual microcomputer (printer, monitor, and such).

**PILOT.** Programmed Inquiry Learning or Teaching—an interactive computer language that employs text editor, graphics editor, and music editor capabilities, thereby enabling teachers without prior computer experience to develop and test dialog programs for classroom application.

**Pixel.** Stands for picture element: an illuminated dot on the monitor screen.

**Port.** The electronic circuitry through which data enters and leaves the computer.

**Printer.** The peripheral device connected to the computer to produce output on paper (hard copy).

**Program.** The sequence of instructions designed to make the computer carry out a given task.

**Random access memory (RAM).** The internal storage area of the computer in which instructions and data are stored temporarily; volatile memory that can be accessed directly and altered by the user; the computer's working memory.

**Read only memory (ROM).** The internal storage area in which programs are placed at the time the computer is manufactured; nonvolatile memory that cannot be changed (though there are exceptions).

**Record.** A collection of fields in a data base.

**Scrolling.** The movement of a program either horizontally or vertically on the display screen.

**Serial.** The method of transmitting data one bit after the other (see also *Parallel*).

**Simulation.** A kind of computer-based instruction that allows students to interact with models of reality that may otherwise be impossible, dangerous, or impractical.

**Software.** The programs that provide instructions to the computer.

**Station.** An area, such as a study carrel, where a microcomputer system is housed for student use.

**Telecommunications.** Communication over distances via the telephone lines or reserved lines.

**Terminal.** A keyboard and monitor used to communicate with a remote computer.

**Thermal printer.** A printer that uses heated wires in a matrix to form characters on sensitized paper.

**Tutorial.** A type of computer-assisted instruction that utilizes the computer to present a concept that a learner does not yet know, presenting the lesson in segmented, individualized steps.

**User friendly.** Used to refer to a computer or program that operates in human terms rather than forcing the user to operate on the machine's terms; also, the tolerance of the system for user mistakes.

**Volatile.** A term used to describe RAM and other memories that lose their contents when power is removed.

**Word.** The unit of data, made up of a specified number of parallel bits, with which the computer works; the size of a word depends upon the kind of computer (e.g., eight-bit, sixteen-bit) being used.

**Word processing.** Using a computer and special software to write and correct various kinds of text materials.

# B

# SOFTWARE PUBLISHERS

Academic Hallmarks
P.O. Box 998
Durango, CO 81301

Academy Software
P.O. Box 6277
San Rafael, CA 94901

Addison-Wesley Publishing Co.
2725 Sand Hill Rd.
Menlo Park, CA 94025

Advanced Ideas, Inc.
2550 Ninth St.
Suite 104
Berkeley, CA 94710

Agricultural Software Consultants, Inc.
P.O. Box 32
Kingsville, TX 78363

Ahead Designs
699 North Vulcan 88
Encinitas, CA 92024

Aims Media
6901 Woodley Ave.
Van Nuys, CA 91406

Alkazar Associates
2638 S. Lynn St.
Arlington, VA 22202

American Educational Computer, Inc.
2450 Embarcadero Way
Palo Alto, CA 94303

American Systems Development, Inc.
403 E. Diamond Ave.
Gaithersburg, MD 20877

Ann Arbor Software Associates
407 N. Main
Ann Arbor, MI 48104

The Answer in Computers
Suite 7
6035 University Ave.
San Diego, CA 92115

Apple Computer, Inc.
20525 Mariani Ave.
Cupertino, CA 95014

Artificial Intelligence Research Group
921 N. La Jolla Ave.
Los Angeles, CA 90046

Artsci, Inc.
5547 Satsuma Ave.
North Hollywood, CA 91601

Artworx Software Co.
150 N. Main St.
Fairport, NY 14450

Atari, Inc.
390 Caribbean Dr.
Sunnyvale, CA 94089

ATC Software
Route 2, Box 475
Estill Springs, TN 37330

A/V Concepts Corp.
30 Montauk Blvd.
Oakdale, NY 11769

Avant-Garde
P.O. Box 30160
Eugene, OR 97403

Barron Enterprises
714 Willow Glen Rd.
Santa Barbara, CA 93105

Basics and Beyond, Inc.
Box 10
Pinesbridge Rd.
Amawalk, NY 10501

Batteries Included
30 Mural St.
Richmond Hill, Ontario
L4B 1B5 Canada

Baudville
1001 Medical Park Dr., S.E.
Grand Rapids, MI 49506

Behavioral Engineering
230 Mt. Hermon Rd., #207
Scotts Valley, CA 95066

BLS, Inc.
2503 Fairlee Rd.
Wilmington, DE 19810

Borland International
4113 Scotts Valley Dr.
Scotts Valley, CA 95066

Brainbank, Inc.
220 Fifth Ave.
New York, NY 10001

Broderbund Software
17 Paul Dr.
San Rafael, CA 94903

The Cactusplot Co.
1442 N. McAllister
Tempe, AZ 85281

Cardco, Inc.
300 S. Topeka
Wichita, KS 67202

Career Publishing, Inc.
936 N. Main St.
P.O. Box 5486
Orange, CA 92667

Centurian Industries, Inc.
1526 Main St.
Redwood City, CA 94063

Children's Computer Workshop
1 Lincoln Plaza
New York, NY 10023

Classroom Consortia Media, Inc.
57 Bay St.
Staten Island, NY 10301

Commodore International
1200 Wilson Dr.
West Chester, PA 19380

COMpress
P.O. Box 102
Wentworth, NH 03282

Compu-tations, Inc.
P.O. Box 502
Troy, MI 48099

Conduit
The University of Iowa
Oakdale Campus
Iowa City, IA 52242

The Continental Press, Inc.
520 E. Bainbridge St.
Elizabethtown, PA 17022

Control Data Publishing Co.
Box O
8100 34th Ave. South
Minneapolis, MN 55440

Counterpoint Software
4005 W. 65th St.
Minneapolis, MN 55435

Courseware, Inc.
10075 Carroll Canyon Rd.
San Diego, CA 92131

Creative Programming
28990 W. Pacific Coast Hwy.
Suite 109
Malibu, CA 90265

Cross Cultural Software
5385 Elrose Ave.
San Jose, CA 93614

Cross Educational Software
1802 N. Trenton
P.O. Box 1536
Ruston, LA 71270

Curriculum Applications
P.O. Box 264
Arlington, MA 02174

Curriculum Associates
5 Esquire Rd.
N. Billerica, MA 01862

Cygnus Software
8002 E. Culver
Mesa, AZ 85207

Data Command
329 E. Court St.
P.O. Box 548
Kankakee, IL 60901

Data Processing Educational
  Corporation (DPEC)
4588 Kenny Rd.
Columbus, OH 43220

Data Transforms, Inc.
616 Washington St., Suite 106
Denver, CO 80203

E. David & Associates
22 Russett Ln.
Storrs, CT 06268

Davidson & Associates
3135 Kashiwa St.
Torrance, CA 90505

DCH Software
D.C. Heath & Company
125 Spring St.
Lexington, MA 02173

DEC Computing
5307 Lynnwood Dr.
West Lafayette, IN 47906

DesignWare, Inc.
185 Berry St., Suite 158
San Francisco, CA 94107

Dorsett Educational Systems
Box 1226
Norman, OK 73070

Educational Activities, Inc.
P.O. Box 392
Freeport, NY 11520

Educational Development Corp.
8141 E. 44th St.
P.O. Box 470663
Tulsa, OK 74145

EduSoft
P.O. Box 2560
Berkeley, CA 94702

Edu-Ware, Inc.
P.O. Box 22222
28035 Dorothy Dr.
Agoura, CA 91301

Electronic Arts
2755 Campus Dr.
San Mateo, CA 94403

Electronic Courseware Systems, Inc.
309 Windsor Rd.
Champaign, IL 61820

Encyclopaedia Britannica Educational
  Corp.
425 North Michigan Ave.
Chicago, IL 60611

Essertier Software Corp.
1020 Manhattan Beach Blvd., Suite 200
Manhattan Beach, CA 90266

Europro
P.O. Box 390605
Mountain View, CA 94039

Fliptrack Learning Systems
999 Main St.
Glen Ellyn, IL 60137

Focus Media, Inc.
839 Stewart Ave.
Garden City, NY 11530

Gamco Industries, Inc.
P.O. Box 1911
Big Spring, TX 79721

Ginn & Co.
191 Spring St.
Lexington, MA 02173

Grolier Electronic Publishing, Inc.
95 Madison Ave., Suite 407
New York, NY 10016

Hartley Courseware, Inc.
123 Bridge St., Box 431
Dimondale, MI 48821

Hayden Software Co.
600 Suffolk St.
Lowell, MA 01854

Hesware
150 N. Hill Dr.
Brisbane, CA 94005

Houghton Mifflin Co.
1 Beacon St.
Boston, MA 02108

Human Relations Media Software
   (HRM)
175 Tompkins Ave.
Pleasantville, NY 10570

HUMANS, Inc.
P.O. Box 82
Evington, VA 24550

IBM (see *International Business Machines
   Corp.*)

Ideaware, Inc.
225 Lafayette St., Suite 607
New York, NY 10012

Individual Software, Inc.
1163-I Chess Dr.
Foster City, CA 94404

Intellectual Software
798 North Ave.
Bridgeport, CT 06606

Interlearn
P.O. Box 342
Cardiff by the Sea, CA 92007

International Business Machines Corp.
   (IBM)
Entry Systems Div.
P.O. Box 1328
Boca Raton, FL 33432

Island Software
Dept. H, P.O. Box 300
Lake Grove, NY 11755

J & S Software, Inc.
14 Vanderventer Ave.
Port Washington, NY 11050

JMH Software of Minnesota, Inc.
P.O. Box 41308
Minneapolis, MN 55441

Kidsware
117 Sheridan St.
Boston, MA 02130

Koala Technologies Corp.
3100 Patrick Henry Dr.
Santa Clara, CA 95050

Krell Software Corp.
1320 Stony Brook Rd., Suite 219
Stony Brook, NY 11790

K-12 Micro Media, Inc.
172 Broadway
Woodcliff Lakes, NJ 07675

L & S Computerware
1589 Fraser Dr.
Sunnyvale, CA 94086

The Learning Company
545 Middlefield Rd., Suite 170
Menlo Park, CA 94025

Learning Technologies
4255 LBJ Freeway, Suite 131
Dallas, TX 75244

Learning Well
200 S. Service Rd.
Roslyn Heights, NY 11577

Lightspeed Software
2124 Kittredge St., Suite 185
Berkeley, CA 94704

MCE, Inc.
157 S. Kalamazoo Mall, Suite 250
Kalamazoo, MI 49007

McGraw-Hill
1221 Avenue of the Americas
New York, NY 10020

Melodian
115 Broadway, Rm. 1202
New York, NY 10006

Metier
P.O. Box 51204
San Jose, CA 95151

Microcomputer Workshops
225 Westchester Ave.
Port Chester, NY 10573

Micro-Ed Inc.
P.O. Box 444005
Eden Prairie, MN 55344

MicroLab
2699 Skokie Valley Rd.
Highland Park, IL 60035

Micro Learningware
Hwy. 66 S., P.O. Box 307
Mankato, MN 56001

Microphys
1737 W. Second St.
Brooklyn, NY 11223

Microsoft Corporation
10700 Northrup Way
Bellevue, WA 98004

Midwest Software
Box 214
Farmington, MI 48024

Milliken Publishing Co.
Computer Products Div.
1100 Research Blvd.
Saint Louis, MO 63132

Mindscape, Inc.
3444 Dundee Rd.
Northbrook, IL 60062

Minnesota Educational Computing
    Consortium (MECC)
3490 Lexington Ave., North
St. Paul, MN 55112

Miracle Computing
313 Clayten Ct.
Lawrence, KS 66044

MUSE Software
347 N. Charles St.
Baltimore, MD 21201

Power Up!
P.O. Box 306
125 Main St.
Half Moon Bay, CA 94019

Practicorp
44 Oak St.
The Silk Mill
Newton Upper Falls, MA 02164

Prentice-Hall
P.O. Box 819
Englewood Cliffs, NJ 07632

Program Design, Inc. (PDI)
95 E. Putnam Ave.
Greenwich, CT 06830

Quark, Inc.
2525 West Evans, Suite 220
Denver, CO 80219

Queue, Inc.
5 Chapel Hill Dr.
Fairfield, CT 06432

Radio Shack Education Div.
1400 One Tandy Center
Fort Worth, TX 76102

Random House School Div.
400 Hahn Rd.
Westminster, MD 21157

The Regents/ALA Co.
2 Park Ave.
New York, NY 10016

Right On Programs
140 East Main
Huntington, NY 11743

Howard W. Sams & Co., Inc.
4300 W. 62nd St.
Indianapolis, IN 46206

Scarborough Systems, Inc.
55 So. Broadway
Tarrytown, NY 10591

Scholastic, Inc.
730 Broadway
New York, NY 10003

Science Research Associates, Inc. (SRA)
155 N. Wacker Dr.
Chicago, IL 60606

Shenandoah Systems
1111 Mt. Clinton Pike
Harrisonburg, VA 22801

Sierra On-Line, Inc.
Sierra On-Line Bldg.
P.O. Box 485
Coursegold, CA 93614

Sight & Sound Music Software
P.O. Box 27
New Berlin, WI 53151

Silver Burdett Co.
250 James St.
Morristown, NJ 07960

Simpac Educational Systems
1105 North Main St., Suite 11-C
Gainesville, FL 32601

Sirius Software, Inc.
10364 Rockingham Dr.
Sacramento, CA 95827

Sliwa Enterprises
2360-J George Washington Hwy.
Yorktown, VA 23692

Society for Visual Education, Inc. (SVE)
1345 Diversey Pkwy.
Chicago, IL 60014

Software Arts
27 Mica Ln.
Wellesley, MA 02181

Software Publishing Corp. (PFS)
1901 Landings Dr.
Mountain View, CA 94043

South-Western Publ. Co.
5101 Madison Rd.
Cincinnati, OH 45227

Spinnaker Software Corp.
One Kendall Square
Cambridge, MA 02139

Springboard Software
7807 Creekridge Cir.
Minneapolis, MN 55435

SubLOGIC Corp.
713 Edgebrook Dr.
Champaign, IL 61820

Sunburst Communications
39 Washington Ave.
Pleasantville, NY 10570

Synapse Software
5221 Central Ave.
Richmond, CA 94804

Synergistic Software
830 N. Riverside Dr., Suite 20
Renton, WA 98055

Teach Yourself by Computer Software
2128 W. Jefferson Rd.
Pittsford, NY 14534

Terrapin, Inc.
222 Third St.
Cambridge, MA 02142

Timeworks, Inc.
405 Lake Cook Rd.
Deerfield, IL 60015

Total Information Education Systems
  (TIES)
1925 W. County Rd., B2
Saint Paul, MN 55113

Touch Technologies
609 South Escondido Blvd., Suite 101
Escondido, CA 92025

Versa Computing Inc.
3541 Old Conejo Rd., #104
Newbury Park, CA 91320

Wadsworth Electronic Publishing Co.
10 Davis Dr.
Belmont, CA 94002

Weekly Reader Family Software
245 Long Hill Rd.
Middletown, CT 06457

John Wiley and Sons
605 Third Ave.
New York, NY 10158

Zephyr Services
306 S. Homewood Ave.
Pittsburgh, PA 15208

# C

# SOURCES OF FREE OR INEXPENSIVE SOFTWARE

American Software Publishing Company
1010 16th Street, N.W.
Washington, DC 20037

Boston Computer Society
Three Central Plaza
Boston, MA 02108

Center for Math Literacy
San Francisco State University
1600 Holloway Avenue
San Francisco, CA 94132

Chicago Public Library
North Pulaski Branch
4041 West North Avenue
Chicago, IL 60639

Commodore International Ltd.
(consult local dealers for public domain
    software)

CONDUIT
P.O. Box 388
Iowa City, IA 52244

COSMIC
112 Barrow Hall
University of Georgia
Athens, GA 30602

Jack Davis
% The Learning Center
College of Education
Gabel 8, Northern Illinois University
De Kalb, IL 60115

Educational Computing Network
12680 Hollyglen
Riverside, CA 92503

"Educational Programs for Children"
Report FP01
P.O. Box 611
Palmyra, NJ 08065

Enrich/Ohaus
2325 Paragon Drive
San Jose, CA 95131
(catalogs for free software for Apple, Atari,
    Commodore and TI99/4A are $8.95
    each)

First Osborne Users Group (FOG)
P.O. Box 11683-A
Palo Alto, CA 94306

FOLLK, Friends of LISP/Logo & Kids
436 Arballo Drive
San Francisco, CA 94132

Georgia Micro Swap
Department of Math Education
University of Georgia
Athens, GA 30601
(users must donate programs in order to
    receive programs)

International Apple Corps
P.O. Box 2227
Seattle, WA 98111
(contact local Apple computer clubs for
    additional information)

International Home Computer Users
    Association (ICA)
P.O. Box 371
Rancho Santa Fe, CA 92067

Micro-Ed
P.O. Box 24156
Minneapolis, MN 55424

Micro X Change
Suite 101
222 East Carrillo Street
Santa Barbara, CA 93101

National LOGO Exchange
P.O. Box 5341
Charlottesville, VA 22905
*(send stamped, self-addressed envelope)*

National Technical Information Service
Springfield, VA 22161

New York Amateur Computer Club
P.O. Box 106, Church Street Station
New York, NY 10008
*(catalog of public domain software for IBM
   personal computer and compatibles)*

Nibble Magazine
P.O. Box 325
Lincoln, MA 01773

North Central Regional Library
Software Library Mail-Order
   Department
238 Olds Station Road
Wenatchee, WA 98801

Northwest Kaypro Users Group
% Charles Hornisher Communications
4700 Southwest MacAdam Avenue
Portland, OR 97201

Oklahoma Educational Computer Users
   Program (OECUP)
University of Oklahoma
601 Elm Street
Norman, OK 73019

PC Software Interest Group
1556 Halform Avenue, Suite 130B
Santa Clara, CA 95051

People's Computer Company
Computertown, USA!
P.O. Box E
Menlo Park, CA 91025
*(consult your local area for additional
   addresses of Computertown, USA!)*

Public Domain Software (for Atari)
297 Missouri Street
San Francisco, CA 94107
*(consult your local dealers for additional
   addresses)*

Queue, Inc.
Five Chapel Hill Drive
Fairfield, CT 06432

Ryan Library
Iona College
New Rochelle, NY 10801

San Francisco Apple Core
1515 Sloat Blvd. #2
San Francisco, CA 94132

SOFTSWAP
% Ann Lathrop, Library Coordinator
San Mateo County Office of Education
333 Main Street
Redwood City, CA 94063

Technology Communications Group
38 Melrose Place
Montclair, NJ 07042

# D

# SOFTWARE GUIDES, CATALOGS, AND REVIEWS

Allenbach Industries (*Software Reports*)
2101 Las Palmas
Carlsbad, CA 92008

American Peripherals
122 Bangor Street
Lindenhurst, NY 11757

*California Library Media Consortium
    Reviews*
San Mateo County, Office of Education
333 Main Street
Redwood City, CA 94063

Computer Information Exchange
P.O. Box 159
San Luis Rey, CA 92068

*The Computing Teacher*
Department of Computer and
    Information Science
University of Oregon
Eugene, OR 97403

*Courseware Report Card*
Elementary and Secondary Editions
Educational Insights
150 West Carob Street
Compton, CA 90220

*Curriculum Products Review*
530 University Avenue
Palo Alto, CA 94301

Data Text Company
Dresden Associates
P.O. Box 246
Dresden, ME 04342

*Digest of Software Reviews*
1341 Bulldog Lane, Suite C
Fresno, CA 93710

DISC Project
IICD Oakland Schools
2100 Pontiac Lake Road
Pontiac, MI 48054

*Dvorak's Software Review*
704 Solano Avenue
Albany, CA 94706

Educational Insights
150 West Carob Street
Compton, CA 90220

EduSoft
Department EE, Box 2560
Berkeley, CA 94702

Edu-Soft
4639 Spruce Street
Philadelphia, PA 19139

Elsevier
Science Publishing Company, Inc.
New York, NY 10017

*EPIE Evaluations*
Educational Products Information
    Exchange
P.O. Box 839
Water Mill, NY 11976

Follett Library Book Company
Microcomputer Division
4506 Northwest Highway
Crystal Lake, IL 60014

*Huntington Computing Catalog*
Box 1297
Corcoran, CA 93212

*ICP Software Directory*
International Computer Programs Inc.
9000 Keystone Crossing, P.O. Box
    40946
Indianapolis, IN 46240

*International Microcomputer Software
    Directory*
420 South Howes Street
Fort Collins, CO 80521

*Instant Software*
80 Pine Street
Peterborough, NH 03458

J. M. Hammett Company
Microcomputer Division
Box 545
Braintree, MA 02184

*Journal of Courseware Review*
The Foundation for the Advancement
    of Computer-aided Education
    (FACE)
20525 Mariana Avenue
Cupertino, CA 95014

*K-12 Micro Media*
P.O. Box 17, Department G
Valley Cottage, NY 10989

Linc Associates
1875 Morse Road, Suite 215
Columbus, OH 43229

Marck
280 Linden Avenue
Brandon, CT 06405

*Microcomputer Corporation Catalog*
34 Maple Avenue, Box 8
Armonk, NY 10504

*Microcomputers in Education Newsletter*
Queue, Inc.
Five Chapel Hill Drive
Fairfield, CT 06432

MicroSift, N.W. Regional Educational
    Library
500 Lindsay Blvd.
710 S.W. Second Avenue
Portland, OR 97204

MicroWorld
*Microcomputer Vendor Directory*
Auerbach Publishers Inc.
6560 North Park Dr.
Pennsauken, NJ 08109

*MISCO, Inc.*
Box 399
Holmdel, NJ 07733

*Online Micro-Software Guide and Directory*
Online Inc.
11 Tannery Lane
Weston, CT 06883

Opportunities for Learning, Inc.
8950 Lurline Avenue, Dept. 6 FM
Chattsworth, CA 91311

*PC: The Buyer's Guide*
Ziff-Davis
One Park Avenue
New York, NY 10016

*PC Clearinghouse—Software Directory*
PC Clearinghouse
Middleburg, VA 22117

*PC Telemart Software Directory*
PC Telemart
11781 Lee Jackson Highway
Fairfax, VA 22033

*PC Telemart/Vanlove's Apple Software
    Directory*
PC Telemart/Vanloves
Suite 108
8575 West 110th Street
Overland Park, KS 66210

*Personal Software*
Hajgden Publishing Company, Inc.
50 Essex Street
Rochelle Park, NJ 07662

*Pipeline—Conduit*
University of Iowa
P.O. Box 388
Iowa City, IA 52244

*Queue*
Five Chapel Hill Drive
Fairfield, CT 06432

*Scholastic Inc.*
904 Sylvan Avenue
Englewood Cliffs, NJ 07632

*School Microware Reviews*
Dresden Associates
Box 246
Dresden, ME 04342

*Series Eighty Software Catalog*
Reston Publishing Company, Inc.
11480 Sunset Hills Road
Reston, VA 22090

*Society for Visual Education (SVE) Catalog*
35 East Wacker Drive
Chicago, IL 60601

Sofsearch
Route 20, Box 3572
Gladiolus Drive
Fort Myers, FL 33908

Softtalk Publisher, Inc.
7250 Laurel Canyon Blvd.
Hollywood, CA 91603

*The Software Catalog*
Elsevier Science Publishing Company
52 Vanderbilt Avenue
New York, NY 10017

*The Software Directory*
Software Central
Box 30424
Lincoln, NE 68503

*Software Reports*
Trade Service Publications
10996 Torreyena Road
P.O. Box 85007
San Diego, CA 92138

*Software Reports*
Allenbach Industries
2101 Las Palmas
Carlsbad, CA 92008

Special Education Technical Online
    Resources
Exceptional Child Center
Utah State University
Logan, UT 84322

*The Specialware Directory*
Oryx Press
2214 North Central at Encanto
Phoenix, AZ 85004

Sterling Swift Publishing Company
P.O. Box 188
Manchaca, TX 78652

*Swift's Educational Software Directory*
Sterling Swift Publishing Company
7901 South IH-35
Austin, TX 78744

*TRS-80 Agricultural Software Sourcebook*
*TRS-80 Educational Software Sourcebook*
*(available at Radio Shack Computer Centers*
    *—consult your local stores)*

*TRS-80 Users Journal*
Box 7112
Tacoma, WA 98407

User's
2520 Broadway Drive
Saint Paul, MN 55113

# E

# COMPUTER MAGAZINES AND NEWSLETTERS

*Apple Education News*
P.O. Box 20485
San Jose, CA 95160

*Apple Educator's Newsletter*
9525 Lucerne
Ventura, CA 93003

*Arithmetic Teacher Magazine*
1906 Association Drive
Reston, VA 22091

*Byte*
70 Main Street
Peterborough, NH 03458

*Classroom Computer Learning*
Peter Li, Inc.
2451 East River Road
Dayton, OH 45439

*Classroom Computer News*
International Education
51 Spring Street
Watertown, MA 02172

*Compute! Magazine*
P.O. Box 5406
Greenshore, NC 27403

*The Computing Teacher*
Department of Computer and
    Information Science
University of Oregon
Eugene, OR 97403

*Creative Computing*
Box 789-M
Morristown, NJ 07690

*CUE Newsletter*
% Don McKell
Computer-Using Educators
Box 18547
San Jose, CA 95158

*Education Computer News*
1300 North 17th Street
Suite 1600
Arlington, VA 22209

*Educational Computer Magazine*
P.O. Box 535
Cupertino, CA 95015

*Educational Resources and Techniques*
    *Magazine*
Texas Association for Educational
    Technology
Eastfield College
3737 Motley Drive
Mesquite, TX 75150

*Educational Technology*
140 Sylvan Avenue
Englewood Cliffs, NJ 07632

*Electronic Education*
Electronic Communications, Inc.
1311 Executive Center Drive, Suite 200
Tallahassee, FL 32316

*Electronic Learning*
Scholastic, Inc.
P.O. Box 644
Lyndhurst, NJ 07071-9985

*Family Computing*
730 Broadway
New York, NY 10003

*MACUL Journal*
Michigan Association for Computer
    Users in Learning
Wayne County, ISD
33500 Van Born Road
Wayne, MI 48184

*Mathematics Teacher*
National Council of Teachers of
    Mathematics
1906 Association Drive
Reston, VA 22091

*Microcomputers in Education Queue*
Five Chapel Hill Drive
Fairfield, CT 06432

*Personal Computing*
P.O. Box 2941
Boulder, CO 90321

*Pipeline*
P.O. Box 388
Iowa City, IA 52244

*Popular Computing*
70 Main Street
Peterborough, NH 03458

*School Microcomputer Bulletin*
Learning Publications, Inc.
P.O. Box 1326
Holmes Beach, FL 33509

*Teaching and Computers*
P.O. Box 644
Lyndhurst, NJ 07071-9985

*Technical Educational Research Centers*
    (TERC)
Monograph Series
1696 Massachusetts Avenue
Cambridge, MA 02138

*T.H.E. Magazine*
Information Synergy, Inc.
P.O. Box 992
Acton, MA 01720

# F

# USER GROUPS

Interested individuals should contact their local dealers for information about user groups involved with specific kinds of computers (International Applecore, for example, specializes in the Apple Computer). The following list of state educational user groups is not complete, but it represents a cross section of active organizations that should be helpful. For additional information contact the various state departments of education.

ACES, Computer Center
205 Skiff Street
Hamden, CT 06514

Board of Cooperative Educational
  Services (BOCES)
Statewide Instructional Computing
  Network
Mexico, NY 13114

Computer Information Exchange
P.O. Box 159
San Luis Rey, CA 92068

Computer Learners, Users, Educators
  Association (CLUES)
50 Nellis Drive
Wayne, NJ 07047

Computer Resources, Inc.
Route 4
Barrington, NH 03825

Computer Users in Education
Box 27561
Phoenix, AZ 85061

Computer Using Educators (CUE)
Box 18547
San Jose, CA 95133

DC AEDS
2216 Rand Place, N.E.
Washington, DC 20002

Educational Computing Consortium of
  Ohio (ECCO)
4777 Farnhurst Road
Cleveland, OH 44124

Florida Center for Instructional
  Computing
College of Education
University of Florida
Tampa, FL 33620

Harvard Graduate School of Education
Monroe C. Gutman Library
Appian Way
Cambridge, MA 02138

HumRRO
300 North Washington Street
Alexandria, VA 22314

Illinois AEDS
Box 128
DeKalb, IL 60115

Indiana Computer Educators
1230 South Clinton
Fort Wayne, IN 46825

Institute for Educational Research (IER)
793 North Main Street
Glen Ellyn, IL 60137

International Institute of Applied
   Technology, Inc.
2121 Wisconsin Avenue, N.W., Suite 400
Washington, DC 20007

Iowa AEDS
Educational Computer Center
500 College Drive
Mason City, IA 50401

Maryland Association for the
   Educational Uses of the Computer
   (MAEUC)
% Catonville Community College
800 S. Rolling Road
Baltimore, MD 21228

Michigan Association for Computer
   Users in Learning
Wayne County ISD
33500 Van Born Road
Wayne, MI 48184

Michigan Educational Resources
   Information Center
Microcomputer Resource Center
Library of Michigan, Dept. of Education
P.O. Box 30007
Lansing, MI 48909

Mid-South AEDS
EBAS, COE, Memphis State University
Memphis, TN 38152

Minnesota Educational Computing
   Consortium (MECC)
2520 Broadway Drive
Saint Paul, MN 55113

National Council of Teachers of
   Mathematics
1906 Association Drive
Reston, VA 22091

Nebraska AEDS
Educational Service Unit #3
4224 South 133rd Street
Omaha, NE 68137

New Hampshire Association for
   Computer Education Statewide
   (NHACES)
Computer Service, Stoke Hall
University of New Hampshire
Durham, NH 03824

New York State AEDS
% Ardsley High School
500 Farm Road
Ardsley, NY 10502

North Carolina AEDS
% Department of Education
116 West Edenton Street
Raleigh, NC 27611

North Dakota Association of School
   Administrators
Divide County School District #1
Box G
Crosby, ND 58730

Northwest Council for Computer
   Education
Computer Center, Eastern Oregon State
   College
LeGrande, OR 97850

Ohio AEDS
6391 Maxtown Road
Westerville, OH 43081

PIE, Corporation for Public
   Information in Education
1714 Illinois
Lawrence, KS 66044

Project Direct
100 Hillside Road
Greenville, DE 19807

South Micro Systems for Educators
P.O. Box 1981
Burlington, NC 27215

Technical Education Resources Center
   (TERC)
Computing Resource Center
8 Eliot Street
Cambridge, MA 02138

Texas AEDS
Box 632
Austin, TX 78767

Texas Computer Educators Association
Box 2573
Austin, TX 78768

UNICOM
297 Elmwood Avenue
Providence, RI 02907

Utah Council for Computers in
    Education (UCCE)
1295 North 1200
West Mapleton, UT 84663

Wisconsin AEDS
Racine Public Schools
Racine, WI 53404

Wyoming Educational Computing
    Council
Laramie County School District #1
2810 House Street
Cheyenne, WY 82001

# G

# TELECOMMUNICATION

CompuServe is located at 5000 Arlington Centre Blvd., Columbus, OH 43222, (614) 457-8650. It costs $39.95 for the initial sign-up, with no monthly minimum charge. The hourly rates run from $6.00 per hour (300 baud) to $12.50 per hour (1,200 baud). Both MicroNet and CompuServe are accessed through the same telephone number.

The Source (Source Telecomputing Corporation), a subsidiary of *Reader's Digest*, is located at 1616 Anderson Road, McLean, VA 22102, (800) 336-3366. The sign-up cost is $100.00, with a $10.00 monthly minimum. The hourly rates are $7.75 (300 baud) to $10.75 (1,200 baud) from 6 P.M. to 5 A.M.; daytime rates (7 A.M. to 6 P.M.) are much higher—$20.75 to $25.75.

Delphi is located at 3 Blackstone Street, Cambridge, MA 02139 (800) 544-4005. Their sign-up cost is $49.95 with no monthly minimum; hourly rates are $6.00 (6 P.M. to 8 A.M.) and $16.00 (peak daytime hours) for both 300 and 1,200 baud.

The headquarters of Dialog Information Services, Inc. is located at 3460 Hillview Avenue, Palo Alto, CA 94301 (800) 227-1972. When using the Dialog service, a subscriber dials their toll-free number and locks on. The sign-up fee of $100.00 gives the subscriber the lock-on code.

The Educational Resources Information Center is part of the large Dialog data base. The addresses for the ERIC clearinghouses are:

ERIC Clearinghouse on Information Resources
Syracuse University, School of Education
130 Huntington Hall
Syracuse, NY 13210      (315) 423-3640

ERIC Clearinghouse of Elementary and Early Childhood Education
University of Illinois
College of Education
Urbana, IL 61801      (217) 333-1386

ERIC Processing and Referencing Facility
4833 Rugby Avenue, 303
Bethesda, MD 20814      (301) 656-9723

The two packet-switching services are:

GTE Telenet
8229 Boone Blvd.
Vienne, VA 22180      (703) 442-1000, customer service (800) 336-0437

Tymnet
2070 Chairbridge Road
Vienne, VA 22180      (703) 827-9110, customer service (800) 336-0149

You can use a BBS to obtain free programs, to leave and read messages, to play games, to order products (books, for example, by calling via modem: PMS, McGraw-Hill, New York (212) 512-2488), or to gather information on movie reviews (Dickenson's Movie Guide, Mission, KS (913) 432-5544).

For the latest listing of the BBSs, you can call (213) 881-6880, twenty-four hours a day. This service is provided by Novation, Inc., of Tarzana, CA, a manufacturing firm that produces modems. Another good first source for information about BBSs is the Peoples' Message System, Santee, CA (619) 561-7277; this system provides an extensive listing of BBSs around the United States.

The following recommended books and newsletters will provide you with a great place to start in your utilization of electronic bulletin boards:

- *The Computer Phone Book,* by Mike Crane. New York: Plume Books (212) 697-8000. A listing of over four hundred on-line BBSs with hours, fees, and general descriptions of services offered.
- *OMNI Online Database Directory,* by Mike Edhart and Owen Davies. New York: MacMillan (212) 702-2000. Descriptions of more than one thousand data bases, with information including telephone numbers and addresses.
- *Computer Shopper,* Jim Cambron, publ. P.O. Box 1000005, Kansas City, MO 64111, (913) 383-2229. Subscription costs $9.95 for one year, $15.95 for two years. A directory of new bulletin boards, with news of interest to BBS users.
- *PLUMB,* Rec Manning, ed. P.O. Box 300, Harrods Creek, KY 40027, (502) 228-3820. Subscription is $26.50 per year (8 issues). This newsletter prints relevant news; lists new bulletin boards with phone numbers, addresses, and services; and lists and reviews telecommunications software.

Following is a listing of specialized national BBSs:

- UFONET, Golden, CO (303) 278-4244, is an exciting system that covers a wide variety of subjects, among them high-technology news with a specialty in space items, and programming tips on Apple, Atari, and Radio Shack microcomputers.
- HEX, Silver Spring, MD (301) 593-7033, is a clearinghouse for information on using technology to aid the disabled and also serves as a message center for deaf microcomputer users. It is a great source of information for students in university and college departments of special education who need contacts and specialized information.

- Energy Tree, Sausalito, CA (415) 332-8115, presents an open forum for anyone interested in the use of alternative energy sources. Users of this BBS exchange data and even documents on various topics relating to alternative energy sources.
- The Kid's Message System, San Diego, CA (619) 578-2646, is a BBS that was set up to encourage children to exchange messages and jokes and to learn about microcomputers. This BBS is utilized by children in school districts all across the country.
- Connection-80, Petersborough, NH (603) 924-7920, specializes in literary criticism. Users can read or contribute poetry, short stories, book reviews, and children's fiction. This BBS has become a valuable source of literary works, with many users willing to critique and referee works for authors.

For those interested in networking, one good networking management software program is the Classroom Monitor, manufactured by Software Connections of Santa Clara, CA. And WICAT Systems, Inc., Orem, UT (801) 224-6400—a notable manufacturer of both hardware and software for networking—has some excellent software programs available.

# H

# WORD PROCESSING

## A WORD PROCESSING EXERCISE USING THE BANK STREET WRITER

Several word processing programs are suitable for general school use. We have selected the Bank Street Writer (Apple version) for the following word processing exercise because of its popularity and ease of use.

One way to understand how a program of this type works is to describe how it corrects different kinds of mistakes. A passage from Melville's classic, *Moby Dick,* was chosen as the material to be edited. Several common errors have been introduced, each of which is identified by referring to its line number; following the passage is a line-by-line description of the key combinations used to make each correction.

(1)      And thus, through the the serene tranquilities of the tropical sea

(2)    among waves whose hand-clappings were supended by exceeding

(3)    rapture, moby dick moved on, still withholding from sight

(4)    the full terrors of his sumberged trunk, entirely hiding the

(5)    wrenchedhideousness of his jaw. But soon the fore part of him

(6)    slowly rose from the water; for an instant his whole marbleized
(7)    body formed a high arch, like Virginia's Natural Bridge, and

(8)    warningly waving his bannered flukes in the sea, the grand god

(9)    revealed himself, soundded, and went out of sight. Hoveringly

(10)   halting, and dipping on the wing,   the white sea fowls longingly

(11)   lingered over the pool agitated he had left.

(12)   With oars apeak, and paddles down, the sheets of their sails

(13)   adrift, the three boats now stilly floated, awaiting Moby Dick's

(14)   reappearance.

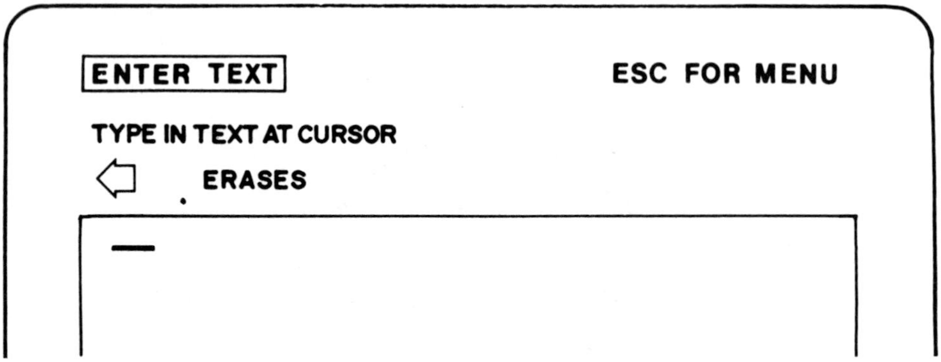

FIGURE 1   Write Mode Menu

Assume that you are sitting at the computer at this moment; you have just finished typing the *Moby Dick* passage, and the cursor (which indicates where the next typed character will appear) is positioned just after the period following *re-appearance* on line 14. The document is filled with errors, and you must now correct them. At the top of the screen is a display called a menu. You have been entering text, so this will be the write mode menu (see fig. 1). The left arrow shown in the menu reminds you that pressing this key will erase the character that has just been typed. Note also that the way to change to the edit mode is indicated (ESC FOR MENU): when you press the escape key, the prompt lines on the screen will change to indicate the new mode.

The edit mode menu (see fig. 2) gives a list of options for making various changes in the document. A diagram of the cursor control keys (the four arrows) is displayed to remind you of the procedure for moving the cursor around on the screen: pressing the I key moves the cursor up one unit; M moves it down, J

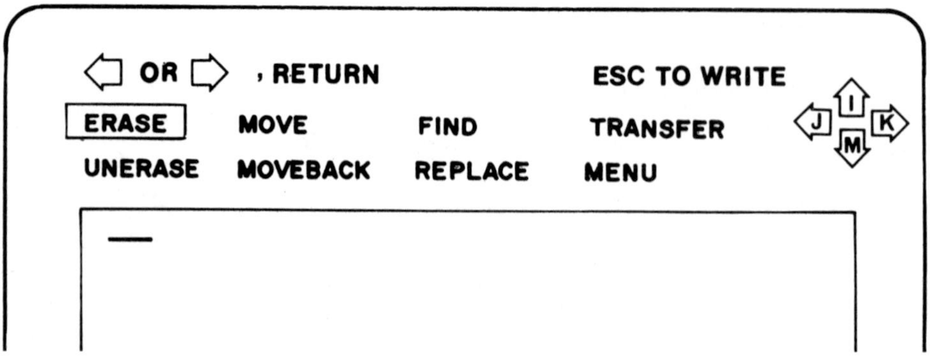

FIGURE 2   Edit Mode Menu

moves it left, and K moves it to the right. (If the Apple IIe is being used, the arrow keys substitute for the letter keys; that is, the right arrow moves the cursor to the right, the up arrow moves it up, and so on.) Before using any of these options, however, you should move to the beginning of the document. To do so, press B; the cursor will appear at the beginning of the first line of text.

There are some slight differences between the commands for the Apple II+ and the IIe; some of these are identified in the following discussion. We should mention that you need not lock the CAPS lock key when using the IIe with the Bank Street Writer. Note also that although some changes can be made in the write mode (you can use the left arrow to delete a character, for example), you must be in the edit mode to make substantial changes.

With the cursor in the upper left-hand corner of the screen, level with the first line, and the program in the edit mode, we will begin correcting the mistakes. Refer back to the original document as needed.

**Line 1.**  To get to the first mistake (an extra *the*), move the cursor along line 1 by pressing the K key (the right arrow on the IIe) until the cursor rests below the space between the two *the*s. Press the escape key and then the left arrow key four times (once for each of the letters and once for the extra space); the word will be deleted. Press ESC to move into edit mode, then continue on to the next line.

**Line 2.**  This line has a misspelled word: *supended* should be *suspended*. Move the cursor until it is under the *p*, press ESC to enter the write mode, and then type the missing *s*; it will be inserted in front of the *p*. Press ESC to change modes, then use the cursor move keys to advance to the third line.

**Line 3.**  By now you are aware of the need to move back and forth between the text and the edit modes. The cursor can be directed to the various parts of the document when the edit mode is in use; to type in the corrections, however, you must be in the write mode. The ESC key is used to change from one mode to the other, and the menu display will remind you which mode you are in. When you are in the write mode, the menu will say ENTER TEXT; as soon as you press ESC, the menu changes to reflect the things that can be done in the edit mode. You can't get lost; just glance at the screen to find out which mode you are in and what functions can be performed. Now, to return to the task of editing, the correction needed in this line is that *moby dick* must be capitalized. Move the cursor until it is under the *o*, press ESC, then the left arrow to delete the *m*. Now press ESC, hold down the shift key and the N key, then release both keys; this tells the computer to capitalize the next letter that is typed (the IIe uses the shift key for this purpose). Next, press the *m*—it will appear in uppercase on the screen, and the first word will be corrected. Use the same procedure for *dick*, then move on to line four.

**Line 4.**  The positions of two letters, the *b* and the *m*, are reversed in the word *sumberged*. This is simple to fix: move the cursor (in edit mode) until it is under the *b*; change to write mode, and delete the *m* with the left arrow. Change to edit mode, move the cursor until it is under the *e*, move back into write mode, and type the letter *m*—the spelling will be corrected.

**Line 5**. A space is needed between the words *wrenched* and *hideousness*. Move the cursor until it is under the *h* in *hideousness*; move into write mode, then press the space bar, and the space is inserted.

**Lines 6 and 7**. A space must be inserted between lines 6 and 7 so they conform to the double-spaced format. Place the cursor after *marbleized* on line 6; enter write mode and then press RETURN—the space will be inserted between the two lines.

**Line 8**. The word *sea* should be *air*. Move the cursor to the space between *the* and *sea*; enter write mode, then press the space bar. Now type the word *air*; move the cursor past *sea*, then, using the left arrow, remove *sea* and the extra space.

**Line 9**. There is an extra *d* in *soundded*. Move the cursor to the second *d*, change modes, and use the left arrow key to remove the first *d*.

**Line 10**. There are two spaces between *wing* and *the*: one must be deleted, using the same procedure you would to delete a character.

**Line 11**. To this point we have been using the erase function in the edit mode. To correct line 11, in which the words *pool* and *agitated* are transposed, we will use the move function in the edit mode. If a IIe is being used, press the open or solid Apple key until the highlight (the bar of light) is over the word MOVE in the menu, then press RETURN. If you are using a II +, the right and left arrow keys move the highlighter horizontally and the space bar moves it vertically. The menu will change at this point, and a set of directions for the move function will be displayed. Following the directions, position the cursor on the first character of the word *pool*, then press RETURN. Now, move the cursor under the space before *agitated* and again press RETURN. Next, move the cursor to a position under the *h* in *he*, then press RETURN; the word *pool* will now be positioned after *agitated*, where it belongs.

**Line 12**. This line should be indented to begin a new paragraph. Position the cursor under the first letter, *W*; enter the write mode, press the space bar three times to move the line (indent it), and you have a paragraph. This concludes the exercise.

The document should now be error-free. To check it, type B to move the cursor to the beginning, then move through a line at a time, reviewing as you go. This is the point at which a document can be saved on a disk, printed out as hard copy, or both.

## SOME WORD PROCESSING PROGRAMS
## SUITABLE FOR GENERAL SCHOOL USE

There are currently so many excellent programs on the market that an entire book would be needed to describe them all. Rather than attempt to cover every suitable title, we have selected a sample of proven, popular programs that reflect different approaches to such functions as cursor moves, screen formatting, and editing. Many outstanding word processors, of course, must be excluded. The intent is not to push specific brands, however, but to present an

overview of word processing software. With this in mind, let us examine Apple-
Writer II, Bank Street Writer, Cut & Paste, HomeWord, Magic Slate, Magic
Window, and Quick Brown Fox, each of which is suitable for various educational
(as well as home) applications.

## AppleWriter II

AppleWriter II is representative of the more sophisticated programs that are
most valuable in the upper grades. Although it lacks some of the special features
that characterize such top-level packages as WordStar and WordPerfect, it is adequate for virtually all conceivable applications. Among its unique features is its
split-screen capability, which permits two documents to be displayed on the
screen at one time. Another useful feature is the user-created glossary: you can
include frequently used words and phrases in the glossary by assigning each
word to a different key.

You will recall that there are two standard techniques for formatting a
document—menu-based and text-embedded; AppleWriter uses both of these
for greater versatility. Another feature is its built-in word processing language
(WPL). Users who desire more control over a document's format can use this feature to create their own tailor-made programs. Although WPL would not have
much utility for the average student or casual user, advanced students and those
in business education classes might find this a challenging and useful option.

The newer version of this best-selling program is designed to take advantage of the features of the Apple IIe—it has an eighty-column display (instead of
forty), and uses the arrow keys to move the cursor rather than the letter keys (see
the preceding text editing exercise for an explanation of cursor moves using
both arrow and letter keys).

AppleWriter uses both menus and direct commands in its operation. A
menu-driven program displays different menus for different modes (see Bank
Street Writer); you select an option from the menu and then follow the subsequent prompts that are displayed. A command-driven program, on the other
hand, lets you type in a command at any time; menus can be displayed if desired,
but they are not required. The latter technique permits the program to operate
more rapidly, but there are more things to memorize. The inclusion of both is a
useful strategy that permits choices based upon the user's need, expertise, and
familiarity with the program.

The menus are called up separately by using various key combinations.
Holding down the CONTROL key while pressing the letter P and ?, for example,
is the command to display the Print Program menu. This command, as well as
most others, is logical and easy to remember. When you type CONTROL-P?
you are essentially saying, "I have a question concerning my print formatting
features—show me what they are."

You can edit text anytime you wish with AppleWriter—a simple keypress
puts you in the edit mode. The various delete options range from the removal of
a single character to that of a full paragraph. An interesting feature of the delete

function is that deleted words and characters are saved in a storage buffer for re-call at a later time if they are needed.

AppleWriter is an excellent all-around tool that would be most valuable in the upper grade levels. Younger students would most likely never use many of its rather sophisticated features. Also, because menus are not constantly displayed, the user must learn procedures for calling up information as it is needed. This can be a difficult task for younger students, but older ones have few problems with it. Finally, many more key combinations must be learned with AppleWriter than is the case with the more simple programs such as Cut & Paste and the Bank Street Writer. (Producer: Apple Computer, Inc., 20525 Mariani Ave., Cupertino, CA 95014)

## The Bank Street Writer

The Bank Street Writer is among the most easily mastered of the current crop of friendly word processing programs. An excellent disk-based tutorial makes the use of the written documentation unnecessary for many students, although the quality of the documentation deserves a word of praise. A student guide and a reference guide are included, as are a question-and-answer segment and a collection of ideas for using word processing in the classroom. Another feature that appeals to young students is the large print format of the screen display. This program also has word-wrap and block movement features, search-and-replace capabilities, and text highlighting features, among others, so it is certainly more than just a bare-bones program.

The virtue of such friendly programs as this lies in their simplicity; they are so easy to learn that beginners (including very young children) are encouraged to engage in creative use virtually from their first exposure.

The Bank Street Writer is menu-driven (see the discussion of Apple-Writer). Although this type of program operates more slowly than does the command-driven variety, the ever-present menus prevent you from ever getting lost or confused—the prompts are always on the screen to give assistance. Also, commands are held to a minimum; all of the functions are performed with very few keys.

There are, however, a few limitations: you cannot underline, nor can you view more than half the line at one time. The formatting options are also some-what limited, but they are generally adequate for most needs. Moreover, since you must move from one mode to another to edit or enter text, the program runs a bit slowly, but for students this is of no real consequence.

In addition to the write or insert mode and the edit mode, there is a third mode—called the transfer mode—which is used to save and print the document. Although space does not permit a detailed description of this mode here, with its addition the Bank Street Writer is able to perform most of the tasks that expensive and complicated programs are capable of (admittedly with fewer niceties). (Producers: home version—Broderbund Software, 1938 Fourth Street, San Rafael, CA 94901; school version—Scholastic Inc., 730 Broadway, New York, NY 10003)

## Cut & Paste

Cut & Paste is another easy-to-use word processing program that emulates the Bank Street Writer but adds several useful features. Menus of commands are used extensively; they keep the user constantly apprised of the available options as well as the current status of the program. The command menu is located along the bottom of the screen; a second line of information displayed across the top indicates what is taking place at any given time (e.g., EDITING MOBY DICK).

In addition to the menus, Cut & Paste uses the technique adopted by AppleWriter: it permits the input of commands without directly accessing a menu. Although menus are very helpful, they tend to slow down processing, so the addition of direct command capabilities is a useful feature. You can use the menu-based approach as a neophyte, then move to the direct approach as your skill level increases.

The process of editing the text is made easy through the use of a unique method of selecting an editing option with cursor moves rather than with typed commands. You select an option from the menu at the bottom of the screen, then move the cursor to that option. For example, if you want to remove a section of text from the document, you define the block with the cursor, then move the cursor to the word CUT in the menu to activate this function.

Cut & Paste lacks certain of the more sophisticated formatting functions (for example, it does not permit underlining), but it is an excellent tool for general school use. (Producer: Electronic Arts, 2755 Campus Drive, San Mateo, CA 94403)

## HomeWord

A current trend is to use icons—small pictures of the objects or processes—in place of words in menus and other information displays. HomeWord makes extensive use of icons, and although they tend to simplify it somewhat, the program is still too advanced for younger students, who would find Bank Street Writer or Cut & Paste much easier to use. Older students, however, should be able to master HomeWord in a short time.

An unusual characteristic is that the menu takes up about the bottom third of the total space, leaving only about two-thirds of the screen available as work space; most users, however, find this adequate for their needs. Since HomeWord offers numerous functions, it provides multiple menus to simplify things. Once you have selected a function from the main menu, a second menu, devoted specifically to that function, is displayed. To make a selection you merely press the arrow keys to move the cursor to the icon that represents the function you wish to use (this process is similar to the one you follow with Cut & Paste, though it uses words rather than icons in the menus).

Whereas Bank Street Writer provides a tutorial on the disk and other programs use a printed pamphlet for this purpose, HomeWord offers a tutorial on audiocassette. It also provides a comprehensive, nicely illustrated manual and a reference card listing commands and other useful information. (Producer: Sierra On-Line, Inc., Sierra On-Line Building, P.O.Box 485, Coarsegold, CA 93614)

## Magic Slate

Magic Slate is unique in that it has three built-in levels of capability, all on one disk: young students just starting out can use the large-letter, twenty-column version; older students and those with some experience will prefer the forty-column version, which offers a selection of different type styles; and for the user who wants all the power of a professional word processor there is an eighty-column advanced version.

The program is quite easy to master in any of the three versions, but the advanced one provides additional features that make it a good choice for the upper grades and administrative-level work. One powerful feature of the advanced version—in keeping with the trend to make application programs more versatile as well as more user friendly—allows you to work on two separate files at once. Both are displayed on the screen in windows where the contents can be viewed, transferred, altered, or added to, as desired.

Some word processing programs make it difficult to move blocks of text, but with this one the process is quick and simple. After deleting the word you don't want, you simply move the cursor to the new position, where the block is repositioned with a single keystroke.

Excellent documentation and instructional print materials are included as part of the courseware package. A workbook for the younger user, various worksheets, a cross section of teaching ideas, teaching guides, and a useful tutorial combine to make this a complete word processing experience. (Producer: Sunburst Communications, 39 Washington Ave., Pleasantville, NY 10570)

## Magic Window

The cursor is used in a unique way in the early version of Magic Window: it remains stationary in the middle of the screen while the text does all the moving, just as on a standard typewriter, where the paper moves while the keys strike in the same spot.

Magic Window has menu-based formatting features only—you cannot use embedded commands as with AppleWriter, for example. The program is also menu-driven: you begin with the main menu and move from one subsystem menu to another as formatting, editing, printing, and so on proceed. The menus guide you every step of the way, so it is difficult to get lost; but moving back and forth between subsystems takes time, and until you get used to the process, it can be a bit frustrating.

Let us examine the process. First, select the desired subsystem from the main menu—filer subsystem, for example. Move the cursor until it rests on this option, then press RETURN. The filer subsystem menu is now displayed. Suppose you wish to save a file: move the cursor to the option Save Formatted File, give the file a name, then press RETURN to save the document on the disk. Next, return to the main menu for another selection. This might seem like a lot of trouble, particularly if you have been working with a program such as Apple-Writer where you merely type CTRL-S anytime you want to save the document on the disk. But you can move through the menus rapidly with a bit of practice, and the extensive options are always there to prompt you.

This program has been popular from the time of its initial release. The updated versions, Magic Window II and IIe, incorporate several improved features, such as a seventy-column display and a moving cursor, but continue to utilize the original program's many capabilities.

Magic Window is too complicated for young children because of its many editing commands and other detailed features. On the other hand, these pose no problems for older students, who typically find such commands as CONTROL-K (for kill a line) and CONTROL-G (for glue a line) fun to work with. (Producer: Artsci, Inc., 5547 Satsuma Ave., North Hollywood, CA 91601)

## Quick Brown Fox

In keeping with our objective of examining a variety of programs with unique features, we will consider Quick Brown Fox for, among other reasons, its editing procedure. Most programs permit full-screen editing of the text; in other words, the cursor is moved up, down, or across until its position corresponds with the point of text insertion or deletion. A few, however—such as Quick Brown Fox—use what is termed line editing, in which the line itself is pulled out of the document and moved to the bottom of the screen for correction. When a mistake is located, you move to edit mode, where the word FROM? is displayed on the screen as the prompt for you to type in the misspelled word. The line containing that word is immediately displayed at the bottom of the screen; when corrections are made the line is returned to its place in the document.

As does Magic Window, Quick Brown Fox makes extensive use of submenus. This program is similar to Bank Street Writer in that it does not permit writing and editing in the same mode—you must change from one to the other as needed.

Many powerful features normally found in more expensive programs are available as part of this economical package. You can create a glossary (see AppleWriter for a discussion), use the search and replace feature, and underline words, among other things. These and other features make this program most useful for general applications by older students and for use in business education classes. (Producer: Quick Brown Fox, 536 Broadway, New York, NY 10012)

# I

# PROGRAMMING AND AUTHORING

## A PROGRAMMING EXERCISE IN BASIC

The following exercise is useful in the early stages of a unit on programming. It has been widely used by a number of students and has been well accepted by them. Note that the lesson should be undertaken only after some discussion and after the student has not only learned the various system commands but also run several disk-based programs. This exercise can be carried out on the Apple II+, Apple IIe, Commodore, Franklin, IBM, TRS-80 and several other machines with few modifications. The major change concerns the word HOME, which is an Apple term used to clear the screen. When you come to this word, change to CLS for the TRS-80 and IBM and to PRINT "CLR/HOME" for the Commodore (note: do not type the words *clr/home*; instead, press the key of that name after typing the first quotation mark, then follow up with the second quotation mark).

1. Type the following (you can change the numbers):

```
PRINT 4 + 5
```

Then press RETURN or ENTER. What did you get?
2. Type the following (use your own name if you wish):

```
PRINT MY NAME IS WHATEVER
```

Then press RETURN/ENTER. What did you get?
3. Type the following:

```
PRINT "MY NAME IS WHATEVER"
```

Press RETURN/ENTER. What did you get this time? Note the difference the quotation marks make.
4. Type LIST. What do you get?
5. Now type the following, then press RETURN/ENTER.

```
10 PRINT "MY NAME IS WHATEVER"
```

What did you get? Can you figure out why?

6. Type:

```
20 PRINT "I LIKE COMPUTERS"
```

(Note: from now on press RETURN or ENTER whenever you complete a line or enter a command.)

What happened? Now type LIST. What did you get? Next, type RUN. Now what do you get? Think about all of this—can you explain it?

7. By now the screen is filled with all kinds of things, so let's see if we can clean it off. Type HOME. What does this command do?

8. Type LIST. What did you get? Can you explain what happened?

9. Next type NEW.

10. Now type LIST. What happens? Why is this listing different from the last one? Explain what NEW does.

11. Type the following short program:

```
10 PRINT "HELLO"
20 PRINT
30 PRINT
40 PRINT
50 PRINT "THERE"

RUN
```

What does PRINT with nothing following it do?

12. Next, type this program:

```
10 PRINT "20 + 5 = " 20 + 5
20 PRINT
30 PRINT "NOW WE'RE ADDING"
40 PRINT "TWO NUMBERS"
50 PRINT "EASY, ISN'T IT"
60 END
```

(Note: from now on type HOME anytime you want to clear the screen.)

13. Now type RUN. How did we get the results on the first line? What do the quotation marks do?

14. Type NEW.

15. Type the following:

```
10 PRINT "I LIKE"
20 GOTO 50
30 PRINT "ICE CREAM AND"
40 PRINT "CAKE AND"
```

```
50 PRINT "COMPUTERS"
60 END
```

16. Type RUN. What happened to lines 30 and 40, ICE CREAM AND CAKE AND?
17. Now type NEW and then the following:

```
20 PRINT "THIS IS"
30 PRINT "AN INFINITE"
40 GOTO 20
50 PRINT "LOOP"
60 END
```

18. Now type RUN. What is happening? Quickly, do you remember how to stop a runaway program? Do it now (press CTRL-C on the Apple, the stop key on the Commodore, the break key on the TRS 80, or the control and break on the IBM). What happened to line 50 (the word LOOP)?
19. Clear both the screen and the memory (do you remember how?).
20. Let's see what a semicolon does. Type in this program:

```
10 PRINT "YOUR NAME";
20 GOTO 10
```

Then run it. Oops, another runaway—better stop it.
21. Clear the screen and the memory, then type the same program with a comma:

```
10 PRINT "YOUR NAME",
20 GOTO 10

RUN
```

Now you know what a comma does. Stop the program and clear the screen and the memory.
22. Let's try the comma and the semicolon again, but this time we won't let the program run away. Type:

```
5 HOME
10 PRINT "HERE ARE THE FISH I HAVE IN MY TANK"
20 PRINT
30 PRINT "TETRAS","ZEBRAS","KOI"
40 PRINT
50 PRINT 12, 4, 6
60 END
```

Now, run it—is it clear what the comma does? Also, did you notice what line 5 did? You can include HOME in a program to clear the screen automatically each time the program is run.

23. Type the fish program again, but this time replace the commas with semicolons (;). What happens when you run this one?

24. Type the following:

```
10 REM ASSIGNING VALUES TO VARIABLES
20 LET X = 5
30 LET Y = 10
40 LET Z = 15
50 PRINT X, Y, Z
60 END
```

Run the program. Notice that the output is not made up of letters (X, Y, Z)—why? See what the commas did? Neat, isn't it? There is a brand new word on line 10 (REM). Did it have any effect on the way the program worked? If you think not, you are correct. It's a remark, and it is included as a reminder; it is useful when programs get very long.

25. Type the following:

```
7 LET X = 5
11 LET Y = 10
19 LET Z = X + Y
40 PRINT Z
56 END
```

Run this program. Explain what it does. Note that you do not have to use 10, 20, 30, and so on as line numbers, but they are fairly standard. Incidentally, in the program above, X, Y, and Z are called variables; they are like memory boxes. The numbers 5 and 10 are values, which are placed in the boxes.

26. Let's try some more stored numbers. Remember that X, Y, and Z are the names of storage spaces (like the boxes in the post office) so we can put numbers in them (this is called assigning a value to a variable). Type:

```
10 HOME
20 LET X = 10
30 LET Y = 5
40 PRINT X, Y
50 PRINT X + Y, X - Y
60 PRINT X * Y, X / Y
70 END
```

What happens when you run this one?

27. A variable such as X, Y, or Z can hold a word if it is changed to a string variable. This is easy to do—just add a dollar sign ($) to the letter and this tells the computer that a word can be stored in that memory space.

```
10 LET A$ = "CHARLES"
20 LET B$ = "BABBAGE"
30 PRINT A$, B$
40 END
```

Now run the program. If you don't like the format, substitute a semicolon for the comma. Do this by typing LIST and then the following at the bottom of the list:

```
30 PRINT A$; B$
```

28. Now type RUN to see the new arrangement. If the spacing between the names bothers you, list the program again and then type this:

```
10 LET A$ = "CHARLES "
```

(leave a space here)

Run the program again. What difference did this change make?

29. Let's try an interactive program. Type this:

```
10 PRINT "HI, WHAT'S YOUR NAME?"
20 PRINT
30 INPUT N$
40 PRINT
50 PRINT "WELL"; N$; "GLAD TO KNOW YOU"
60 END
```

30. Run this program. When the computer stops and asks HI, WHAT'S YOUR NAME? type your name. What happens? How does the computer know your name? Note the crowded spaces next to your name. Retype this line (number 50) and fix it.

31. Here's an IF-THEN statement using relational symbols ( > < = ). Type the following:

```
5 PRINT
10 PRINT "HOW MANY INCHES IN ONE YARD?"
20 PRINT
30 INPUT I
```

```
40 PRINT
50 IF I = 36 THEN 90
60 IF I > 36 THEN PRINT "TOO HIGH, TRY AGAIN"
70 IF I < 36 THEN PRINT "TOO LOW, TRY AGAIN"
80 GOTO 5
90 PRINT "YOU GOT IT"
100 END
```

When you run this one, try putting in wrong answers as well as right ones. Analyze the program to see how it works.

32. Remember our program that ran away? It looked like this:

```
10 PRINT "YOUR NAME"
20 GOTO 10
```

One way to get it to stop is to use a FOR-NEXT loop. Type this:

```
10 FOR X = 1 TO 6
20 PRINT "YOUR NAME",
30 NEXT X
40 END
```

How many times did the program print your name? Why? Can you figure out why it stopped at this number?

33. For our last program we'll combine several of the statements we have learned to create a new program that permits only so many guesses before the computer moves on to another question. Type this:

```
10 REM MULTIPLICATION PROGRAM
20 HOME
30 REM THREE TRIES
40 FOR T = 1 TO 3
50 PRINT "WHAT IS 7 X 9?"
60 PRINT
70 INPUT A
80 PRINT
90 REM CHECK THE ANSWERS
100 IF A = 63 THEN 160
110 IF A > 63 THEN PRINT "TOO LARGE"
120 IF A < 63 THEN PRINT "TOO SMALL"
130 PRINT
140 NEXT T
150 GOTO 170
160 PRINT "GOOD, YOU GOT IT"
170 PRINT "LET'S TRY ANOTHER"
```

(Continue adding lines as desired.) When you run this program, you'll get three tries, then you will move on to line 170. But if you get the right answer before the three tries have been used, you will move to line 160, then to line 170 for the next question (which you will need to add). Try tracing this through to see that it all makes sense.

## A SAMPLE PROGRAM IN THE PILOT AUTHORING LANGUAGE

A program written in PILOT has a much different appearance than one written in BASIC. The following material is provided to help you gain a feel for the structure of this language. More information can be found in various texts and journals, but one of the best sources is the manual that comes as part of the PILOT programming package.

The PILOT instruction set consists of a total of about forty-five abbreviated commands, the bulk of which would not be used until you had become quite familiar with the language. Some common commands follow.

| Symbol | Meaning | Function |
| --- | --- | --- |
| T: | Type | Displays text on the screen. |
| R: | Remark | Serves the same function as its equivalent in BASIC; the information is for the author's use and is not executed. |
| A: | Accept | Accepts the student's response. |
| M: | Match | Causes the items included after M: to be checked against the input the student entered after A: to see if they match. |
| J: | Jump | Causes a jump to a subprogram. |
| C: | Compute | Calls for a computation. |
| *(name) | Label | Identifies a label (*COLOR1, for example); a label is a kind of subprogram to which other parts of the larger program refer. |

As mentioned earlier, there are many more instructions in the PILOT language than the few listed here. It is possible, however, to write simple programs with an amazingly limited number of PILOT instructions. The following brief (and incomplete) program follows the traditional question-and-answer format. Remember that the simplest drill-and-practice PILOT lesson can be made much more interesting by using the outstanding graphics and sound capabilities.

| *The Program* | *Comments* |
|---|---|
| R: REPTILES AND AMPHIBIANS | Remark; not executed, but used for reference. |
| T: | |
| T: | Type; using T: alone creates a space. |
| D: N$ (20) | Dimension (see note following the program). |
| T: HI, WHAT'S YOUR NAME? | |
| A: $N$ | Accept; the storage space $N$ holds the name of the student. |
| T: | |
| T: MY, $N$, THAT'S A NICE NAME. | Displays the student's name, which is in memory space $N$. |
| *ANIMAL | Label; identifies a program section. |
| T: DO YOU WANT TO LEARN ABOUT REPTILES OR AMPHIBIANS? (CHOOSE ONE OR THE OTHER) | |
| A: | |
| M: REPTILES | Match: does the student's answer match *reptiles*? |
| T: | |
| TY: GOOD CHOICE, $N$, LET'S STUDY ABOUT REPTILES. | Type with a modifier (Y for yes): if there is a match, display this text. |
| JY: REPT | Jump with a modifier: if there is a match, jump to the label *REPT. |
| M: AMPHIBIANS | If there is not a match on the first M: instruction (M: reptiles), continue to this M: instruction and look for a match between the student's input and *amphibians*. |
| T: | |
| TY: SO YOU WANT TO LEARN ABOUT AMPHIBIANS, $N$ ! | If there is a match, display this. |
| JY: AMPHIB | If there is a match, jump to the label *AMPHIB. |

```
T:

T: NO, YOU MUST TYPE EITHER        If there has not been a match to this
   REPTILES OR                     point, display this text.
   AMPHIBIANS--
   BE SURE THAT THE
   SPELLING IS CORRECT.

J: ANIMAL                          Jump: in the absence of a match,
                                   jump back up to the label *ANIMAL,
                                   and go through this part again.

*AMPHIB                            Label.

T: DO YOU KNOW WHAT AN
   AMPHIBIAN IS?
_____    Continue adding lines to the pro-
_____    gram as needed.

_____
E:                                 End.

*REPT                              Label.

T: DO YOU KNOW WHAT A
   REPTILE IS?
_____    Continue adding lines to the pro-
_____    gram as needed.

_____
E:                                 End.
```

The dimension statement, which appears as D: N$ (20) in the program, tells the computer to set aside a storage area in memory to hold a word of up to twenty characters. The N$ symbol identifies a string variable; this concept is discussed in detail in the section on BASIC. Note that each of the instruction symbols is followed by a colon (:). This is a characteristic of PILOT that must be observed for the program to operate properly.

Now let's run the program. Here is how it will look.

```
HI, WHAT'S YOUR NAME?
```
REBECCA
```
MY, REBECCA, THAT'S A NICE NAME.
DO YOU WANT TO LEARN ABOUT REPTILES OR AMPHIBIANS?
(CHOOSE ONE OR THE OTHER)
```
REPTILES
```
GOOD CHOICE, REBECCA, LET'S STUDY ABOUT REPTILES.
DO YOU KNOW WHAT A REPTILE IS?
```

The program is complete to this point only, but you can see how it could be made to continue if more instructions were to be added.

Let's try an incorrect response to the query, "Do you want to learn about reptiles or amphibians?"

```
HI, WHAT'S YOUR NAME?
```

PATRICIA

```
MY, PATRICIA, THAT'S A NICE NAME.
DO YOU WANT TO LEARN ABOUT REPTILES OR AMPHIBIANS?
(CHOOSE ONE OR THE OTHER)
```

BIRDS

```
NO, YOU MUST TYPE EITHER REPTILES OR AMPHIBIANS--
BE SURE THAT THE SPELLING IS CORRECT.

DO YOU WANT TO LEARN ABOUT REPTILES OR AMPHIBIANS?
(CHOOSE ONE OR THE OTHER)
```

AMPHIBIANS

```
SO, YOU WANT TO LEARN ABOUT AMPHIBIANS, PATRICIA!
DO YOU KNOW WHAT AN AMPHIBIAN IS?
```

Now that one of the two alternatives has been selected, the program can continue.

# INDEX

## DATE DUE

| | | |
|---|---|---|
| RETURNED | | |
| | | |
| | | |
| | | |
| | | |
| | | |
| | | |
| | | |
| | | |
| | | |
| | | |
| | | |
| | | |
| | | |
| | | |
| | | |
| | | |
| | | |